WORKING WITH PIAGET

Working with Piaget

Essays in honour of Bärbel Inhelder

edited by

Anastasia Tryphon and Jacques Vonèche

Archives Jean Piaget,
University of Geneva, Switzerland

First published 2001 by Psychology Press
27 Church Road, Hove, East Sussex, BN3 2FA

www.psypress.co.uk

Simultaneously published in the USA and Canada
by Taylor & Francis Inc
325 Chestnut Street, 8th Floor, Philadelphia PA 19106

Psychology Press is part of the Taylor & Francis Group

British Library Cataloguing in Publication Data
A catalogue record for this book is available from the British Library

Library of Congress Cataloging in Publication Data
Working with Piaget : essays in honour of Bärbel Inhelder / edited by Anastasia Tryphon
and Jacques Vonèche.
    p. cm.
Includes bibliographical references and index.
ISBN 0-86377-621-3 (alk. paper)
    1. Psychology—History—20th century. 2. Piaget, Jean, 1896–3. Inhelder, Bärbel. I.
Inhelder, Bärbel. II. Tryphon, Anastasia. III. Vonèche, J. Jacques.

BF105.W63 2001
150'.92—dc21   00-045799

ISBN 0-86377-621-3

Cover design by Terry Foley
Typeset in Times by Facing Pages, Southwick, West Sussex
Printed and bound in the United Kingdom by Biddles, Guildford and King's Lynn

Contents

List of contributors

Trevor G. Bond, School of Education, James Cook University, Townsville, QLD 4811, Australia.

Terrance Brown, 3530 N. Lakeshore Dr. 12-A, Chicago, IL 60657, USA.

Peter Bryant, University of Oxford, Department of Experimental Psychology, South Parks Road, Oxford OX1 3UD, UK.

Michael Chandler, University of British Columbia, Department of Psychology, 2136 West Mall, Vancouver, BC V6T 1Z4, Canada.

Wolfgang Edelstein, Max Planck Institut für Bildungsforschung, Lentzeallee 94, 14195 Berlin, Germany.

Patricia M. Greenfield, University of California at Los Angeles, Department of Psychology, Los Angeles, CA 90095, USA.

Jean-Louis Paour, Université de Provence, Département de Psychologie Développementale et Différentielle, 29, av. Robert Schuman, 13621 Aix-en-Provence, France.

Eberhard Schröder, Universität Potsdam, Postfach 601553, 14415 Potsdam, Germany.

Anastasia Tryphon, Université de Genève, Archives Jean Piaget, Uni-Mail, 40 Blv. Du Pont d'Arve, 1205 Genève, Switzerland.

Jacques Vonèche, Université de Genève, Archives Jean Piaget, Uni-Mail, 40 Blv. Du Pont d'Arve, 1205 Genève, Switzerland.

Ernst von Glasersfeld, Scientific Reasoning Research Institute, Hasbrouck Laboratory, University of Massachusetts, Amherst, MA 01003, USA.

Figure acknowledgement

We would like to thank the following for permission granted.

Figure 5.1. From page 99 in Edelstein, W. (1996). The social construction of cognitive development. In G. Noam & K. Fischer (Eds.), *Development and vulnerability in close relationships.* Mahwah, NJ: Lawrence Erlbaum Associates Inc. Copyright © Lawrence Erlbaum Associates Inc. Reprinted with permission.

Where necessary every effort has been made to trace copyright holders and obtain permissions. Any omissions brought to our attention will be remedied in future editions.

Introduction

Jacques Vonèche and Anastasia Tryphon
Archives Jean Piaget, University of Geneva, Switzerland

This book has two aims: one is to distinguish Bärbel Inhelder's scientific contribution from that of Piaget in the movement of the so-called School of Geneva in developmental psychology. The second is to have the various sites of Bärbel Inhelder's endeavour revisited by scholars expert in these fields of research.

There are many possible ways of accomplishing these two goals. Our strategy in this book is not to try to elucidate—by what sort of scrutiny?—the respective contributions of Jean Piaget and Bärbel Inhelder in their joint writings, researches, and preoccupations. The necessary pieces of evidence are presently lacking for such an undertaking. Moreover, who could tell, even among those of us who had a glimpse of their most intimate scientific collaboration, how they really worked together when no-one else was there? It would be like trying to decide whether a falling tree makes a noise in the forest when no-one is there to hear it. Piaget and Inhelder certainly produced a lot of research papers and books together, but it would be an exercise in futility to try to separate Inhelder's contribution entirely from that of Piaget's, especially as Inhelder had the singular elegance to present the public with a unified front over a dispute (in the medieval sense of *disputatio*) and to settle it in a satisfactory way for both of them.

Instead, we have isolated from the Genevan heritage those aspects to which Bärbel Inhelder made a personal contribution distinct from that of Piaget: reasoning in mental retardation, space and the three mountains experiment, adolescent logic and formal operations, longitudinal methodology, mental imagery, learning, cross-cultural studies, strategies and procedures. Some of these aspects resulted in collaborative books with Jean Piaget, but as Trevor Bond aptly shows in his contribution, the discovery of the stage of formal operations does belong to Bärbel Inhelder. Similarly, Vonèche shows in his chapter in mental imagery that there was some difference between Piaget and Inhelder over the status of the mental image.

However, mental retardation, longitudinal methodology, learning, cross-cultural studies and strategies are the sole endeavours of Bärbel Inhelder, with the help of her own set of collaborators in the great Genevan tradition of cooperative research.

This volume opens with a chapter by Vonèche describing the place in the history of psychology of Bärbel Inhelder as a person separate from Piaget—especially as a woman doing science at a moment in history and in a European country not particularly propitious to women. We have to think of what it meant for that generation of women to sacrifice a possible family life to a scientific career and, in the case of Inhelder, to be constantly considered as the second in command, and never the captain of the ship. Nevertheless, as not only Vonèche but also Bond and Brown show in their respective chapters, she was the psychologist behind the epistemologist. She not only ran the subjects and organised the young staff of research assistants and the invited group of research associates and visiting professors, but she was also in touch with the state of the art in world psychology, keeping a keen eye open for novelty in the behaviour of children. Her eye was keen enough to discover the last and most complex stage of formal operations during the course of her studies on chance and stochastic processes.

Jean-Louis Paour's chapter on mental retardation deals with Inhelder's doctoral dissertation on the topic (published in 1943), with a special interest in the methodological strategies Inhelder developed in that dissertation. The chapter questions the opposition between the developmental and the deficit approaches in mental retardation in contemporary psychology, and concludes that a truly constructivist approach is the only way to solve the dilemma of this difficult field of research.

Michael Chandler, in a review of the literature about the three mountains task devised by Inhelder and Piaget, shows how this task has been diverted from its initial function—i.e., as a test of the construction of objective space and a measure of the passage from egocentrism to decentration (a truly Copernican revolution in the child's mind)—into a different type of evidence in favour of the so-called "theory of mind". Ironically enough (and Michael Chandler is indeed a master of irony)—the author considers that, after 50 years of all sorts of manipulations and alterations dreamed up by various interested researchers, Inhelder's and Piaget's views still remain valid.

The next chapter by Trevor Bond marks a change of approach. Instead of a review of the vast literature on the topic of formal operations, Bond embarks on a detective-like quest into the area of formal operations. Does the discovery of the ultimate stage of mental operations belong to Inhelder or to Piaget? Bond gathers evidence, discusses alternative views, scrutinises the texts available in published form, looks at the archives, and comes to his conclusions, for the reader to read and discuss, without further disclosure by us here.

Once again a change of approach: The next two chapters are devoted to longitudinal studies. Instead of reviewing and analysing the classical longitudinal research initiated by Inhelder into cognitive development, Edelstein and Schröder describe their own longitudinal study of individual development and social structure in Iceland. What is stressed here is the determinant role played by social constraints in cognitive development. According to the authors it is the social group that tempers and moderates cognitive development, and it does so by regulating the amount of opportunities available to the growing mind at any moment in the form of experiences, interactions, and stimulation of all kinds.

In their longitudinal study of deductive reasoning in 9- to 17-year-olds, Schröder and Edelstein show that belonging to a specific social class, and to one sex rather than the other, provides differences in exposure to cognitive socialisation, giving rise in turn to differences in the formation of cognitive structures.

Restating Inhelder's position on mental imagery, Vonèche shows, in his review of the current state of affairs, that some of the discoveries of neuroscientists were largely anticipated by the School of Geneva, and that cognitive psychologists of today have failed to understand fully the role of action and more specifically the role of *schèmes d'action* in the genesis of mental imagery.

Dealing with learning, Peter Bryant discusses the role of language in the development of conservation. He points out that the Piagetian hypothesis that action precedes operation without a strong mediation by language has not been appropriately tested by the Genevan School, with damaging consequences of which everyone in the field is aware. The Piagetians have underrated the so-called pre-operational stage of development and the semiotic function in general by concentrating on its deficits and not its successes.

The next chapter, by Ernst von Glasersfeld, discusses the classic tenets of constructivism. Radical constructivism (which is the position held by the author) drives a middle course between Platonic idealism and British empiricism as far as learning is concerned. Platonic idealists such as Fodor and Bereiter postulated that no learning is possible unless one assumes the previous existence of innate, ideal, and perennial forms. This is the famous anamnesis theory of learning. The great merit of Ernst von Glasersfeld is to show that the very notion of *schème*, introduced by Piaget and Inhelder, demonstrates the inanity of both idealism and empiricism as well as the necessity of constructivism.

Patricia Greenfield tackles another aspect of Inhelder's career: intercultural research into sensory-motor development in Baoulé children from the Ivory Coast of Africa. As Greenfield points out, the scope of cross-cultural studies in cognitive development is to test the hypothesis of the possible generalisation of the stages of mental development discovered in Geneva. In other words, the question is: Are there universals in mental development or is it culture-specific? Basing her model on specific studies of a Mayan culture in Mexico, Patricia Greenfield offers an interpretation of "stage": A stage is neither universal nor specific. Or rather, more appropriately, it is both general and specific. It is universal to the extent that it offers a general sensitivity for specific cultural stimulation and learning. In Greenfield's model, a stage is a critical period at three levels: maturational, socio-cultural, and ecological-historical, and not simply maturational as in ethology, socio-cultural as for Vygotsky and his followers, or ecological and historical only. This new interactionism promises to be very encompassing and integrative.

The last contribution by the psychiatrist Terrance Brown, in a bold metaphor, compares Bärbel Inhelder to Brünhilde, Wagner's heroine, to the extent that Inhelder's work with Piaget is seen as a progressive farewell party to genetic epistemology, moving towards the shores of pragmatic, individual psychology. Brown observes in Inhelder's *oeuvre* an increasing focus on procedures and strategies instead of structures and stages, on microgenesis instead of macrogenesis, on differences instead of resemblances, and on biological and cultural backgrounds, all culminating in her last book.

Finally to round off this review of Inhelder's various endeavours and their spin-offs, the reader is offered, thanks to Trevor Bond's efforts and initiative, the first English translation of a paper by Inhelder herself on the experimental approach in children and adolescents, to be read in conjunction with Bond's and Brown's chapters.

This volume illustrates the fecundity and the vitality of Bärbel Inhelder's contribution to science. As Piaget pointed out at the creation of the Jean Piaget Society, the thing is not to build a chapel but a place for open discussion, which we hope this book will prove to be.

CHAPTER ONE

Bärbel Inhelder's contributions to psychology

Jacques Vonèche
Archives Jean Piaget, University of Geneva, Switzerland

BEGINNINGS

Bärbel Inhelder was born in 1913 in the small German-speaking town of St Gallen in north-eastern Switzerland, a quiet place with an interesting history, having once been an important European intellectual centre. In 1932, at the age of 19, she made her first trip to Geneva, to improve her French. There she attended the Institut Jean-Jacques Rousseau. With some exceptions, Bärbel Inhelder spent the next 65 years in Geneva as Piaget's student and chief collaborator. Thus, from an early time she became and remained committed to a rich and powerful ideal, the creation of a new discipline, genetic epistemology. This was a monumental undertaking and Inhelder's role in it was seminal and crucial, as she set for herself the task of justifying her epistemology by her psychological research. But she had her own view of things, as we shall see in the rest of this chapter.

It should be mentioned that there were other, more senior psychologists in the Institut who were important in encouraging Inhelder to explore a variety of intellectual perspectives—Pierre Bovet and Edouard Claparède. The latter's work on hypothesis formation (Claparède, 1933) and problem solving, often using the think-aloud method, played a role in Inhelder's functionalism. Her personal brightness and psychological presence endeared her to the younger staff: Edith Meier, Alina Szeminska, André Rey, and Marc Lambercier to mention just a few.

Setting aside Piaget's own very great accomplishments, together Inhelder and Piaget produced a series of six volumes of research on stage theory and the development of operational thought, two volumes on the development of figurative thought, and one work of synthesis. Working alone or with collaborators other than Piaget, Inhelder pioneered the application of genetic epistemology to the study of mental deficiency, and to two other pathologies later with the psychiatrist Julian de Ajuriaguerra: cross-cultural research, and the field of learning. She and her team also produced several studies on the development of cognitive strategies and procedures. Her work played an essential part in the "cognitive revolution" in psychology, in ensuring that developmental research and theory would be a fundamental part of that movement.

The bulk of her work was done independently and largely on her own initiative. In other words through her own activity she grew rapidly from the status and role of eager neophyte to that of effective intellectual leader. She exemplified the most distinguished version of the very influential role of women in the Institut Jean-Jacques Rousseau. Inhelder and Piaget saw each other or spoke on the telephone almost daily. Consequently, the best characterisation of their work should be: "independence in interdependence" as the French have it.

Although she never mentioned it publicly (she was in many ways a very private person) her career was distinct from that of Piaget, right from the beginning of their collaboration in 1933 when she was working on the problem of conservation in physics, in contradistinction as well as complement to Szeminska's studies of number. We will devote much of this chapter to these distinctions and to the originality of Inhelder's work.

CONSERVATION 1936

Rereading now her 1936 paper on the genesis in the child of the conservation of physical quantities (Inhelder, 1936), we can make at least three observations. First, we see the anticipation of the secondary mechanisms of equilibration: the famous alpha, beta, and gamma types of reactions, later to be described by Piaget in *The equilibration of cognitive structures* (1975/1985).

The alpha type of reactions simply neutralises the perturbation of the level of equilibrium reached by the child and thus restores the equilibrium between assimilation and accommodation. The beta type begins to integrate the perturbation under the form of a variation within the system leading to an equilibration of the subsystems. The gamma type is an anticipation of possible variations within the system with a balance between differentiations and an integration of the variations in the whole system. In each instance, equilibration is constructive. Neutralisation can go from merely disregarding the perturbation, as is usual in young children, to partial compensation, as when they make special provision for exceptions in their classifications of objects. Integration supposes a full compensation by assimilation of the perturbation and not a cancellation of the perturbation; that is to say that integration means a displacement of the equilibrium in order to maximise the gain through internalisation of the variation. In the gamma type of reactions, all the possible transformations are anticipated. It corresponds to virtual works in physics or to competence in linguistics.

This triple distinction corresponds to the intra-, inter-, and trans-levels in *Psychogenesis and the history of science* (Piaget & García, 1983/1989), about the mechanisms common to progress in science and to cognitive development in the child. A good example of these processes is given by the history of geometry: Euclidean geometry is intra-figural; projective geometry is inter-figural; and Kleinian geometry is trans-figural. In child development, intra- corresponds to the discovery of the properties of an object, inter- to class inclusion, and trans- to formal operations of the INRC type, where I stands for identical, N for negation, R for reversibility, and C for correlative.

The first two of these mechanisms were described by Piaget and Inhelder in their book *The child's conception of space* (Piaget & Inhelder, 1948/1967). But the point of origin lies in this 1936 paper which anticipates more the "trans-" dimension of the 1980s; a solo paper by Inhelder and not one co-authored with Piaget.

To return to our three observations; second, Inhelder's method is original too. Her approach is qualitative, but her qualitative findings are drawn from representative samples of population, and fit in factor analysis and Rasch analysis of scaling. Inhelder was a strong believer in the daily interviewing of children on many different topics at the same time. In other words, she did not favour the massive and singular intakes of information that are so fashionable in present-day psychology. She did not even like the method used by many of Piaget's collaborators, that is, one weekly interview of children on one specific question. She thought that pursuing several inquiries at the same time gave a much better overview of children's thinking processes in general and thus guaranteed benefits to all these simultaneous inquiries.

MENTAL RETARDATION

Third, the way in which Inhelder described the problem of conservation shows that she had a clear idea of the differences between her own psychological approach and Piaget's epistemological one. Once again, we will not dwell on this point, as it is well made by Terrance Brown later in this book (see Chapter 11).

Another difference between Inhelder's position and Piaget's is perceptible when Inhelder came back to Geneva to a permanent position at the university, after having written her doctoral dissertation on mental retardation (Inhelder, 1943/1968) in the canton of St Gallen. Mental retardation is a psychological problem not an epistemological one. That is, it is epistemological to the extent that Inhelder was able to show that these individuals go through the same stages as normal and gifted children do, but more slowly and not equally far, thus supporting the view that mental development is a universal, stage-like process. However, mental handicap is also a psychological question. By her own admission, (1998) Inhelder grew interested in the problem because she was alone in St Gallen in 1939 starting psychological services there. Mental retardation presented one last advantage: It was a topic Piaget was not interested in, so she could study it without unwanted interference from him, and capitalise on her daily clinical experience.

In Inhelder's book on the diagnosis of mental handicap (1943/1968), one can discern a strong functionalist train of thought that differed radically from Piaget's structuralism. The contrast between them was especially evident because, at the time, Piaget was dedicating all his energies to the problem of mental operations and their logical structure. In addition, Inhelder used diagnostic tools based on André Rey's tests of learning and adaptation (Rey, 1935) plus some tests invented by herself and Piaget for the work reported in the book on *The child's construction of quantities* (Piaget & Inhelder, 1941/1974). This was because her purpose was psychological in contrast to epistemological, and theoretical in contrast to empirical, in the sense that she did not believe in hodge-podge testing "à la Binet-Terman" which she aptly compared to random cuts in anatomical tissues. Already then, she favoured an approach that broadly surveys the mental processes at work in problem-solving situations.

SPACE

This survey approach is continued in the book *The child's conception of space* (Piaget & Inhelder, 1948/1967) where Inhelder's thorough knowledge of the history of geometry is apparent. She compared the development of the notion of space in the child and in the history of geometry in such a way as to show that the crucial moment of development in the genesis of geometrical notions is the passage from intra-figural considerations to inter-figural ones. In the former case, the child's knowledge is limited to a sort of putting-together of the parts of the same figure or of the same object. In the latter, the relationships among figures or objects are actively sought by the child who understands space as a general form against which the constructed properties and relations are mapped. In other words, the passage from topology to projective and Euclidean geometries is made possible by the synthesis of the topological substratum into a system of relations organised according to certain rules. By following all the meanderings of children's thinking, Inhelder was able to show the passage, in the construction of space, from sensory-motor placements and displacements to their representation in mental imagery and their consolidation into a logico-mathematical group.

The child's conception of space was, according to both Piaget's and Inhelder's independent accounts, largely prepared by Inhelder alone, unlike its sister volume in geometry (*The child's conception of geometry*, Piaget, Inhelder, & Szeminska, 1948/1960). This is apparent in the wording of the questions. There are significantly more variations of wording in *The child's conception of space* than in *The child's conception of geometry*, and the role of student assistants seems more important in the former than in the latter. Inhelder was adept at working with others, although she lived alone and liked her privacy in everyday life.

Inhelder remarked in her *Autobiography* (1998) that the book on the representation of space was her favourite work. It is worth noting that the English translation gives the title as *The child's conception of space*.

"Conception" has the ring of attainment; "Representation"—the key word in the original French title—has the ring of process, which is better attuned to Inhelder's way of thinking. There is another reason for Inhelder's preference for this book on space: The geometry book was based on a series of experiments made before World War II with Alina Szeminska. Thus, the space book was more her own book.

CHANCE

After *The child's conception of space*, Inhelder's next project was to study chance, randomness, and probabilities, because she had been struck by the fact that chance was almost totally absent from children's explanations of physical phenomena. As Inhelder put it in a private conversation with Vonèche, "they were hypercausative". So she attended classes on probability and chance at the University of Geneva, read Cournot and others, and acquired an entire education on the topic. This study of probability theory showed her that, contrary to her initial intuition, chance was not a simple notion based on elementary mental operations. Thus, the question arose: Is chance a natural outcome of the concept of number and as such a rather precocious concept (as she expected at first), or is it an elaborate notion that appears only in adolescence? Inhelder raised this question before the stage of formal operations had been discovered. In fact, it is this preoccupation with random processes and their relationship to logic, reversibility, and the idea of mixture so central to Cournot's thinking that led her to the famous discovery of formal thinking.

The general intuition about chance as a lay concept in children's and adolescents' explanations was indeed discussed with Piaget in a most interesting way: Inhelder and Piaget each had a notebook in which they jotted down their theoretical and experimental ideas and their criticisms of each other. By comparing notes and discussing them first together, then with students, they formed the project of the book to be written on the basis of experiments imagined during their summer vacation in the Alps. Inhelder started experimenting alone and consulted Lucien Feraud, the eminent Professor of Probability and Calculus at the university, on the nature of the concept of chance in mathematics. Then students came in and ran subjects for all the experiments presented in *The origin of the idea of chance in children* (Piaget & Inhelder, 1951/1975). This group of students was important because they were very able and enthusiastic. At that time, Piaget was engrossed in his *Introduction à l'épistémologie génétique* (1950), three volumes that he had discussed extensively with Inhelder, though he considered the final product his own private affair.

Discovering that chance is a concept that needs time to be elaborated by her subjects, Inhelder had to make what was a very bold move at the time—to interview children in the secondary school, not just in the elementary school. Interviewing primary school pupils was acceptable in the wave of modern pedagogy at that time and it was standard practice at the Institut Jean-Jacques Rousseau. But disturbing students in the Collège Calvin was daring and even considered arrogant and ridiculous. Nevertheless Inhelder persisted, in spite of the scepticism of both students and professors of the Collège. Rather quickly, scepticism gave way to respect and keen interest, because of the intelligence of the experimenters (Rutschmann, Morf, Aebli, Noelting, Vinh-Bang, among others). Piaget was not interested during the experimental part of the study. He was busy with epistemology and theoretical issues in physics, mathematics, biology, psychology, and sociology (in this declining order).

Inhelder's intention, at the time, was already to study strategies, procedures, goals, and means, in problem solving from childhood to adolescence. This project was organised like the previous space project, with two sister volumes. But now, one volume would deal with experimental induction and the other with experimental attitude, including chapters on the nature of observables, evidence, discovery, and validation in spontaneous scientific thinking.

As one can see, in the early 1950s, the preoccupations and interests of Bärbel Inhelder and Jean Piaget were clearly separate: Piaget was concerned with structures in perception—he wrote *The mechanisms of perception* (Piaget, 1961/1969) while in residence at the Institute for Advanced Studies in Princeton, USA. Inhelder was involved in developing a functionalist viewpoint and was concerned with procedures.

FORMAL OPERATIONS

In the course of experiments on flexibility, pendulum movement, and other hypothetico-deductive areas, Inhelder and her brilliant collaborators found that they had invented a new stage of mental development. Piaget was pleased with the discovery and immediately projected his INRC group onto it (Piaget, 1952), or group of quaternality linking together the four mental operations mentioned earlier.

In the mid-1950s the atmosphere in Geneva changed considerably, because of the conjunction of three factors: the discovery of formal operations,[1] the creation of the International Center for Genetic Epistemology, and large grants from the Rockefeller and Ford Foundations. This brought an influx of researchers of high quality from all over the world and shed some additional light on the ensemble of studies undertaken in Geneva. From this time on, Inhelder began to recede from centre stage. Inhelder had already undertaken, as requested, to fill a gap in Piaget's system by studying the early growth of logic in children, resulting in *The growth of logical thinking from childhood to adolescence* (Inhelder & Piaget, 1955/1964), a book that she never liked because she felt the experiments were too perfunctory. Now she was organising research, and helping students and visiting professors.

In spite of this new "housekeeping" role, Inhelder managed to study stages longitudinally with the help of G. Noelting, and to show that each stage is characterised by a double movement: closure of the previous structure assigning it to oblivion, and opening of novelties that advance the entire system of thinking.

MEMORY AND IMAGERY

Inhelder also studied mental imagery and memory from a personal viewpoint (Piaget & Inhelder, 1966/1971). Piaget insisted on the primacy of mental operations upon images, whereas Inhelder considered imagery as the material props for mental actions: For her a mental image was the figurative aspect of an operative activity.[2] By insisting on the role of representation of reality as the material support of the interiorised actions of the child, Inhelder paved the way for her future study of procedures and strategies in the course of cognitive growth. This new approach was a turning point in Inhelder's intellectual life.

MICROGENESIS IN THE CHILD AND IN CULTURES

After the division of labour established around 1957 between the epistemic Piaget and the strategic Inhelder, their respective domains of specialisation were well defined, as we have already seen. She was no longer interested in longitudinal studies demonstrating the universality of stage-like cognitive development. She concentrated on microgenesis. Three volumes written independently of Piaget marked the change: one book on learning (Inhelder, Sinclair, & Bovet, 1974), one on cultural differences (Dasen, Inhelder, Lavallée, & Retschitzki, 1978), and one on strategies (Inhelder & Cellérier, 1992).

In the 1960s, when Inhelder was at the Harvard Center for Cognitive Studies, George Miller and Jerome Bruner had shown some interest in the Genevan theory of mental development. But they had also presented Inhelder with their own work. The "subjective behaviorism" advocated by Miller, Galanter, and Pribram in *Plans and the structure of behavior* (1961) had caught her keen eye. Bruner's studies of cognition had persuaded Inhelder that she needed to use more powerful techniques, essentially the study of micro-processes and local strategies, to show that Bruner was misled when he believed that one could learn anything at any age provided that one hits the right communication channel. She was convinced then that Piaget could not gain the approval of psychologists in favour of his epistemological ideas, mainly because the genesis of cognitive structures had not been clearly explicated and unfolded. She wanted to mark all the obstacles and detect all the difficulties met by children in the passage from one stage to the next one, in order to show the differences between constructivism and other approaches in developmental psychology. The 1959 Woods Hole conference which she attended on Cape Cod was another stimulus because it accentuated the possibility of accelerating the speed of development. A further incentive to change was, once again, methodological: Inhelder believed that her longitudinal studies, as well as those of others, were too descriptive and not experimental enough.

LEARNING AND DEVELOPMENT

Consequently, with two junior colleagues, Hermine Sinclair-de Zwart and Magali Bovet, she undertook the immense task of studying the affiliation of processes and strategies by means of which growing children really develop. Sinclair-de-Zwart was a Dutch linguist who had studied the relationship between language and mental operations. Bovet is a Swiss with an extensive background as an experimental and cultural psychologist. The three of them and their assistants spent a long time analysing the development of mental structures in children. The book, *Learning and the development of cognition* (Inhelder et al., 1974), was poorly reviewed and unfairly represented, perhaps because of a misunderstanding about the use of the word "learning", which was infelicitous and too loaded with behaviouristic connotations for the Piagetians and Gestaltists, and too reminiscent of the book on logic, learning, and probability by Apostel, Jonckheere, and Matalon (1959). The aim of Apostel et al.'s book was to show that any form of learning, including spontaneous development, amounts to a general algebra of so-called "learning operations" corresponding to logical classes, relations, and judgements typical of genetic epistemology. The book by Inhelder, Sinclair, and Bovet was quite different in intention as well as in scope. The interest of the work comes from the analysis of the role of experience, language, and action, which is clearer than in Piaget's own books.

CROSS-CULTURAL DEVELOPMENT

Another domain touched by Inhelder at the time was the cross-cultural study of mental development (Dasen et al., 1978), in which she compared the rate of development in Baoulé children (Ivory Coast) and in Genevans, with the expected conclusion that sensory-motor development is more rapid in Africa than in Europe whereas representational and operational stages are more beneficial to European children. She was never satisfied with the book that came out of these studies, and she learned to her cost how difficult it is to write about cultural differences when they deal with intelligence: One has to watch for the politically correct as well as for the psychologically true.

STRATEGIES FOR DISCOVERY

In the meantime, Inhelder had organised a new team of collaborators whose enthusiasm and dynamism, according to her own account, worked wonders in a fashion similar to the team with which she discovered the stage of formal operations. These young people wanted a break from Piaget, both methodologically and theoretically, and they came up with the idea that Inhelder should go back to her older project about strategies and the study of discovery in scientific thinking.

From 1970 to 1992, Inhelder and this team worked together, producing a number of doctoral dissertations and a fair number of papers. All the doctoral dissertations stemming from this project were co-directed by Inhelder and Cellérier. She was the senior partner and he was the often invisible theoretical mentor. The protracted publication of *Le cheminement des découvertes de l'enfant* (1992), summarising all this research, was due not so much to maturation as to the duty Inhelder felt to edit Piaget's posthumous books as tribute of recognition to the last paper they published on structures and procedures (Inhelder & Piaget, 1979).

Not working in the team just described, but closely related in their work, were Christiane Gilliéron, who was closely allied to Inhelder, and David Leiser. All these people were interested in the idea that Inhelder had so long promoted, that the study of cognitive structures should be extended to the study of related procedures and strategies. In other words, mental structures do not stand alone, they survive and develop through action, and these actions are specific procedures governed by discernible strategies.

In her Foreword to Leiser and Gilliéron's book on the many variations on the operation of seriation, Inhelder (1990, p. vi) aptly characterised the theoretical issue at stake:

> Leiser and Gilliéron explore the passage from [structural] atemporality to [procedural] temporality and the construction of normative structures. They raise the fundamental problem of how a new procedure is invented, and how a successful procedural invention can lead to an understanding that goes beyond its specificity.

The essentials of Inhelder's perspective on developmental psychology are expressed in her last book, *Le cheminement des découvertes de l'enfant* (Inhelder & Cellérier, 1992). The book, which was published when she was almost 80 years old, is functionalist at heart and it tries to evaluate, demonstrate, and justify the explanatory virtues of Piagetian theory. This was her life-long preoccupation and research strategy. Unlike others around and against Piaget, she was not concerned with the logical truth of Piaget's theory, but was worried about its capacity to generate refutable hypotheses. Although she was by no means a Popperian, she often expressed her interest in Popperian philosophy in private conversations. As she used to say, "at least, what we have learned in German-Swiss secondary school is the art of experimenting" (personal communication). She even said that she wanted to restore "experimental morality" among psychologists.

Another point that she wanted to make in this book, which she knew would be her last, was to solve the functional problems of developmental psychology. To her this did not mean re-opening the debate opposing functionalism to structuralism. Nor did it mean coming back to the concrete, real subject after having flirted for so many years with the elusive epistemic subject, following a salutary detour through the maze of aseptic laboratory experiments. It meant for her, essentially *testing the categories of analysis.* This was her answer to the question of what is a cognitive structure. Is it an abstract construct representing a competence attested by a set of various and synchronic performances? Or is it a more or less realistic representation of the tools used by real thinking subjects to organise reality or, at least, successive subjective representations of reality by a sort of ideal subject? If the latter is the case, then the question becomes: "How does the subject put these cognitive tools to work?" Hence her emphasis on the shrewdness of questioning and on the subtleties of the experimental apparatus to unearth the tools that the subject is unconsciously using. But this approach raises more questions than it solves. As a matter of fact, if the subject interviewed by Inhelder and her collaborators instantiates a structure in the process of solving the problem presented, is this instantiation an operation, in the Piagetian sense of the term? However, if this is so, then, as Inhelder used to tell her assistants: "it is one thing to have a cognitive structure, another to use it". In this case, what are the users' instructions and where are they located, in memory or mental imagery or in both? Does the subject unfold schemata one after the other until satisfaction is reached? Are there rules governing the correct application of these schemata? If this is the case, what is their locus? In the tools themselves? In social practices? Or are they kits that have to be constructed?

Each of these last three questions corresponds to a specific epistemological bias: Mere unfolding of schemata one after the other up to satisfaction means a nativistic stand. If the locus of the schemata lies in social practices, it is social learning. If it is in the tools themselves, then it is empiricism. If they are kits to construct, then it is constructivism. Indeed, Inhelder's preference was constructivism in a qualified form, as, along with learned algorithms and tested routines, the growing child's instrumentation comprises tools that are not a ready-made tool-box but a kit to be constructed. This standpoint allowed Inhelder to shed some new light on what a structure really is in cognitive development. It is the expression of the compatibility of pieces with (and their likely relevance to) a class of coded problems, demonstrating the validity of Piaget's phrase that "intelligence is structured by its own functioning".

Therefore, the fastidious observation of all the functioning of children in Inhelder and Cellérier's *Le cheminement des découvertes de l'enfant* (1992) is not the mere narrative of the historicity of intellectual labour in context, but one of the best ways to complete and renew the analytic categories by entering the mechanisms themselves. By so doing, Inhelder managed to close the great gap between epistemology and psychology that had been pointed out by Piaget.

NOTES

1. See Chapter 7 of this volume, by Jacques Vonèche, for a fuller treatment of this question.
2. See Chapter 4 of this volume by Trevor Bond for a better analysis of the discovery.

REFERENCES

Apostel, L., Jonckheere, A.R., & Matalon B. (1959). Logique, apprentissage et probabilité [Logic, learning and probability]. *Études d'épistémologie génétique, Vol. VIII*. Paris: Presses Universitaires de France.

Claparède, E. (1933). La genèse de l'hypothèse: Étude expérimentale [The genesis of hypothesis: An experimental study]. *Archives de Psychologie, 24* (93/94), 1–154.

Dasen, P.R., Inhelder, B., Lavallée, M., & Retschitzki, J. (1978). *Naissance de l'intelligence chez l'enfant baoulé de Côte d'Ivoire* [The growth of intelligence in Baoulé children of the Ivory coast]. Berne: H. Huber.

Inhelder, B. (1936). Observations sur le principe de conservation dans la physique de l'enfant [Observations on the principle of conservation in children's physics]. *Cahier de pédagogie expérimentale et de psychologie de l'enfant, 9*, 3–16.

Inhelder, B. (1968). *The diagnosis of reasoning in the mentally retarded* (W.B. Stephens et al., Trans.). New York: John Day. (Original work published 1943)

Inhelder, B. (1990). Foreword. In D. Leiser & C. Gilliéron, *Cognitive science and genetic epistemology: A case study of understanding* (pp. ix–xii). New York, London: Plenum Press.

Inhelder, B. (1998). Autobiographie de Bärbel Inhelder, rédigée à partir d'entretiens avec Jacques Vonèche, 1985–1992 [Bärbel Inhelder's autobiography, based on interviews with Jacques Vonèche, 1985–1992.] *Archives de Psychologie, 66*, 155–168, 258–259.

Inhelder, B., & Cellérier, G. (Eds.). (1992). *Le cheminement des découvertes de l'enfant: Recherche sur les microgenèses cognitives.* Neuchâtel: Delachaux & Niestlé. [To appear in English as *Children's journeys of discovery*, T. Brown, E. Ackermann, & M. Ferrari (Eds.), Hillsdale, NJ: Lawrence Erlbaum Associates Inc.]

Inhelder, B., & Piaget, J. (1964). *The growth of logical thinking from childhood to adolescence: An essay on the construction of formal operational structures* (A. Parsons & S. Milgram, Trans.). London: Routledge & Kegan Paul. (Original work published 1955)

Inhelder, B., & Piaget, J. (1979). Procédures et structures [Procedures and structures]. *Archives de Psychologie, 47* (181), 165–176.

Inhelder, B., Sinclair, H., & Bovet, M. (1974). *Learning and the development of cognition.* London: Routledge & Kegan Paul.

Miller, G.A., Galanter, E., & Pribram, K.H. (1960). *Plans and the structure of behavior.* London: Holt, Rinehart & Winston.

Piaget, J. (1950). *Introduction à l'épistémologie génétique* (3 vols). Paris: Presses Universitaires de France.

Piaget, J. (1952). *Essai sur les transformations des opérations logiques: les 256 opérations ternaires de la logique bivalente des propositions* [Essay on the transformations of logical operations: The 256 ternary operations of bivalent propositional logic]. Paris: Presses Universitaires de France.

Piaget, J. (1969). *The mechanisms of perception* (G.N. Seagrim, Trans.). London: Routledge & Kegan Paul. (Original work published 1961)

Piaget, J. (1985). *The equilibration of cognitive structures* (T. Brown & K.J. Thampy, Trans.). Chicago: University of Chicago Press. (Original work published 1975)

Piaget, J., & García, R. (1989). *Psychogenesis and the history of science* (H. Feider, Trans.). New York: Columbia University Press. (Original work published 1983)

Piaget, J., & Inhelder, B. (1967). *The child's conception of space* (F.J. Langdon & J.L. Lunzer, Trans.). New York: W.W. Norton. (Original work published 1948)

Piaget, J., & Inhelder, B. (1971). *Mental imagery in the child: A study of the development of imaginal representation* (P.A. Chilton, Trans.). London: Routledge & Kegan Paul. (Original work published 1966)

Piaget, J., & Inhelder, B. (1974). *The child's construction of quantities: Conservation and atomism* (A.J. Pomerans, Trans.). London: Routledge & Kegan Paul. (Original work published 1941)

Piaget, J., & Inhelder, B. (1975). *The origin of the idea of chance in children* (L. Leake, P. Burrell, & H.D. Fishbein, Trans.). London: Routledge & Kegan Paul. (Original work published 1951)

Piaget, J., Inhelder, B., & Szeminska, A. (1960). *The child's conception of geometry* (E.A. Lunzer, Trans.). London: Routledge & Kegan Paul. (Original work published 1948)

Rey, A. (1935). *L'intelligence pratique chez l'enfant. Observations et expériences* [Practical intellience in the child: Observations and experiments]. Paris: Félix Alcan.

CHAPTER TWO

From structural diagnosis to functional diagnosis of reasoning: A dynamic conception of mental retardation

Jean-Louis Paour
University of Aix-en-Provence, France

> ... *the retardate who has reached the elementary forms of operatory organisation is capable of remaining at this level for years. It is as though he lacked the interest, the curiosity, and the general activity which, in the normal child lead the subject to ask new questions and to find the solutions, both of which lead him to superior levels*
>
> —Inhelder 1943/1968, p. 291

More than 50 years ago, Bärbel Inhelder published *The diagnosis of reasoning in the mentally retarded* (Inhelder, 1943/1968). This book, which influenced developmental approaches to mental retardation for many years, had a dual objective: to validate the Piagetian model by proving its utility in psychiatric practice; and to unravel the dynamics of development by analysing its retardation. Inhelder's first aspiration was entirely fulfilled. References to stages of conceptual development have indeed allowed different levels of retardation to be recognised and enabled the definition of each stage according to specific modes of thought. Inhelder's work was therefore critical in promoting a psychological view of mental retardation and special education. The appeal of referring to stages of epistemic development made researchers lose sight of her second objective, which ultimately led Piagetian approaches of mental deficiency down a structural dead-end. Yet Inhelder's functional analyses point towards original research perspectives, whose prospects still remain attractive today. As we assess the twentieth century's worth of research on mental retardation, it may be useful to reread Inhelder.

We shall do so by following the structure of her book. After reviewing both Inhelder's intentions and methods, we shall re-examine her data, organising them according to the three kinds of similarity (sequence, structure, response) underlying developmental conceptions of mental retardation (Zigler, 1967). Then, we shall

13

show that the learning of Piagetian concepts can help revitalise the Piagetian approach to mental retardation and reinforce its utility. We shall also evaluate the validity of Inhelder's diagnostic criteria. Finally, we shall explain how her functional analysis of reasoning may contribute to our understanding of mental retardation.

INHELDER'S INTENTIONS AND METHODS

The diagnosis of reasoning in the mentally retarded covers the thesis content Inhelder presented for her PhD (in pedagogy) at the University of Geneva, Switzerland. This work, first published in 1943, was re-edited with a substantial new introduction in 1963, then translated into English by Beth Stephens in 1968. Following the first publication, Inhelder, either alone or with colleagues, wrote numerous articles and book chapters regarding the application of operational diagnosis to other pathologies (dysphasia, dyspraxia, psychosis, senile dementia; a synthesis of this work can be found in Inhelder, 1966). However, her thesis remains her only contribution to the study of mental retardation.

Its four chapters can be organised into three distinct sections, which are of varying interest for contemporary readers. The first section (Chapter I: "Genetic theories and the diagnosis of mental development"), focusing essentially on the problems in measuring and diagnosing intelligence, has only historical value. The second section (Chapters II and III: "Fixations of reasoning at stage I" and "Fixations of reasoning at stages II and III") represents Inhelder's essential contribution to the Piagetian approach of mental retardation. It remains empirically pertinent, and the numerous studies that later followed this perspective did not challenge her original observations. Inhelder provided many protocol excerpts to support her analysis and these enhance the usefulness of both chapters. However, it is the third section of Inhelder's thesis (Chapter IV: "Abnormal intellectual oscillations", and "Conclusions") that presents her most stimulating writing, as she explains how she understands the retardation of reasoning. Although this last section is based on clinical intuitions, and is therefore empirically more controversial than the previous one, it has two main qualities. First, it reveals Inhelder's originality with respect to Piaget: her interest in how psychological functioning is related to epistemic construction. Piaget explicitly acknowledges her originality in his preface to the first edition of the book; he writes that, according to Inhelder, "operations and their groupings appear as components ... of a vivid reality full of significance for the dynamism of concrete development" (Inhelder, 1943/1968, p. 12). Thus, *The diagnosis of reasoning in the mentally retarded* is a preview of Inhelder's later contribution to research: studies on experimental reasoning (Inhelder & Piaget, 1955/1958), on structural learning (Inhelder, Sinclair, & Bovet, 1974), and on the micro-genetic transformations of problem-solving procedures (Inhelder & Cellérier, 1992). Second, Inhelder's interest in function lies at the root of her subtle, non-reductionist, developmental perspective of mental retardation, which may transcend the "delay vs deficit" debate that polarised opinions for a long time, and still does.

Intentions

The diagnosis of reasoning in the mentally retarded fully justifies the arguments put forth in the present chapter and elsewhere in this book. In the preface to her first publication, Inhelder points out that her research responded to a need expressed by the Public Instruction Department of St Gallen, Switzerland. As a school psychologist, she was expected to evaluate the intellectual capacities of pupils experiencing important difficulties, in order to give advice regarding future educational and vocational choices. She considered classic intelligence and mental retardation diagnostic tools inadequate for this purpose, and preferred to use the developmental markers of the genesis of physical quantities, which she had helped define (Piaget & Inhelder, 1941/1974). In her eyes, this method had two key advantages. First, it helps overcome the empiricism of definitions based on mental age (MA; abbreviation used throughout this chapter) and IQ, by replacing them with an intrinsic measure of intelligence which is based on the stages in its structuring. Second, it provides more useful information regarding educational and vocational orientation than classic intelligence tests, as reasoning is observed in situation. In other words, Inhelder suggested replacing a static measure with a dynamic measure, based on the extended observation of chains of reasoning. We would like to highlight this innovative characteristic of Inhelder's work, as it anticipates the current movement towards "dynamic" evaluations of intellectual potential (Feuerstein, Rand, & Hoffman, 1979; Haywood & Tzuriel, 1992). It is noteworthy that Inhelder's method addresses the three essential dimensions of this "dynamisation": It changes the nature of examiner–examinee interactions by using the "method of open dialogue"; it focuses on the functioning observed in reasoning produced "before our eyes"; it takes learning potential into account by giving participants the opportunity to perform empirical controls (weighing, checking, going back to the initial state). Although Inhelder's ideas were not sufficiently explicit to enjoy immediate practical success, she remains a pioneer, and so-called "operational" exams have since been added, as a dynamic complement, to the more traditional static evaluation procedures. These practical objectives later led Inhelder to address two key theoretical questions. The first question is built in to her approach: by advocating the use of operational construction stages for the diagnosis and differentiation of levels of retardation, she attempts to establish their validity as "mental level indices". The second issue is the relationship between psychological functioning and developmental dynamics. Following Wallon, who considered that "the normal child is discovered in the pathological child" (Wallon, 1925, p. 309), Inhelder hypothesises that mental retardation may be a natural experiment for exploring developmental processes. Indeed, by being slowed down, they permit the experimenter to analyse their mechanisms and connect construction with different psychological factors and maybe even distinguish different types or levels of retardation.

Method

Tasks and interviewing method. In order to attain her objectives, Inhelder uses three of the four tests described in *The development of physical quantities in the child: Conservation and atomism*: substance, weight, and volume conservation of continuous physical quantities; sugar dissolution; weight transitivity. She explicitly justifies this choice by her desire to study the homogeneity of reasoning. It allows her to compare tests whose semantic content is relatively poor (e.g., conservation) with tests that are likely to activate empirical and factual knowledge (about sugar, and its behaviour in liquids; about the properties of different materials: lead, candle wax, etc.); it also allows her to confront logical reasoning (conservation and transitivity) with results from the dissolution problem, which can be tackled experimentally. Clearly, Inhelder chose to use such a set-up—which can activate different types of rationality (logical and empirical)—in an attempt to dissociate operational mechanisms from daily experience in the subject's reasoning.

Reading Inhelder's protocols shows that she administered tests with a lot of freedom, in order to identify levels of conceptualisation as closely as possible: She was inventing the "Genevan clinical method". It is worth emphasising clearly that this method has a prosthetic effect on the typical difficulties in adaptation to test situations experienced by subjects who are poorly efficient. The test's dynamic character (open dialogue, use of counter-arguments, and empirical learning attempts) allows Inhelder to contribute to the optimisation of cognitive functioning. Thus, paradoxically, her focus on the clinical method prevents Inhelder from observing the autonomous functioning of mentally retarded subjects when they are left to their own means. We shall discuss this important issue later.

Population. Inhelder examined 159 individuals (96 male, 63 female), both children and adults, whose IQ varied between 42 and 105 (average: 73), and who were between 7;5 and 52 years old (see Table 2.1; 14 subjects were 18 years old and above). On the basis of current criteria, approximately half of these subjects would be considered mentally retarded. The case descriptions provided by Inhelder further reveal a broad diversity of aetiologies as well as socio-familial and educational conditions: Our conclusion is that some of these mentally retarded subjects have an organic aetiology. As Inhelder does not provide the MA of her subjects, we considered it useful to estimate MA on the basis of IQ and chronological age (CA; abbreviation used throughout this chapter), with an upper CA of 16. This calculation shows that MA is widely distributed between 5;5 and 14 years. Broad IQ variance and aetiology heterogeneity were necessary for Inhelder's enterprise, as she was not aiming to evaluate a subject's reasoning on the basis of IQ, but instead was trying to create a new kind of diagnosis. Thus, it was essential for her to have a population whose variation was much broader than the IQ criteria she was challenging.

TABLE 2.1
Inhelder's participants: CA, IQ, and extrapolated MA*

	Minimum	Mean	Maximum	SD
Chronological age (years)				
Males + Females (n = 159)	7,5	13,2	52	5,5
Males (n = 96)	7,5	13,2	38	4,92
Females (n = 63)	7,8	13,1	52	6,36
IQ (from various intelligence tests)				
Males + Females (n = 159)	42	73.7	105	11.5
Males (n = 96)	45	74	105	11.7
Females (n = 63)	42	73.4	101	11.2
MA (years), extrapolated from IQ				
Males + Females (n = 159)	5,7	8,9	13,8	1,8
Males (n = 96)	5,9	9	13,1	1,9
Females (n = 63)	5,5	8,6	13,6	1,8

*See the text.

Inhelder met most subjects 2–3 years later, without presenting them with operational tests a second time: She was only trying to confront the diagnosis of reasoning she had made with a subject's subsequent educational and vocational evolution. Therefore, her study remains cross-sectional. Of course, we regret that she did not re-evaluate at least a few of the subjects she described as having fluctuating reasoning abilities.

SIMILARITY OR DEFICIT?

To understand Inhelder's contribution we must refer to the debate between development (delay) and deficit conceptions of mental retardation at a psychological level. This controversy mirrors the dual nature of mental retardation: difference (less efficiency at a given CA) and delay (similarity with younger children). The difficulty in reconciling delay and difference explains why both conceptions are still presented as antagonists. According to the delay hypothesis (Zigler, 1969), mental retardation is simply characterised by slow and incomplete intellectual development; IQ would therefore express developmental speed and, at a given MA, retarded and non-retarded subjects would not use different cognitive processes to reason and to learn. Zigler wrote in 1962 (p. 157): "As such, retarded individuals are not different in kind from individuals of normal intelligence; they do not suffer from rigidity or any single defect that causes their retardation." On the other hand, according to the deficit concept, mental retardation emerges from one (or several) constant and irreversible central cognitive deficits (e.g., memory or attention deficit), which distinguish retarded from non-retarded individuals of the same MA: Here, IQ would stand for information treatment efficiency. The delay conception has been operationalised according to three distinct hypotheses: the similar sequence hypothesis, based on the order in which new behaviours appear

(Weisz & Zigler, 1979); the similar structure hypothesis, based on the homogeneity of behaviour in different domains (Weiss, Weisz, & Bromfield, 1986; Weisz & Yeates, 1981); and the similar response hypothesis, based on modes of adaptation to environmental variation (Hodapp & Zigler, 1990). At first, the delay conception only pertained to non-organic retardation, but its sequential aspect was later extended to certain organic aetiologies, including Down's syndrome.

It would have been useful for the proponents of this conception to inquire where Inhelder fits in. At a first glance, her work seems to conform to the developmental conception: It is clear that Piagetian indicators provide the most empirical support for this position. However, Inhelder's concepts of "false equilibrium" and "genetic viscosity", which both characterise the cognitive functioning of mentally retarded subjects, should prevent us from prematurely assuming an absence of deficit when observing similar sequence or structure.

Similar behaviour

Before considering the similar sequence and similar structure hypotheses, we would first like to emphasise the behavioural similarity observed in response justifications and in reactions to counter-arguments. In her (1943/1968) Chapters II and III, which address fixations of reasoning, Inhelder repeatedly expresses her surprise when witnessing behavioural similarity: "... surprising to find in this psychological analysis the same primitive functioning of thought" (p. 97) , "... common logical structure and identical psychological functioning" (p. 87), "...almost word for word the same judgements and reasoning ..." (p. 92), "reply with the same eloquence as younger normal children" (p. 104), "The stage was homogeneous to the first stage ..." (p. 86), "the certitude with which the child suddenly confirmed the conservation ..." (p. 142). We are not surprised at Inhelder's insistence, as her diagnosis method implies that both populations are truly comparable. But her surprise is unexpected to us, and reminds us of Binet's amazement (Binet & Simon, 1908), when he could not distinguish whether written test responses came from subjects with or without delay. Such surprise seems to underline how robust developmental processes can be: capable of producing similar cognitive acquisitions—despite detrimental conditions and pathologies.

Although response and argument similarity is overwhelming, Inhelder points out several specificities, throughout the two chapters, which are only observed in retarded subjects: differences in commitment, seen in fluctuating attention, which require more effort from the examiner to engage retarded subjects in activities; certain specific responses in tests with the richest semantic content; oscillations in reasoning that go beyond those observed in normal children. When summarising these qualitative differences in the third section of her book, Inhelder proposes an analysis of the cognitive functioning of retarded individuals.

These differences remain marginal compared with the striking number of similarities (90% of the protocols record behaviour that is not distinguishable from behaviour observed in non-retarded children). Inhelder was thus able to demonstrate —and has not been challenged to date—that mentally retarded subjects use reasoning that is entirely homologous with that of younger, non-retarded children. In other words, she showed that they were rational! This discovery had two important consequences. First, it enabled a positive description of mental retardation by referring to a level of rationality, which was equivalent to a stage in normal genesis. Second, it established the framework for the cognitive education of mentally retarded individuals, based on a hierarchy of developmental indicators. Later, Woodward (1959, 1963) authoritatively demonstrated the usefulness of Piagetian indicators for diagnosis and education, when she applied them to severe mental retardation: She recognised in stereotypies and motor perseverations, which at the time were considered abnormal, the circular conducts typical for very young children. In the area of special education, references to general action and reasoning structure were instantly more useful than intelligence test results.

Similar sequence

Table 2.2 shows the distribution of subjects among the seven levels distinguished by Inhelder: 88% are in so-called "completed" stages, 12% in so-called "intermediate" ones. This distribution reflects the variance in intellectual levels apparent in the mental ages listed earlier, and some protocols (9%) even show pre-formal and formal levels. Although this result may seem quite trivial nowadays, we should not underestimate its importance at the time. The idea that the development of mentally retarded individuals follows normal stages and stops earlier was not original when Inhelder published it (a few studies had even been based on early Piagetian research: Abel, 1941; Lane & Kinder, 1936). However, referring to an explicit and coherent developmental hierarchy gave it further credibility: Well beyond the reference to a succession of mental ages, it described degrees of retardation using general modes of thought (Maier, 1993). It appears that the factors responsible for mental retardation respected the normal pattern of

TABLE 2.2

Distribution of Inhelder's participants (numbers and percentages) in the seven stages

Stages		Males + Females (n = 159)		Males (n = 96)		Females (n = 63)	
		Number	%	Number	%	Number	%
I	Non conservation	50	31.4	27	28.1	23	36.5
I/II	Intermediate	8	5.0	6	6.2	2	3.1
II	Conservation of substance	47	29.5	25	26.0	22	34.9
II/III	Intermediate	2	1.2	1	1.0	1	1.5
III	Conservation of weight	38	23.8	26	27.0	12	19.0
III/IV	Intermediate	9	5.6	7	7.2	2	3.1
IV	Conservation of volume	5	3.1	4	4.1	1	1.5
Sum I, II, III, IV		140	88.0	82	85.4	58	92.0
Sum intermediates		19	11.4	14	14.5	5	7.9

developmental sequences. Inhelder therefore helped establish one of the fundamental ideas in this area of research. Baumeister (1997) wrote, when taking stock of this century's progress: "There is a definite sequence to developmental characteristics of the human species that applies to most individuals, no matter what their intellectual status and the source of mental disability" (p. 29).

As Inhelder's work provides empirical evidence in favour of the developmental conception, we are surprised that its advocates have made so little use of it. For example, Weisz and Zigler (1979) judge that Inhelder's conclusions are hard to evaluate, because the procedure was not entirely standardised, and results were not formally analysed. Inhelder could have put together a table summarising her findings, as we have done. Yet once it is clear that the clinical method's aim is to associate, as unambiguously as possible, observed behaviour with developmental stages, Inhelder's data can be organised into a perfect scalogram, which demonstrates their hierarchical nature. Weisz and Zigler (1979) criticise authors whose quantifying methods do not allow hierarchical analysis. In her Chapters II and III and her conclusion, Inhelder repeatedly emphasises the importance of similar sequence, which she believes justifies the psychological validity of structural indicators, and enables the diagnosis of mental retardation. Similar sequence was never challenged by the numerous ensuing studies (Bolton, Haller, & Gourlay, 1987, cite more than 200 items linked to mental retardation in the Jean Piaget Archives). Throughout the replication studies, numerous operational tests were used to explore various conceptual domains (number, relations, and classes; spatial relationships; space, time, speed; chance; logic; moral development, etc.). We do not yet have a complete review of these studies, only incomplete and outdated syntheses (Robinson & Robinson, 1976; Wilton & Boersma, 1974; Woodward, 1963, 1979). Among them, we would like to highlight Weisz and Zigler's (1979) meta-analysis, which cites only high-quality research that generally allows scalogram construction. These essentially cross-sectional data have been confirmed by Stephens and McLaughlin's longitudinal study (1974) and by the longitudinal sensorimotor development follow-up of mentally retarded children (in particular, with Down's syndrom: Cichetti & Mans-Wegener, 1987; Dunst, 1990). The scale developed by Uzgiris and Hunt (1975), based on the Piagetian description of sensorimotor development, has now become a tool for the evaluation of severe retardation levels.

Similar structure

The study of similar structure is based on the examination of intra-individual homogeneity in reasoning, either observed between different tests within the same conceptual domain (as in Inhelder's work), or between different conceptual domains. This brings us back to the famous issue of horizontal décalages in mental retardation. Observing uneven performances, associated with mental retardation, could help pinpoint domains in which determinants have differential effects. This line of research has been heuristic for the study of conceptual construction in sight-, hearing- or physically disabled children (see for example Hatwell, 1966). However, it has not yet caught the attention of authors dealing with mental retardation for three reasons: (1) Inhelder's postulation of relatively homogeneous reasoning; (2) the absence of a hypothesis likely to direct research on specific differences; (3) the complexity of the theoretical debate on interpreting inter- and intra-subjects horizontal décalages.

We must point out that when trying to connect various psychological factors (suggestibility, impulsiveness, social dependency) with modes of reasoning, Inhelder purposely uses different kinds of tests. She refers to the conservation test to evaluate the behaviour she observes in the two other tests (transitivity and sugar dissolution). Inhelder probably did not itemise her results (test by test) because of the strong overall intra-individual homogeneity of reasoning. In her preface to the second edition of her 1943 book (1963), she also refers to results from a whole series of tests in different conceptual domains which confirm her first observation: the homogeneity of inter-test and inter-domain behaviour seems to be more developed in mentally retarded subjects.

Again, Inhelder does not minimise qualitative differences and points out two kinds of discrepancies. First, she noticed that some older subjects, particularly adults, achieve better results in the transitivity and sugar dissolution tests than in the conservation test (however, she only picks out one "clear" case of discrepancy between the conservation test and the sugar dissolution test). She then points out that mentally retarded subjects seem to reap less benefit from empirical observations (using scales in the weight conservation test, for example) than non-retarded subjects observed under the same conditions.

These cases of heterogeneity in reasoning, which we shall further interpret shortly, remain marginal compared with the homogeneity revealed in Inhelder's overall results, and in later research by other authors. Kahn (1985), for example, was able to show this homogeneity by using a series of tests involving elementary logic, numerical and physical invariance, and moral reasoning. However, we must admit that these authors were less concerned with similar structure than with similar sequence. Even Weisz and Yeates' (1981) meta-analysis, which explicitly aims to test the similar structure hypothesis, is not directly pertinent in this case, as it focuses on the relationship between MA and operational level, and does not address structural coherence in a Piagetian sense.

The study of sensorimotor development leads to a much subtler conclusion, which needs to be differentiated according to aetiology. Such research has focused on the study of local homologies between general sensorimotor abilities (looking for an object that has disappeared, using intermediaries, for example), and the appearance of more specific, yet crucial cognitive abilities (social and linguistic) seems promising. On the one hand, strong links between the level of sensorimotor functioning and affective, motivational, and temperamental development have been observed (Dunst, 1990). On the other hand, certain local homologies found in normal children (means–end distinction and pointing, for example) do not always appear in retarded subjects (Mundy, Seibert, & Hogan, 1984). The existence of deficits that are specifically associated with certain aetiologies (like Williams syndrome, for example) lead us to recognise the vulnerability of developmental synchronies. Therefore similar structure, as anticipated by Inhelder and as was later confirmed, must be restricted to the development of general conceptual structures, which do not seem to be significantly desynchronised by mental retardation.

Similar response

Only recently have Hodapp and Zigler (1990) suggested a third hypothesis, which addresses the adaptation of mentally retarded individuals to social, familial, and educational characteristics of their environment and changes thereof: the similar response hypothesis. According to this hypothesis, mentally retarded subjects who are confronted with the same conditions as non-retarded individuals (deprivation, abandonment, institutionalisation, various kinds of support, etc.), should react globally according to the same adaptation processes. However, similar response may often be overlooked, as mentally retarded individuals are more often exposed to unfavourable environments. This hypothesis is very stimulating, because it leads us to compare developmental processes, and not just their product. We believe it is the only way to address the delay vs deficit debate. On the one hand, it seems logically and psychologically inadequate to reject the deficit conception by simply observing similar sequence and similar structure: The identity of the product (stages of conceptual development) is strongly constrained by quasi-universal physical and rational regularities. On the other hand, only relatively long interventions can guarantee that differences in favour of non-retarded subjects are not linked to variables (knowledge, emotion, motivation, etc.) other than treatment ability.

This hypothesis has not yet been empirically tested. One way of doing so, in the area of conceptual development, involves exploring various learning experiences of Piagetian concepts in mentally retarded subjects. This paradigm allows the observation of how subjects with and without mental retardation, at the same developmental stage, react to identical interventions that are conceived to stimulate the transition to the next higher level of reasoning.

The learning of logical structures is an area of research that grew out of the epistemological debate on the origin of logico-mathematical knowledge (see various of the *Études d'Épistémologie Génétique*: Goustard, Gréco, Matalon, & Piaget, 1959; Gréco & Piaget, 1959; Morf, Smedslund, Vinh-Bang, & Wohlwill, 1959). Trying to identify to what extent, and under which conditions, logical abilities can be stimulated to appear earlier has become a privileged method for investigating the equilibration process postulated by Piaget. In the context of his operational theory, the paradigm of "operational learning" has been invoked in favour of opposite conceptions regarding the existence and status of logical structures.

According to one line of thought, which follows in Inhelder's footsteps, Inhelder, Sinclair and Bovet (1974) tried to define the nature of, and the conditions for, reflective abstraction (initial level, cognitive conflict, precursory schemes). Guided by a constructivist conception of development and learning, they essentially proposed cognitively conflicting situations, which were likely to trigger a transformation process of the original reasoning schemes. A second line of thought attempted instead to challenge the concept of logical structures and the model of their equilibration, essentially by having subjects: learn to discriminate between pertinent dimensions of Piagetian tests; learn by instruction; repeat empirical observations; verbally learn notions; and socially model behaviour. This research led to numerous controversies regarding which criteria should be used to evaluate the structural aspect of learned acquisitions. Problems with defining these criteria finally halted this area of research. Also, the observation of early rational behaviour seemed sufficient to challenge the Piagetian model, and made such research appear useless, both difficult to interpret and expensive to implement. It is interesting to note that certain kinds of operational learning, organised into genuine educational curricula, seem to have found a second wind in the context of "cognitive" education and school failure prevention (Adey & Shayer, 1994; Griffin & Case, 1997; Paour, Cèbe, & Haywood, 2000).

Of course, the paradigm of learning Piagetian concepts has also been used with mentally retarded subjects. Many of these studies (see for example Boersma & Wilton, 1976; Brison & Bereiter, 1967; Field, 1974; Lister, 1972) involved subjects with various levels of retardation and aetiologies. The same diversity of conceptual domains, learning techniques, and evaluation criteria as with non-retarded children can be observed. The educational pertinence of such studies explains why they have not completely disappeared with operational learning issues (see for example the recent studies by McCormick, Campbell, Pasnak, & Perry, 1990; Perry, Pasnak, & Holt, 1992; Williams, 1996). Although these studies cover the whole area of cognitive development, sensorimotor organisation, and pre-formal reasoning schemes, most of them involve learning concrete concepts (numerical, physical, and logical).

Beyond the general debate on the nature of behaviour induction, it is particularly interesting to conduct these types of learning activities with mentally retarded subjects because they aim at triggering fairly general transfers. Given that transfer difficulties are characteristic of mental retardation (Campione & Brown, 1984), it is quite pertinent to study transfer abilities in a paradigm that: (1) is explicitly conceived to trigger them; and (2) takes each subject's conceptualisation level into account. In a constructivist perspective, we feel somewhat cautious (as do Case, Sandieson, & Dennis, 1986) towards research that attempts to promote cognitive strategies (including memorisation) without taking into consideration either the conceptual dimension of the promoted strategy, or the conceptual dimension of the new knowledge whose learning/memorisation is supposed to be promoted by the aforementioned strategy. We believe that the hypothesis of a strategic or meta-cognitive deficit has been hastily put forward in order to explain how fragile the transfer of newly learned cognitive strategies can be, without having seriously looked into the necessary conditions for implementing functional integration.

We have conducted more than a dozen such experiments (for a synthesis see Paour, 1992). Our objective was to induce the construction of relatively general conceptual frameworks (e.g., notion of couple, compensation scheme), which we believed could condition access to concrete operational thought. Thus, compared with other forms of operational learning—constructivist and empiricist—our experiments had the major advantage of proposing training tasks that were totally different from the Piagetian pre- and post-tests. This condition ensures that observed progress does not represent the acquisition of specific responses, but instead stands for real structural learning. In order to check how solid these acquisitions were (another criterion of the structural aspect of learning), we systematically proposed delayed post-tests, long after the end of training sessions. Certain experiments also involved subjects without mental retardation, both trained and untrained, whose initial levels of reasoning were the same as in the mentally retarded subjects.

This area of research has not yet been entirely reviewed. However, on the basis of data from the literature, as well as from our own research, it seems that, in general, operational learning is fairly efficient in mentally retarded subjects, if we exclude attempts to teach them formal reasoning schemes. Overall, we observe a significant progression between trained and untrained control groups, and progress is both fairly general and relatively stable in the delayed post-tests. The fact that some types of learning seem more efficient than others, and that effects vary with subject condition, does not challenge our general observation. Overall results are even more significant as they arise from diverse learning techniques and involve very different populations, representing a wide range of intellectual levels, ages, and aetiologies. Of course, the extent and the nature of progress are linked to the level of retardation and to the initial level of development. A deeper examination of the similar response hypothesis requires research comparing subjects with and without mental retardation. In our experiments, we observed similar progression in both populations at the first post-test. However, at the delayed post-test, non-retarded subjects gradually outdistanced retarded participants, without the latter falling back.

Paradoxically, both in our research and in the literature, it is not the progress observed in trained groups that is noticeable, but the fact that spontaneous evolution is extremely rare in retarded control groups. This phenomenon is especially striking when using very delayed post-tests. For example, in one of our experiments, we were able to follow our experimental and control groups over four years; the control subjects hardly progressed along Piagetian indicators between the pre- and post-tests. Perhaps such fixations are specific to a sub-population, in the sense that we excluded subjects from our experiments if they were too close to the targeted conceptual level. It would be very interesting to investigate differences between subjects who, for a given MA, achieve different levels in Piagetian tests.

These data provide important information for understanding mental retardation. At a micro-genetic level, they validate observations of similar sequence and similar structure, as retarded subjects appear to reap equal benefit when they are given learning occasions. These data also resolve the meaning of fixations: Whatever their level of retardation or their aetiology, mentally retarded subjects seem to have a developmental potential that can be drawn out by learning activities. The solidity of progress and its relative generalisation lead us to believe that it represents genuine ability acquisition.

Developmental plasticity is nonetheless limited, as retarded subjects do not spontaneously attain higher levels of reasoning. Thus, fixation phenomena emerge from the interaction between concept complexity and weaknesses in cognitive functioning, as witnessed in the stagnation of control groups: It is difficult to overcome fixations without very specific educational interventions.

As the learning of Piagetian concepts does not aim at acquiring specific answers, but instead at triggering relatively general competencies, it is clear that the help provided basically promotes cognitive functioning: (1) by focusing a subject's attention on pertinent problem dimensions—we know that mentally retarded individuals tend to focus their attention on dimensions that are external to the task (Zigler & Yando, 1972); (2) by inducing cognitive activities (anticipation, explicitation, verification) that mentally retarded subjects seem to have trouble implementing when left to their own devices. This analysis emphasises chronic cognitive under-functioning: At all levels of mental retardation, retarded individuals have trouble efficiently mobilising their cognitive potential. Cognitive under-utilisation is shown in Inhelder's analyses, when she highlights how difficult it is for retarded subjects to take advantage of experiments. We shall examine the nature of this cognitive under-functioning later when discussing the meaning of abnormal reasoning oscillations.

Overall, research on operational learning leads to mixed results: While these do reinforce the similar sequence hypothesis, they also clearly show that retarded and non-retarded subjects experience different cognitive functioning. Thus, we believe that such functional differences may play a non-negligible role in the construction of mental retardation. But we also suggest that individuals with mental retardation possess developmental potential and can, with adequate help, go beyond their current level of development. If, as believed by Piagetians and neo-Piagetians, the indicators that are provided by Piagetian tests really stand for cognitive abilities and are therefore useful for dealing in an efficient manner with a wide variety of tasks and situations, then this research is of great interest for the science of education.

DIAGNOSIS OF REASONING OR DIAGNOSIS OF INTELLIGENCE?

Based on the similarities just described, Inhelder proposed new criteria of mental retardation and its degrees which reflect the stages of operational development (1943/1968, p. 293):

...mental deficiency begins when the subject will never be able to make up his retardation of operatory construction [italics in original]. 1. the idiot never outgrows the sensory-motor compositions (previous to language). 2. the imbecile is capable of intuitive thought (egocentrism, irreversibility, but no operation). 3. the retardate is capable of operatory construction which he is incapable of completing, i.e., "concrete operations" as opposed to formal operations. 4. the slow learner is capable of achieving formal operations and thus in time of reaching the full development of a normal child.

Inhelder's work could be described as the practical failure of a theoretical success, in the sense that these criteria have never been used for diagnostic purposes. This is especially surprising as French-speaking authors have often referred to her work to criticise psychometric definitions of mental retardation (see Perron, 1979). We must, however, admit that the meaning of operational diagnosis is not clear when compared to IQ-based diagnoses: Does it measure intelligence? Inhelder does not explicitly address this essential issue. Although she never formally assimilates intelligence with reasoning, her criticism of intelligence tests implies that she considers operational diagnosis a central measure of intellectual potential. It is unfortunate that she did not try to link it with the intelligence test results she had to hand.

Long after the publication of Inhelder's work, Zazzo (1972, 1973) thought of comparing both measures. He showed that reasoning levels lead to harsher diagnoses than IQ. We have repeated this kind of comparison in Table 2.3: In 37% of cases, Inhelder's diagnosis is more strict than IQ-based diagnoses. However, by considering IQ without taking CA into account, differences tend to be exaggerated, as in Zazzo's study, as the level of reasoning in younger subjects may still progress. Taking MA into account reduces the number of discrepancies, but they do not completely disappear. However, having to correct the diagnosis of reasoning with MA reveals the limits of Inhelder's approach; like MA, operational diagnosis is only really valid for adults. The impossibility of developing an operational development scale, and thus calculating an IQ equivalent for reasoning, was the fatal blow to the diagnosis criteria proposed by Inhelder.

TABLE 2.3

Comparison of diagnostics based on IQ vs Inhelder's criteria (percentages of cases)

Diagnostic based on IQ*	Inhelder's diagnostic			
	Normality	Mild MR	Moderate MR	Severe MR
Normality	26.91	27.00	1.87	–
Mild MR	0.62	16.97	7.54	–
Moderate MR	0	4.40	13.20	1.25

*Based on the AAMD's definition of mental retardation (Grossman, 1983).
Concordance of the two diagnostics: 57.08%.
Inhelder's diagnostic more severe: 37.69%.
Inhelder's diagnostic less severe: 05.02%.

Her objective may have been misinterpreted, as she might have intended that her diagnosis should be considered along with other indicators, including IQ. In fact, she repeatedly emphasises that operational diagnoses should only be one of several information items within the whole clinical examination. She also advocates care when integrating operational diagnosis to all the other aspects of mental life. However, her criticism of intelligence tests and her definition of degrees of mental retardation leave little room for doubt: Inhelder did not realise that mental retardation is not to be defined psychologically but socially. Although her reference to an explicit developmental model helps to clarify the nature of retardation, it cannot, on its own, provide a diagnosis, which clearly depends on social expectations. Obviously, this objection is invalid when there is a perfect correspondence between social expectations and the cognitive abilities that address them. This is the case in early stages of development, which explains the generalised use of Uzgiris and Hunt's scale for young retarded children and severe retardation.

LINKS WITH MENTAL AGE AND IQ

Grading subjects between 1 and 7 (depending on the 7 levels of conservation) allows us to calculate a correlation between CA, MA, and IQ (see Table 2.4). As expected, the correlation between operational reasoning and the two other measures of intelligence is highly significant ($p < .0001$). As may also be expected, the correlation with MA (.70) is stronger than with IQ (.56), a relationship that persists after calculating partial correlations (.63 with MA and .43 with IQ). Pasnak, Willson-Quayle, and Whitten (1998) have recently reported similar results using three Piagetian tests (categorisation, seriation, and conservation of discrete quantities): They found correlations of .66 with IQ and of .77 with MA.

The link between reasoning levels and MA can be observed in Table 2.5: Operationality score increases as a function of MA. This confirms, if necessary, that the diagnosis of reasoning is, in fact, a developmental indicator. More interestingly, Inhelder's data show an IQ effect, which can easily be picked out in Table 2.5 by distinguishing three IQ levels. Robinson and Robinson (1976) mention an obvious 1- to 2-year operational delay between retarded and non-retarded subjects (matched for MA). This observation was not confirmed by Weisz and Yeates' (1981) review,

TABLE 2.4
Correlations between operational reasoning #, CA, MA, and IQ (n = 159)

	Operational reasoning	IQ	MA
CA	.09	−.32**	.20*
MA	.70**	.40**	−
IQ	.56**	−	−

#see the text.
*significant at $p < .01$.
**significant at $p < .0001$.

TABLE 2.5

Links between the score of operational reasoning (out of 7) and MA, in three levels of IQ

MA	IQ 105–85			IQ 84–65			IQ 64–41		
	n	Mean	SD	n	Mean	SD	n	Mean	SD
6	1	3	–	18	1,6	0,9	6	1	–
7	5	2,8	1,5	20	2,2	1,1	13	1,4	1,1
8	6	3,7	1,5	19	2,6	0,9	6	1,7	1
9	3	5	0	12	4,3	1,5	4	2	1,1
10	6	5	1,3	20	4,6	1,4	1	5	–
11	8	5,6	0,7	11	4,6	1,4			

which assembled 30 different studies allowing 104 comparisons of equal MA on 18 different conceptual domains (moral judgement, decentration, space, physical quantities, logic, probabilities, etc.). Their analysis shows that when subjects are sorted by aetiology, there are too few cases where, for a given MA, normal subjects perform better than retarded subjects of non-organic aetiology. On the basis of this analysis, Weisz and Yeates conclude that similar structures exist, which leads them to propose that mentally retarded subjects do seem to use the same cognitive processes. Inhelder's data do not necessarily contradict these findings. The effect of IQ on level of reasoning only seems to be apparent below a certain level of intelligence at which IQ weakness and organicity are confounded. Thus, it seems that the extent of retardation dissociates the relationship between MA and level of reasoning. This observation hints towards sensorimotor development dis-synchronies, mentioned earlier. In other words, while operational diagnosis is a clearly developmental measure, it measures something other than is measured in intelligence tests (see Carroll's factorial analyses, 1993).

Weisz and Yeates' meta-analysis data are especially interesting in the light of a second meta-analysis which was based on very diverse cognitive tasks, some of which were problem-solving tasks. Weiss, Weisz, and Bromfield (1986) observe that matching for MA does not always balance retarded and non-retarded performance: In several cases, retarded subjects were less efficient than non-retarded pairs. Haywood's (1987) review came to the same conclusion: He calls this phenomenon "mental age deficit". We will also cite Spitz's work (1987) which mentions striking efficiency differences in the solving the Tower of Hanoi problem, as well as Paour and Asselin de Beauville's research (1998) which shows that mentally retarded subjects are spontaneously less capable of abstracting a relational system when using free exploration computer-simulation tasks.

Such reduced efficiency has been interpreted either in favour of the deficit hypothesis (Spitz, 1987) or as the consequence of motivational differences (Burack, Hodapp, & Zigler 1990): the more motivating character of Piagetian tests would tend to minimise differences between ability and performance. In the light of the operational learning data, we tend to interpret the lower efficiency of mentally retarded people in problem-solving situations as the consequence of cognitive under-functioning, rather than being a deficit. We believe it is not the motivational character of Piagetian tests that explains their lower sensitivity to cognitive under-functioning, but their nature. We shall further discuss this issue when addressing the functional characteristics Inhelder pointed out.

What is left from the practical use of operational reasoning diagnosis? Essentially two things. First, it provides useful information to complete intelligence test data. This is particularly interesting when results diverge, either between different cognitive indicators (reasoning and IQ for example) or between different conceptual domains (Gibello, 1984; Schmid-Kitsikis, 1985, 1990). Second, information from operational tests seems more useful than traditional indicators to implement psycho-pedagogical interventions: It designates targets and provides a developmental guide.

FROM REASONING OSCILLATIONS TO A DYNAMIC CONCEPTION OF MENTAL RETARDATION

The conceptual development of mentally retarded people is thus essentially characterised by slowness and incompleteness: (1) It follows the normal sequence of developmental stages and expresses the same forms of synchronies; (2) the achievement of each stage leads to abilities that are comparable with those found in non-retarded children of the same level; (3) the sequence of developmental stages allows us to pinpoint levels of reasoning and subsequently adapt cognitive education; (4) the final level of reasoning allows us to evaluate the extent of retardation.

Inhelder, however, went beyond this striking demonstration. She understood that structural analysis as a psychological explanation leads to a dead-end: Delay cannot explain itself. Thus, in the last chapter of her thesis she attempted to complete this perspective with a functional analysis of reasoning.

With this in mind, Inhelder associated the qualitative differences just mentioned with certain protocols that seemed to illustrate pathological reasoning oscillations. By this we mean modifications to answers observed during identical quantity conservation tests; Inhelder characterises such answers as progressive, retrograde, or oscillating (see Table 2.6). In fact, oscillations themselves are not pathological, as non-retarded children also sometimes change their answers during tests, but the extent of the oscillations may be pathological: either through the magnitude of the differences between reasoning levels or through oscillation persistence. Like the other qualitative differences we have mentioned previously, such phenomena are fairly rare (15 out of 159 cases, barely more than 9%) and are mainly found in older subjects.

On the basis of these data, Inhelder (1943/1968) proposes an original hypothesis—that the slowness of development affects the nature of logical abilities and their implementation: "His mental level, which reflects very slow maturation, remains fragile. ... Even when he has attained a superior level, his thought bears the

TABLE 2.6

Pathological reasoning oscillations and other forms of equilibrium
(fixations at a stage and intermediate answers)

Forms of equilibrium	Males + Females (n = 159)		Males (n = 96)		Females (n = 63)	
	n	%	n	%	n	%
Fixation at a stage	125	78.6	73	76	52	82.5
Intermediate answers	19	11.9	14	14.5	5	7.9
Fixations + intermediate	144	90.5	87	90.6	57	90.1
Oscillations	4	2.5	2	2	2	3.1
Progressive oscillations	8	5.0	4	4.1	4	6.3
Retrograde oscillations	3	1.8	3	3.1	–	–
Oscillations total	15	9.4	9	9.3	6	9.5

imprint of a system or reasoning he has just outgrown. ... he runs a much greater risk than the normal child of hesitating between two systems of thought, which therefore coexist" (p. 290); "... traces of the previous level will persist much longer ... It is possible to be simultaneously confronted with two heterogeneous system in the same individual ..." (p. 292); "... the operation, not yet being pure ..." (p. 304).

The slowness of equilibration processes ("genetic viscosity") leads to a "false equilibrium" that weakens reasoning by making it more sensitive to perceptual factors, or to the intrusion of empirical knowledge and non-cognitive determinants (shyness, dependency, suggestibility, etc.). Oscillations are thus the result of changes in treatment mode or of treatment mode alternation. Retrograde oscillations, for example, would thus arise from abandoning empirical treatment, which leads to higher-level, non-logical answers, instead of applying a logical treatment that would bring the answer back down to the level of a subject's reasoning abilities. Cases of inter-test discrepancies would thus stand for the implementation of different types of rationality (logical or empirical), depending on the nature of the supports that were used and on the test progression. By selectively activating different treatment modes and modifying this activation during the test, non-cognitive factors can affect reasoning efficiency.

We can only be surprised at how contemporary Inhelder's functional analysis is regarding two essential issues. On the one hand, she explicitly postulates the existence of several treatment levels linked to the coexistence of heterogeneous results. Besides logical treatments, Inhelder pinpoints more pragmatic treatments, which rely on factual or empirical knowledge. In certain cases, the activation of factual knowledge provides answers that go beyond logical abilities: Even when subjects don't understand the logic of the conservation of matter, they will have had many occasions to observe the behaviour of sugar in water, especially the older subjects. On the other hand, the available logical treatments can be set aside by the uncontrolled activation of dangerous factual knowledge. Inhelder further postulates that the activation of these different levels of rationality are rooted in non-cognitive determinants, beyond perceptual factors, which exert their influence by centring attention. Depending on personal histories and emotional and motivational characteristics (Zigler & Balla, 1979), the reasoning of mentally retarded individuals is more exposed to fluctuations due to the ill-controlled activation of different treatments.

However interesting they may be, the concepts of pathological oscillation, false equilibrium, and genetic viscosity have not received much attention, despite the recurrence of issues like learning fragility or regression in special education. For example, Zigler and his colleagues have repeatedly ignored this "deficit perspective" of Inhelder's conception. This omission is especially noticeable because, in their evaluation of the similar sequence hypothesis, Weisz and Zigler (1979) illustrate the deficit hypothesis with a quotation from Milgram (1969) that could be straight out of Inhelder's last chapter: Mentally retarded subjects "are more likely to contain traces of developmentally earlier levels and more likely to show regression to those earlier levels" (p. 835). The lack of attention given by Stephens (1974) to Inhelder's most original contribution in her preface to the English translation of her (Inhelder's) book is another example.

It is true that in the absence of a non-retarded control group, Inhelder's observations remain anecdotal, and the described phenomena remain fairly discrete. Their rarity has been confirmed by later studies, which do not often mention oscillation phenomena. In her comparative longitudinal study, Stephens (1974; Stephens & McLaughlin, 1971, 1974) indicates, for example, that from one evaluation to the next regression phenomena seem more marked in retarded subjects, but the coding methods she used make it difficult to appreciate this observation. This is why research by Schmidt-Kitsikis (1976) is valuable, as it explicitly addresses the issue of reasoning oscillations. Comparing the behaviour of mentally retarded and psychotic children in a series of operational tasks, Schmidt-Kitsikis shows that oscillations observed in retarded children are perfectly rational compared with psychotic children. It seems that, unlike psychotic children, mentally retarded individuals show progress after short learning periods, which is perfectly compatible with genetic hierarchy. However, sensorimotor follow-ups seem to emphasise regression phenomena from one evaluation to the next more frequently in mentally retarded subjects (Dunst, 1990; Hodapp & Zigler, 1997). Results of such tasks led Hodapp and Zigler to recognise Inhelder's pioneering role in describing the fragility of reasoning.

Globally speaking, regression and oscillation phenomena are relatively rare in Piagetian tasks. This does not mean they should be of no interest to us. First, these tasks deliberately do not include much semantic content, in order to require the treatment of "logical" dimensions. Let us remember that it is tasks with more semantic content (weight transitivity and sugar dissolution) that lead to intra-individual discordances, and that it is mainly in the weight conservation task, which involves the most semantic content, that Inhelder observes the most oscillation cases. Later, in an intercultural comparison, Bovet (1968) demonstrated that answers regarding the concept of mass can be "contaminated" by social practice.

In addition, the type of interaction taking place, which optimises functioning, can lead subjects to operate rational problem treatments. We have already mentioned that the clinical method Inhelder chose to use led her to witness only the best kind of reasoning in her subjects. Under such conditions, it is indeed remarkable that she was able to notice the few available manifestations and understand their importance despite their rarity.

These few qualitative differences and striking oscillations can be associated with low efficiency of mentally retarded subjects in problem-solving situations. Inhelder provides a good example of this aspect in the preface to the second edition of her thesis, published in 1963: After mentioning that mental retardation appears to be characterised by strong homogeneity between reasoning domains, she cites an exception. This involves a combinatory task in which mentally retarded subjects show much lower levels of reasoning than they show in other Piagetian tasks. A similar efficiency differential is observed by Spitz with the Tower of Hanoi problem. We think that the combinatory test is a genuine problem-solving task for subjects without pre-formal logical abilities, which is generally not the case for operational tasks. Thus we do not consider that the equal efficiency of mentally retarded subjects in Piagetian tasks is due to the motivating character of the tasks, but rather to the fact that they are not really problem-solving tasks. As they require minimal control, they hardly enable the expression of differences in functioning. They were not constructed for such a purpose, but instead to rapidly activate previously existing conceptual levels.

Differences in cognitive efficiency are only occasionally apparent in operational tasks, and the fact they may be due to emotional and motivational factors must not lead us to minimise them. In fact, operational learning data tell us that cognitive under-functioning prevents mentally retarded subjects from fully developing their intellectual potential. It may even be possible that its cumulative effect throughout development contributes non-negligibly to the formation of mental retardation. Inhelder does not defend a psychogenetic hypothesis of mental retardation: She does not consider genetic viscosity to be the cause of retardation; however, she postulates that, as in non-retarded children, functional dynamics contribute to cognitive development. This is how we interpret the quotation from Inhelder at the beginning of this chapter. We must emphasise that, generally speaking, attempts to use Piagetian models in psychopathology have neglected such dynamics in favour of structural analysis. Schmid-Kitsikis and Ajuriaguerra (1973) emphasised that such work rarely achieves explanatory levels precisely because they favour the study of structural aspects (searching for stages and their appearance) rather than functional issues (studying structure transformation processes and their implementation in various activities). This is especially to be regretted because, as we have tried to demonstrate, Inhelder had opened an avenue for the functional analysis of conceptual development. We also believe that developmental conceptions of mental retardation, as expressed by Zigler, do not completely cover this key constructivist dimension.

Must we then place Inhelder's hypothesis among the deficit theories, due to her insistence on "unusual" aspects of reasoning? This question involves determining the status (normal or pathological) that reasoning fragility should be given. Inhelder is not clear about this issue and the concepts of false equilibrium and genetic viscosity have been criticised for being ambiguous in this respect (Perron, 1979). It is true that Piagetian conceptions of equilibration hardly account for oscillation and regression (including retrograde) phenomena. Fragility would be considered a deficit if it remained permanently ingrained in constructed conceptual elaborations. It would only be considered functional if it remained temporary, and disappeared before final conceptualisation. The imposing aspect of sequential identity, and especially the operational learning data, lead us to reject the hypothesis that fragility definitively affects cognitive abilities. According to Inhelder's functional analysis (which we described earlier) we think that reasoning fragility is permanently functional but temporarily structural: Permanently functional because, throughout development, slowness due to mental retardation merges with cognitive under-functioning to permanently impair conceptualisation processes; temporarily structural because it does not influence conceptual stages, once they are achieved.

Distinguishing several stages in conceptualisation processes (Bang & Gillièron, 1983; Karmiloff-Smith, 1992; Piaget, 1974)—attentional success, followed by understanding this success, which leads to genuine conceptualisation—allows us to consider reasoning fragility to be relatively permanent each time a subject fails to achieve his or her development and go beyond the phase of attentional success. Under such circumstances, reasoning remains potentially fragile because it is exposed to interferences of the kind Inhelder mentioned (dangerous empirical knowledge, motivation) and depends on attention levels. We can expect the transition from attentional success to comprehension to be particularly vulnerable in mentally retarded individuals. It requires the implementation of both a relatively efficient cognitive treatment for the abstraction of relational systems, and the adoption of intrinsic motivation (task-oriented, and especially towards functioning within the task). We know that mentally retarded individuals: (1) tend to use associative learning strategies instead of relational ones (Achenbach & Zigler, 1968); and (2) are rather extrinsically motivated (Haywood & Switzky, 1986) and tend towards outer-directedness (Zigler & Burack, 1989).

This attempt to pursue Inhelder's functional analysis leads us to emphasise, in conclusion, the key idea we were struck by when re-reading *The diagnosis of reasoning in the mentally retarded*: it is essential to bring developmental approaches to mental retardation into a genuinely constructivist perspective. This can be achieved by integrating two aspects into our psychological conceptions of mental retardation: the possible structural limitations weighing on development, and daily cognitive functioning, on which fortunately we can have a positive influence.

ACKNOWLEDGEMENTS

This chapter was translated from French by Nadine Allal. Many thanks to Sylvie Cèbe and Marie-Thérèse Paour for revising this chapter's manuscript.

REFERENCES

Abel, T.M. (1941). Moral judgments among subnormals. *Journal of Abnormal and Social Psychology, 6*, 378–392.

Achenbach, T., & Zigler, E. (1968). Cue-learning and problem-solving strategies in normal and retarded children. *Child Development, 39*, 827–848.

Adey, A., & Shayer, M. (1994). *Really raising standards: Cognitive intervention and academic achievement.* London/New York: Routledge.

Bang, V., & Gillièron, C. (1983). Pourquoi les lampes ne s'allument-elles pas? Conscience du but et conscience des moyens [Why can't the lamps be turned on? Being conscious of the goal or of the means]. *Archives de Psychologie, 51*, 111–115.

Baumeister, A.A. (1997). Behavioral research: Boom or bust? In W.E. MacLean, Jr. (Ed.), *Ellis' handbook of mental deficiency, psychological theory and research* (3rd ed., pp. 3–46). Mahwah, NJ: Lawrence Erlbaum Associates Inc.

Binet, A., & Simon, T. (1908). Le développement de l'intelligence chez les enfants [The development of intelligence in children]. *L'Année Psychologique, 14*, 1–94.

Boersma, F.J., & Wilton, K. (1976). Eye movements and conservation acceleration in mildly retarded children. *American Journal of Mental Deficiency, 80*, 636–643.

Bolton, S., Haller, O., & Gourlay, T. (1987). *Jean Piaget Archives bibliography on mental retardation.* Calgary: The Vocational and Rehabilitation Research Institute.

Bovet, M. (1968). Études interculturelles du développement intellectuel et processus d'apprentissage [Intercultural research into intellectual development and learning processes]. *Revue Suisse de Psychologie Pure et Appliquée, 27*, 89–200.

Brison, D.W., & Bereiter, C. (1967). Acqusition of conservation of substance in normal, retarded and gifted children. In D.W. Brison & E.V. Sullivan (Eds.), *Recent research on the acquisition of conservation of substance.* Toronto: The Ontario Institute of Studies in Education.

Burack, J.A., Hodapp, R.M., & Zigler, E. (1990). Technical note: Toward a more precise understanding of mental retardation. *Journal of Child Psychology and Psychiatry, 31*, 471–475.

Campione, J.C., & Brown, A.L. (1984). Learning ability and transfer propensity as sources of individual differences in intelligence. In P. Brooks, H.R. Sperber, & C. McCauley (Eds.), *Learning and cognition in the mentally retarded.* Hillsdale, NJ: Lawrence Erlbaum Associates Inc.

Carroll, J.B. (1993). *Human cognitive abilities: A survey of factor-analytic studies.* Cambridge: Cambridge University Press.

Case, R., Sandieson, R., & Dennis, S. (1986). Two cognitive-developmental approaches to the design of remedial instruction. *Cognitive Development, 1*, 293–333.

Cicchetti, D., & Mans-Wagener, L. (1987). Sequences, stages, and structures in the organization of cognitive development in infants with Down syndrome. In I. Uzgiris & J.M. Hunt (Eds.), *Infant performance and experience: New findings with the ordinal scales* (pp. 281–310). Urbana: University of Illinois Press.

Dunst, C.J. (1990). Sensorimotor development of infants with Down syndrome. In D. Cicchetti & M. Beeghly (Eds.), *Children with Down syndrome: A developmental perspective* (pp. 180–230). New York: Cambridge University Press.

Feuerstein, R., Rand, Y., & Hoffman, M. (1979). *The dynamic assessment of retarded performers: The Learning Potential Assessment Device, theory, instruments and techniques.* Baltimore: University Park Press.

Field, D. (1974). Long term effects of conservation training with educationally subnormal children. *Journal of Special Education, 7–8,* 449–461.

Gibello, B. (1984). *L'enfant à l'intelligence troublée* [The child with disturbed intelligence]. Paris: Le Centurion.

Goustard, M., Gréco, P., Matalon, B., & Piaget, J. (Eds.). (1959). *La logique des apprentissages* (vol. X). Paris: Presses Universitaires de France.

Gréco, P., & Piaget, J. (Eds.). (1959). Apprentissages et connaissance (vol. VII). Paris: Presses Universitaires de France.

Griffin, S., & Case, R. (1997). Re-thinking the primary school math curriculum: An approach based on cognitive science. *Issues in Education, 3,* 1–49.

Grossman, H.J. (Ed.). (1983). *Classification in mental retardation.* Washington DC: American Association on Mental Deficiency.

Hatwell, Y. (1966). *Privation sensorielle et intelligence. Effets de la cécité précoce sur la genèse des structures logiques élémentaires* [Sensory deficit and intelligence: Effects of early blindness on the genesis of elementary logical structures]. Paris: Presses Universitaires de France.

Haywood, H.C. (1987). The mental age deficit: Explanation and treatment. *Upsala Journal of Medical Sciences, Suppl. 44,* 191–203.

Haywood, H.C., & Switzky, N.H. (1986). Intrinsic motivation and behavior effectiveness in retarded persons. In N.R. Ellis & N.W. Bray (Eds.), *International review of research in mental retardation* (pp. 1–46). New York: Academic Press.

Haywood, H.C., & Tzuriel, D. (Eds.). (1992). *Interactive assessment.* New York: Springer-Verlag.

Hodapp, R.M., & Zigler, E. (1990). Applying the developmental perspective to individuals with Down syndrome. In D. Cicchetti & M. Beeghly (Eds.), *Children with Down syndrome: A developmental perspective* (pp. 1–28). New York: Cambridge University Press.

Hodapp, R.M., & Zigler, E. (1997). New issues in the developmental approach to mental retardation. In E. MacLean, Jr (Ed.), *Ellis' handbook of mental deficiency, psychological theory and research.* Mahwah, NJ: Lawrence Erlbaum Associates Inc.

Inhelder, B. (1966). Cognitive development and its contribution to the diagnosis of some phenomena of mental deficiency. *Merrill-Palmer Quarterly of Behavior and Development, 12,* 299–319.

Inhelder, B. (1968). *The diagnosis of reasoning in the mentally retarded* (B. Stephens, Trans.). New York: The John Day Company. (Original work published 1943).

Inhelder, B., & Cellérier, G. (Eds.), (1992). *Le cheminement des découvertes de l'enfant.* Neuchâtel: Delachaux & Niestlé.

Inhelder, B., & Piaget, J., (1958). *The growth of logical thinking from childhood to adolescence.* London: Routledge & Kegan Paul. (Original work published 1955).

Inhelder, B., Sinclair, H., & Bovet, M. (1974). *Learning and the development of cognition* (S. Wedgwood, Trans.). Cambridge, MA: Harvard University Press.

Kahn, J.T. (1985). Evidence of the similar structure hypothesis: Controlling for organicity. *American Journal of Mental Deficiency, 89,* 372–378.

Karmiloff-Smith, A. (1992). *Beyond modularity: A developmental perspective on cognitive science*. Cambridge, MA: MIT Press.

Lane, E.B., & Kinder, E.F. (1936). Relativism in the thinking of subnormal subjects as measured by certain of Piaget's tests. *Journal of Genetic Psychology, 54*,107–118.

Lister, C. (1972). The development of E.S.N. children's understanding of conservation in a range of attribute situation. *The British Journal of Educational Psychology, 42,* 14–22.

Maier, R. (1993). Imbecility, feeble-mindedness and normality: The diagnosis enterprise of Inhelder and its consequences. *Archives de Psychologie, 61,* 173–179.

McCormick, P.K., Campbell, J.W., Pasnak, R., & Perry, P. (1990). Instruction on piagetian concepts for children with mental retardation. *Mental Retardation, 28,* 359–366.

Milgram, N.A. (1969). The rationale and irrational in Zigler's motivational approach to mental retardation. *American Journal of Mental Deficiency, 73,* 527–532.

Morf, A., Smedslund, J., Vinh-Bang, & Wohlwill, J.F. (Eds.). (1959). *L'apprentissage des structures logiques* (vol. XIX). Paris: Presses Universitaires de France.

Mundy, P., Seibert, J., & Hogan, A. (1984). Relationship between sensorimotor and early communication abilities in developmentally delayed children. *Merrill-Palmer Quarterly, 30,* 33–48.

Paour, J.-L. (1992). Induction of logic structures in the mentally retarded: An assessment and intervention instrument. In H.C. Haywood & D. Tzuriel (Eds.), *Interactive assessment* (pp. 119–166). New York: Springer-Verlag.

Paour, J.-L., & Asselin de Beauville, É. (1998). Une étude de la flexibilité du fonctionnement cognitif chez des adolescents présentant un retard mental léger [A study on flexibility of cognitive functioning in children with a mild mental retardation]. In F. Büchel, J.-L. Paour, C. Courbois, & U. Scharnhorst (Eds.), *Attention, mémoire, apprentissage. Études sur le retard mental* (pp. 153–166). Lucerne: Edition SZH/SPC.

Paour, J.-L., Cèbe, S., & Haywood, H.C. (2000). Learning to learn in preschool education: Effect on later school achievement. *Journal of Cognitive Education and Psychology, 1*(1). (On-line publication, www.iace,coged.org/journa)

Pasnak, R., Willson-Quayle, A., & Whitten, J. (1998). Mild retardation, academic achievement, and piagetian or psychometric tests of reasoning. *Journal of Developmental and Physical Disabilities, 10,* 23–33.

Perron, R. (1979). Le concept de déficience mentale. Évolution des théories, des attitudes et des pratiques [The concept of mental deficiency: The evolution of theories, attitudes and practice]. *Archives Suisses de Neurochirurgie et de Psychiatrie, 124,* 113–127.

Perry, P., Pasnak, R., & Holt, R.W. (1992). Instruction on concrete operations for children who are mildly mentally retarded. *Education and Training in Mental Retardation, 27,* 273–281.

Piaget, J. (1968). Foreword to the first edition. In B. Inhelder, *The diagnosis of reasoning in the mentally retarded* (pp. 9–12). New York: The John Day Company. (Original work published 1943).

Piaget, J. (1974). *Success and understanding* (A.J. Pomerans, Trans.). London: Routledge & Kegan Paul.

Piaget, J., & Inhelder, B. (1974). *The child's construction of quantities: Conservation and atomism* (A.J. Pomerans, Trans.). London: Routledge & Kegan Paul. (Original work published 1941).

Robinson, N., & Robinson, B.B. (1976). *The mentally retarded child: A psychological approach*. New York: McGraw-Hill.

Schmid-Kitsikis, E. (1976). The cognitive mechanisms underlying problem-solving in psychotic and mentally retardate children. In B. Inhelder & H. Chipman (Eds.), *Piaget and his school* (pp. 234–255). New York: Springer-Verlag.

Schmid-Kitsikis, E. (1985). *Théorie et clinique du fonctionnement mental* [Theory and practice of mental functioning]. Bruxelles: Mardaga.

Schmid-Kitsikis, E. (Ed.). (1990). *An interpersonal approach to mental functioning; Assessment and treatment.* New York: Springer-Verlag.

Schmid-Kitsikis, E., & Ajuriaguerra J. de (1973). Aspects opératoires en psychopathologie infantile [Operatory aspects in infant psychopathology]. *Revue de Neuropsychiatrie Infantile, 21,* 7–21.

Spitz, H.H. (1987). Problem-solving processes in special populations. In J.G. Borkowski & J.D. Day (Eds.), *Cognition in special children: Comparative approaches to retardation, learning disabilities, and giftedness* (pp. 153–193). Norwood: Ablex Publishing Corporation.

Stephens, B. (1974). Symposium: Developmental gains in the reasoning, moral judgment, and moral conduct of retarded persons. *American Journal of Mental Deficiency, 79,* 113–115.

Stephens, B., & McLaughlin, J.A. (1971). Analysis of performances by normals and retardates on piagetian reasoning assessments as a function of verbal ability. *Perceptual and Motor Skills, 32,* 868–870.

Stephens, B., & McLaughlin, J.A. (1974). Two years gains in reasoning by retarded and nonretarded persons. *American Journal of Mental Deficiency, 79,* 16–126.

Uzgiris, I.C., & Hunt, J.M. (1975). *Assessment in infancy: Ordinal scale of psychological development.* Urbana: University of Illinois Press.

Wallon, H. (1925). *L'enfant turbulent. Étude sur les retards et les anomalies du développement moteur et mental* [The turbulent child: A study on retardation and anomalies in motor and mental development]. Paris: Alcan.

Weiss, B., Weisz, J., & Bromfield, R. (1986). Performance of retarded and nonretarded persons in information-processing tasks: Further tests of the similar structure hypothesis. *Psychological Bulletin, 100,* 157–175.

Weisz, J., & Yeates, K. (1981). Cognitive development in retarded and nonretarded persons: Piagetian tests of the similar structure hypothesis. *Psychological Bulletin, 90,* 153–178.

Weisz, J., & Zigler, E. (1979). Cognitive development in retarded and nonretarded persons: Piagetian tests of the similar sequence hypothesis. *Psychological Bulletin, 86,* 831–851.

Williams, K.C. (1996). Piagetian principles: Simple and effective application. *Journal of Intellectual Disability Research, 40,* 110–119.

Wilton, K.M., & Boersma, F.J. (1974). Conservation research with the mentally retarded. *International Review of Research in Mental Retardation, Vol. 7.* New York: Academic Press.

Woodward, W.M. (1959). The behavior of idiots interpreted by Piaget's theory of sensori-motor development. *British Journal of Educational Psychology, 29,* 60–71.

Woodward, W.M. (1963). The application of Piaget's theory to research in mental deficiency. In N.R. Ellis (Ed.), *Handbook of mental deficiency, psychological theory and research* (pp. 297–324). New York: McGraw-Hill.

Woodward, W.M. (1979). Piaget's theory and the study of mental retardation. In N.R. Ellis (Ed.), *Handbook of mental deficiency, psychological theory and research* (pp. 169–196). Hillsdale, NJ: Lawrence Erlbaum Associates Inc.

Zazzo, R. (1972). La pratique des tests dans l'examen des débiles mentaux [The use of tests in the examination of the mentally retarded]. In J. Petit (Ed.), *Les enfants et les adolescents inadaptés et l'Éducation Nationale*, Vol. 1. Paris: Armand Colin.

Zazzo, R. (1973). Les débiles mentaux [The mentally retarded]. In M. Reuchlin (Ed.), *Traité de psychologie appliquée*, Vol. 7. Paris: Presses Universitaires de France.

Zigler, E. (1962). Rigidity in the feebleminded. In E. Trapp & P. Himelstein (Eds.), *Readings on the exceptional child* (pp. 141–162). New York: Appleton-Century-Croft.

Zigler, E. (1967). Familial mental retardation: A continuing dilemma. *Science*, *155*, 292–298.

Zigler, E. (1969). Developmental vs. difference theories of mental retardation and the problem of motivation. *American Journal of Mental Deficiency*, *73*, 536–556.

Zigler, E., & Burack, I.A. (1989). Personality development and the dually diagnosed person. *Research in Developmental Disabilities*, *10*, 225–240.

Zigler, E., & Balla, D. (1979). Personality development in retarded persons. In N.R. Ellis (Ed.), *Handbook of mental deficiency, psychological theory and research* (pp. 143–168). Hillsdale, NJ: Lawrence Erlbaum Associates Inc.

Zigler, E., & Yando, R. (1972). Outerdirectedness and imitative behavior of institutionalized and noninstitutionalized younger and older children. *Child Development*, *43*, 413–425.

CHAPTER THREE

Perspective taking in the aftermath of theory-theory and the collapse of the social role-taking literature

Michael Chandler
University of British Columbia, Vancouver, Canada

Collectively, the several chapters that make up this volume are intended to assemble a mosaic of Bärbel Inhelder's long and distinguished career, and to bring out the ways in which her work continues to inform and steer the course of contemporary research and theory. The particular part of this larger undertaking that is taken up in this chapter is the task of following that thread of her programme of research concerned with the development of children's abilities to adopt the perspectives of others. Although, as a matter of historical obligation, this assignment naturally sets Piaget and Inhelder's 1948 book *La représentation de l'espace chez l'enfant* (*The child's conception of space*) as my primary text, and requires that I give pride of place to their key chapter on "The co-ordination of perspectives", I will not make this the only, or even the central business of what follows. Rather, my job, as I have read it, is to view this classic text with an eye towards its continuing impact on the ongoing efforts of the discipline to understand how it is that young persons gain some mature understanding of the perspectival character of all knowledge. However, as I hope to make plain, doing just this is not at all the same thing as relegating *The child's conception of space* to the status of some cobwebbed footnote of merely historical interest. Instead, I hope to show that history—in this case the history of research into the perspective-taking process—once again threatens to come full circle, as 50 years of interim work now appear to be leading us back to a set of insights already more or less explicitly contained in Piaget and Inhelder's original text. Perhaps there is some room for talking spirals here but, if so, their coils are wound exceedingly tight, and it is hard to escape the impression that those of us who have spent many years investigating one or another aspect of the development of perspective-taking competence may well have been wasting a lot of your and our precious time.

With or without evidence of genuine progress there is, nevertheless, a real story to be told here and, as with canonical stories more generally, it begins with a mystery and meanders towards some plot resolution, while managing to sandwich a whole lot of "trouble" in between (Bruner, 1990; Burke, 1945). The mystery here is plain enough. Adults obviously operate in a world that constantly requires that they mark the differences between their own and others' perspectives, or the difference between their own dated and now more current perspectives, and, of course, most of us regularly comply. Very young children, just as obviously, do none of these things, but, as essentially every celebrated student of human development has remarked (e.g., Baldwin, 1906; Piaget, 1926), behave instead as though all the world operated with reference to their own idiosyncratic viewpoint. Exactly *how* and *when* we all, by and large, manage to make it from point A to point B is clearly the puzzle, and attempts to work out how this is accomplished form the plot of our story. The "trouble", as I will be at some pains to show, is that each time our collective research community seems to be on the verge of getting some piece of explanatory machinery suitable for this purpose up and running, its wheels always seem to fall off in a dramatic fashion. The debris from these crash sites is the stuff of which the balance of this chapter is constructed.

AGENDA

As told here, this story unfolds in four parts. *Part One* is really a prologue, and is meant to say something quick and synoptic about Piaget and Inhelder's catalytic research using the now famous three mountains procedure, and to highlight important aspects of this work that have often been obscured in the retelling. *Part Two* concerns the decade covering the late 1960s and early 1970s, describes work done in direct reaction to the 1956, 1963, and 1967 English-language translations of *The child's conception of space*, and is all about a rising tide of research into every conceivable aspect of children's emerging perspective-taking competence. Here the narrative divides into two streams. The first of these, a mere trickle in comparison to the second, comprises what eventually became roughly 100 more or less ugly, brutish, and short parametric variations on the three mountains procedure. The second and broader of these streams is altogether more meandering and constitutes a current of work that formed an eventual flood of nearly 1000 analogical research efforts, all concerned with documenting the developmental course of sundry things variously referred to as "egocentrism", "sociocentrism", and "role-taking competence", as well as "conceptual", "social", and "affective" perspective taking. Although occasional sightings are still reported, both of these streams of work effectively dried up in the late 1970s and early 1980s, when their respective research programmes fell into incoherence.

Part Three addresses the so-called "theory-of-mind" literature which, while a bona fide chapter in this same story, is so regularly told in a different voice, and is so full of claims about having emerged fully grown from the heads of comparative ethologists and contemporary philosophers of mind, that it is often imagined to be about something else entirely. Notwithstanding, then, its ahistorical claims to be only about such things as "theory-theory" and the possibility of false belief, I mean to suggest that this work is the natural heir to the earlier and now moribund perspective-taking tradition, out of whose ashes it has arisen like some amnesic phoenix. Although clearly the apple of the new cognitive science's otherwise jaundiced eye, it too, I will allege, is bobbing in a sea of "troubles", all of its own making. That is, like the spoiler notions that brought down the role- and perspective-taking enterprise a decade earlier, this new research enterprise also rests on a fundamentally non-developmental, "one-miracle" view of cognitive growth—a view according to which children who are thought to initially lack any capacity for recognising "representational diversity" somehow transform themselves, in one fell swoop, into the proud owners of a new and fully representational or "interpretive" theory of mind.

Finally, in *Part Four* I report on a recent second generation of studies of representational diversity that, while still masquerading in the livery of the theory-theory cult, is nevertheless hard at work laying out a developmental course concerning the emergence of beliefs about beliefs that, in the end, comes remarkably close to a similar story told 50 years ago by Inhelder and by Piaget.

PART ONE:
"THE COORDINATION OF PERSPECTIVES"—A PROLOGUE

Chapter 8 of Piaget and Inhelder's *The child's conception of space* is a slim document consisting (in its most recent English-language translation) of only 37 printed pages. Although I have no intention of attempting yet another close exegesis of this largely self-explanatory work, I do mean to make room for three remarks, mostly about certain of its originally sharp features that, over the decades, have been largely worn away as a consequence of repeated rough handling.

First, anyone bothering to re-read this document with fresh eyes would, I think it is worth saying, be impressed by just how thoroughly and uncharacteristically modern the whole thing is. Notwithstanding Piaget and Inhelder's usual practice of giving over large chunks of texts to verbatim reports of their subjects' exact remarks, the document is not very different from something that might easily have just landed on the desk of this or that contemporary journal editor. A nicely rounded sample of 100 subjects aged 4–12 was enlisted; the particular stimulus materials and assessment procedures employed are painstakingly described; and the exact scoring criteria employed are all laid out with sometimes mind-numbing modern precision.

Second, although the original text is filled with detailed descriptions of precisely what children think they and others are actually "seeing", the chapter, and in fact the whole book, ends up having surprisingly little to do with perception, spatial or otherwise. Instead, as Piaget and Inhelder are at considerable pains to point out, the coordinated system of perspectives that the child builds up in the course of the several "substages" is not really "perceptual" at all, but is instead fundamentally "conceptual in character" (Piaget & Inhelder, 1948/1963, p. 245). If, over the last 50 years, more attention had actually been paid to this important fact, then a lot of lambs otherwise sacrificed on the altar of "perceptual vs conceptual perspective taking" might well have been spared.

Third—and this is perhaps my main point about this wellspring chapter—Piaget and Inhelder's text is not, as is frequently imagined, an "either–or" story about how children start off being profoundly egocentric, and then, as if by magic, suddenly end up perspectival. Rather, their work on the "coordination of perspectives" is, if anything, a detailed itinerary of that slow, step-wise developmental process by which children are eventually led to some better understanding of those "real coordinations" that actually obtain among the multiple perspectives afforded by "one and the same" experiential event. What it is not at all about, as many subsequent "replication" studies have mistakenly alleged, is the business of locating some precise, singular, and salutary moment of onset when the scales of egocentrism fall abruptly and completely from young children's eyes. In fact, Piaget and Inhelder are at great pains throughout their chapter to point out that children of all ages are constantly en route towards some eventually unqualified relativism of thought. Even by the end of the first year, they point out (p. 218), "the child has already arrived at a constancy of shape for small objects ... [and] ... by the end of his third year (during Stage I) has already achieved some sort of representational constancy for large objects such as buildings, mountains, and so on." Similarly, children as young as 3 or 4 are credited with the realisation "... that mountains [actually] look different from different places" (p. 216), and so rightly ascribe such "apparent changes of shape to changed point of view" (p. 218). Consequently, Piaget and Inhelder are quite explicit in their claim that even the youngest of their subjects, who were all capable of understanding their questions (i.e., Substage IIA), were "perfectly well aware that the appearance of the group of mountains changed together with the observer's point of view" (p. 216), and so by 6 or 7 were "already aware that the observer will experience an image different from his own ..." (p. 218). What justifies this dense thicket of direct quotations is the fact that, having otherwise overlooked all of these plain words, whole generations of latter-day psychologists have managed to work themselves into an outrage over the mere prospect that children as old as 10 or even 12—children on the very doorstep of adulthood—might still somehow be egocentric. Swiss children, it is allowed, might well drag their developmental feet in this fashion, but certainly not children of the "new world", who, it is generally assumed, all become perspectival at a much more tender age.

Leaving aside all such ethnocentric rhetoric, what Piaget and Inhelder did actually claim was that, well into middle childhood, young persons typically continue to show "vestiges" (p. 231) or "residual traces of spatial egocentrism" (p. 233) that interfere with their ability to "fully" (p. 231) distinguish their own and others' points of view. The ongoing problems in perspective taking that plague such school-age children, they argued, centre around their continuing inability to appreciate that, in addition to simply presenting different faces to differently situated observers, the actual internal *relations* that obtain among the elements of any complex display will also "vary with each vantage point taken" (p. 233). Consequently, simply appreciating that different people see different things, or that a given picture could not be taken from "just anywhere", is one thing; it is quite another to "logically multiply" the internal, multiple, projective relations that obtain between such objects, and to do so in a way that permits them to be welded into a unified, homogeneous and coordinated system "that permits one to see the correspondences that exist between all possible points of view" (p. 242).

The prospect that children might typically prove to be 9 going on 12 before mastering these lofty accomplishments should not, it can be argued, be surprising. The real surprise, if there is one, is that children of any age actually manage to accomplish such feats at all. Of course, Piaget and Inhelder insisted that they did, and had the last 50 years of related research really resulted in a serious test of their claims, then we might now be in a position to weigh such evidence. As it is, the literature to which I now turn has been, by and large, about something entirely different. Rather than sharing in Piaget and Inhelder's enthusiasm for working out the long details of what is involved in becoming fully perspectival, what subsequent inquiring minds have apparently been most interested in is precisely when young persons can safely be said to have put "childhood egocentricism" comfortably behind them. The recurrent answer to this threshold question, you will see, is that it always occurs earlier than experts of an earlier generation would ever have imagined, even in their wildest dreams.

PART TWO:
THE DECADE OF PIAGET AND INHELDER'S "RE-BIRTH"

For almost 20 years following its publication, *The child's conception of space* lived in that quaint backwater that at least North American psychology once reserved for the whole of Genevois psychology. Then, along with the demise of classical behaviourism, the arrival of Sputnik, the "new look" in psychology, the free-speech and desegregation movements, and the general waning of colonialism on every front, the rest of the psychological world finally began to grasp that one epistemology might not actually fit all. One result of all of this was the onset, in the 1960s, of what Kessen (1996) has dubbed "the decade of the rebirth of Piaget". Suddenly new life began to be breathed into the attendant idea that problems in perspective taking were worthy of study, and stock in the three mountains task began to rise dramatically. As already hinted at in the introduction, the resultant outpouring of new research eager to trace its intellectual roots back to *The child's conception of space* quickly divided into two streams. The discussion of the larger of these, the one that came to concern itself with the broad topics of "conceptual", "social", and "affective" perspective taking, will be the subject of a later section. For the moment, I mean to restrict attention to the smaller of these separate currents of research, by first considering only those studies that had as their narrow purpose somehow "replicating" or otherwise extending Piaget and Inhelder's original work dealing with "visual" or "spatial" perspective taking in general, and the three mountains task in particular.

"Replications" of the three mountains task

Both early and all along the way, there have been a surprisingly large number (something in the order of 100) of attempts to directly "replicate", or otherwise "extend", Piaget and Inhelder's classic findings with respect to the three mountains task. Before going on to examine some of the details of this work, it seems useful to reflect on the often dim prospects held out for such replication efforts and why, given the general absence of professional incentives for ever doing anything twice, there are any such studies to be found at all. The problem, of course, is that whatever else we may have heard about the virtues of "replication" as a mainstay of the scientific method, the hard reality is typically something quite otherwise: In a professional world where only novelty really sells, any optimistic attempt to replicate anyone's work, including one's own, is likely to prove a poor investment. Consequently, when they do appear, what end up being billed as "replications" are rarely the work of one's "friends" (who wisely suspect that their efforts will be treated dismissively), and are instead much more likely to be the work of one's professional "enemies" (who often see some profit in gainsaying claims that differ from their own). Given this, much of what tends to be listed under the broad banner of replication studies often ends up looking more like some form of "bear baiting", better suited to further inciting already committed nay-sayers than actually helping to adjudicate anything. That, I am sorry to report, is not only how things are generally, but also in the present instance, where the bulk of writing about the three mountains task both begins and ends with the premise that the whole of Piaget and Inhelder's project is so cumbersome and fundamentally flawed that nothing short of beginning again with some other less unruly, or more "minimally complex", assessment strategy could possibly do.

That aside, there were, of course, a few early friends in court who, in their initial flush of excitement over their discovery (or re-discovery) of Piaget and Inhelder's work, undertook what amounted to straight-up attempts at replication (e.g., Elkind, 1985; Flavell et al., 1968; Laurendeau & Pinard, 1970). By and large, these earliest efforts at replication met with the sort of general success that always serves to further incite one's critics, and to backlight one's work as a target for their less friendly fire. While the odd result did continue to appear that lent further strength to one or another of Piaget and Inhelder's original findings (e.g., Fishbein, Lewis, & Keiffer, 1972; Flavell, Everett, Croft, & Flavell, 1981a; Flavell, Flavell, Green, & Wilcox, 1981b; Gzesh & Surber, 1985; Liben, 1978; etc.), the majority of so-called "replication" studies that appeared after the early 1970s were done by those who were already set on demonstrating just how seriously mistaken it was to imagine that children went on being egocentric beyond their tender years.

What followed was a long and still ongoing series of parametric studies, all meant to demonstrate that something or other about the original three mountains task worked to obscure children's true perspective-taking talents. Forgetting that the Salève, which served as the model for Piaget and Inhelder's stimulus materials, was as familiar as an old shoe to most Genevois children, some argued that the standard display actually lacked familiarity, and so attempted to substitute stimulus arrays composed of various nursery-school toys. Others (e.g., Nigl & Fishbein, 1974) found the original procedure altogether too dependent on the ability of young children to deal with two-dimensional representations of three-dimensional space, or to take the point of view of hypothetical persons, and so asked children to respond with reference to three-dimensional models, or substituted real people for the doll sometimes used by Piaget and Inhelder. Others, worried that the irregular character of the original three mountains display might cause children to adopt initially helpful, but ultimately limiting "non-spatial strategies" (e.g., Jacobsen & Waters, 1985), substituted more symmetrical geometric shapes. Others still, concerned that children's unfamiliarity with the procedures of the three mountains task might work to obscure their real abilities, introduced various drills or training sessions meant to help subjects over the initial shock of the unfamiliar. Many researchers, forgetting that Piaget and Inhelder's primary concern was with children's abilities to coordinate the various internal relations among the several elements of their own display, set out to minimise or eliminate what they regarded as unnecessary complexities by either: (a) reducing (often to one) the number of display items to which children were exposed (e.g., Gzesh & Surber, 1985; Jacobsen & Waters, 1985; Salatas & Flavell, 1976); or (b) providing "simpler" response alternatives by inviting subjects to rotate the display rather than predicting the view of a moving observer (e.g., Borke, 1975; Fishbein et al., 1972; Horan & Rosser, 1983; Huttenlocher & Presson, 1973, 1979). This last practice, as Silverman (1994) pointed out, is fundamentally misleading because it automatically preserves the very internal spatial relations among the elements of the display that Piaget and Inhelder assumed were the Achilles heel for young children. Others still, operating out of concern that the original three mountains procedure might throw children into a tail-spin of intellectual realism, conducted their own inquiry only after having draped or otherwise covered the display.

It is not, at first blush, altogether self-evident exactly what sort of sense to make out of all these and many other like-minded studies. It would have been, at best, a happy coincidence if, in their first foray, Piaget and Inhelder had stumbled upon the one thing that would forever stand as the "minimally complex" assessment paradigm, so it is perhaps not surprising that various others have found that children actually do acquire certain perspective-taking abilities at a younger age than was originally alleged in *The child's conception of space*. Certain recent publications (e.g., Silverman, 1994) have suggested—and there is no serious reason to doubt—that, through the introduction of various innovative assessment techniques (e.g., clearly marking subjects' hands to minimise right/left confusions), some of the best available studies may well have succeeded in pushing back the threshold of various putative perspective-taking abilities by one or two years. Just as obviously, other investigators seem to have succeeded so well in their efforts to simplify the original three mountains procedure that they ended up measuring something else entirely. It is difficult to imagine, for instance, how one could succeed in measuring children's ability to coordinate the projective relations that obtain among the various elements of a complex array while using only a single display item, as did, for example, Jacobsen and Waters (1985), or how it would be possible to detail what Piaget and Inhelder alleged to be a long and variegated course of perspective-taking development while using only a simple pass–fail coding scheme, as did, among many others, Flavell et al. (1968).

So where, you might well ask, have the last 50 years of wandering about in search of procedural rigour actually got us? The answer, it would seem, is that the terrain all looks discouragingly familiar. A once elaborate developmental trajectory is again reconstrued as a single and sovereign threshold competence. What was once a texturally rich, if somewhat Byzantine, assessment strategy has now been deconstructed into a perhaps more civilised subset of parametric variations that, in all likelihood, are no longer measures of anything like the same thing.

Although there should be nothing especially surprising in the discovery that, after being hammered away at for over a half a century, yet another "big" idea has been reduced to a seemingly random heap of parametric rubble, it is, perhaps, a mistake to code the confusion that surrounds our current understanding of children's spatial perspective-taking abilities as just another case in which the wheels of "normal science" have ground exceedingly fine. Instead, some have felt that systematic confusions and motivated misunderstandings on the scale just described demand some interpretation in depth. My own, somewhat less clinical, reading of the habitual misunderstanding to which *The child's conception of space* is heir, is that Piaget and Inhelder's account was written under the sway of an epistemology so sharply different from that of its critics that what we have here is more akin to a paradigm clash between warring epistemologies, with text and counter-text steaming past one another like proverbial ships in the night. Piaget and Inhelder's research into the child's conceptual understanding of projective space, like their research efforts more generally, was conceived and carried out against a backdrop of an unremittingly "constructivistic" epistemology. By contrast, the majority of those psychologists from North America and elsewhere who used this work as a springboard for their own programmes of empirical research, did so from an epistemological frame of reference openly reliant on a brand of naïve or metaphysical realism that is completely unapologetic about its objectivist assumptions (Bickhard, 1992). What followed from these sharply different epistemic orientations, I mean to argue, was a long list of inevitable and mostly negative consequences that effectively guaranteed that Piaget and Inhelder's work would be found seriously wanting. I suggest that outlining a few of these differences will prove a useful framework on which to pin some of the otherwise loose details of the research literature just sampled.

For Piaget and Inhelder the presumably hard-to-acquire, and so late-arriving, insight that they sought to document was the gradual realisation that experience (in this case perceptual experience) is inevitably situated such that the *relations* thought to obtain among the various touchstones of possible understanding are always at least potentially relative to the situated stance of the knower. With this in mind they: (a) built perceptual displays that were rich in such potential internal relations; (b) regarded the simple intuition that not everyone sees everything in precisely the same way as a uniformly early insight; and (c) treated their young subjects as still unformed until (usually well into their middle school years) they manifested a clear understanding that the actual *relations* that obtain among the elements of any perceptual display vary as a function of an observer's physical location.

As seen through the more objectivist eyes of Piaget and Inhelder's critics, however, intellectual maturity is naturally understood to be measured by the degree of correspondence obtaining between one's mental representations and the real-world events of which intellectual life is thought to be only a faint and often imperfect copy (Bickhard, 1992; Chandler & Carpendale, 1998; Chandler & Sokol, 1999). By these lights, interpretation is seen to be equivalent to misinterpretation, and maturity as coming to a series of decision heuristics or matching rules of the sort: "same position–same view", "different position–different view", etc. (e.g., Flavell et al., 1981b; Gzesh & Surber, 1985; Yaniv & Shatz, 1990). Investigators caught in the grip of such an untempered correspondence theory of truth naturally equate knowledge with having mental representations that "match" reality as it really is (Chapman, in press), leaving little or no room for the prospect that understanding could be improved by access to more and more powerful "forms" of knowing. Consequently, such objectivistic views offer very little in the way of toeholds where development could potentially gain any real purchase. Little wonder, then, that most students of perspective taking who have subscribed to such views have found it hard to imagine how anyone who already appreciates that reality presents a different face to different observers could be expected to improve on what seems to be a picture-perfect match between the world and its unencumbered representation. Nor is it surprising that investigators of this objectivist stripe: (a) would naturally favour the use of a "minimally complex" assessment strategy meant to spare children the necessity of wading through a lot of incidental display complexity en route to demonstrating what amounts to an either–or ability; and (b) would automatically gravitate towards a "one-miracle view" (Chandler & Carpendale, 1998), according to which perspective taking is a singular achievement, grasped by children at a much younger age than Piaget and Inhelder ever dreamed. As such, then, these constructivistic and objectivistic epistemologies naturally conspire towards sharply different research strategies, and what are already shaping up as incommensurable conclusions. For these reasons, I argue, the available literature on visual perspective taking is best read as the fallout of a paradigm clash, and is not, as some would have you believe, a just-so story about how, with growing scientific precision, we have come to a new and improved understanding of the errors of a now dead generation of perspective-taking pioneers.

Viewpoints and visual rhetoric: Egocentrism, role taking, social perspective taking, affective perspective taking, and social cognition in general

An electronic search of the 1968–1998 PsycINFO database, using only common variations on the term "perspective taking" as sorting criteria, yielded well over 1000 "hits", only a few of which were about other than direct psychological matters, and nearly half of a sample 100 of these directly cited *The child's conception of space* in their reference lists. In addition to serving as a benchmark of how central Piaget and Inhelder's work on perspective taking has been in jump-starting one of psychology's most productive research enterprises, two other things leap off the pages of this search. One is that, while these books, chapters, and journal articles are all about perspective taking in everything from "autism" to "xenophobia", only the smallest fraction actually involve anything that could reasonably be counted as yet another procedural variation on the original three mountains task. Rather, the main line of this work moves off in quite different directions that, when not specifically about some clinical or applied matter, at least tend to be about the course of socio-cognitive development in general, rather than about visual perspective taking in particular.

The second message delivered by this long reference list is that the heyday of role- and perspective-taking research of any sort appears to have passed—replaced, it would seem, with new smart talk about children's so-called "developing theories of mind". Similarly, a much more focused review of 20 years of *Psychological Abstracts* shows that, whereas new articles on the specific subject of "social role taking" were once appearing at a rate of 30–40 a year during the late 1970s and early 1980s, only three such articles are cited in the 3-year period between 1995 and 1997. A comparable review of the programmes of the biennial meetings of the Society for Research in Child Development for the same period shows a similar pattern. Throughout most of the 1970s, how children become perspectival was the talk of the town, but in the last two SRCD meetings there have been only two presentations that listed "role or perspective taking" among their key index terms.

Although it is probably no surprise that the discipline has grown rather cool towards endless rounds of techno-tinkering with the three mountains task, it is a good deal less obvious: (a) how the narrow study of spatial perspective taking managed to become the detonator for the explosion of research in the domain of social perspective taking, or (b) how it came to pass that this once incendiary enterprise stalled so completely, only to be entirely eclipsed by something as cryptic as the study of children's developing theories of mind. Trying to find answers to these two questions will make up the balance of this section.

Surfing from spatial to social perspective taking on a wave of metaphoric excess. Although it would undoubtedly be a mistake to try to put the whole of the so-called "social-cognitive revolution" down to such metaphoric excess, one thing seems clear. Some part of the responsibility for the suspect efforts to knit together both Piaget and Inhelder's earlier work on spatial perspectives and the later-arriving studies of social perspective taking does seem to be legitimately owed to what Gallup and Cameron (1992) describe as our peculiar predisposition to "equate sight with understanding" (p. 97) and "to use visual terms as metaphors to describe or capture mental events" (p. 93). According to their research there is, in most contemporary and ancient languages, a linguistic bias towards conflating visual and mental terms in ways that promote easy metaphoric leaps between appropriately narrow talk about literal vantage-points or line-of-sight perspectives, and fully symbolic talk, for example, about your perspective on the war in Vietnam, or my vantage-point on the abortion issue. As an apparent consequence, many have found it perfectly natural to mix the properly perceptual subject of visual perspective taking with just about anything else having to do with the situatedness of social roles, or the ineluctably subjective nature of the knowing process. From there it has proved to be only a short step to the common confusion of making a single conceptual piece out of the otherwise disparate matters of visual perspective taking, social role taking, narcissism, self-absorption, empathy, and a hundred other things having to do with the fact that knowing, like seeing, lends itself to being discussed in the language of coordinated perspectives. The result has been a whole dog's breakfast of seriously incommensurable bits and pieces of theory and practice that, as I suggest in the next section, prove to be indigestible.

Who or what is responsible for the eclipse of the role- and perspective-taking literatures?   Although, as the boom–bust numbers cited earlier are meant to demonstrate, fate eventually proved rather unkind to the broad-band consortium of perspective-taking studies that arose in the 1970s, there is, on the brighter side, the fact that before their eventual fall into ignominy their rise was, as such things go, rather spectacular. In those halcyon days, at least, perspective-taking research was clearly the done thing. In addition to a long queue of investigators promoting their own particular brands of "conceptual" or "social" perspective taking, there was also available a whole *pharmakeia* of spin-off studies having to do with the supposed developmental course of such things as "affective" role taking (e.g., Kurdek & Rodgon, 1975; Rotenberg, 1974), referential communication (e.g., Shatz & Gelman, 1973), and "moral" perspective taking (e.g., Selman, 1971), as well as a spate of more "applied" studies relating perspective taking to a broad range of socialisation issues and clinical matters (e.g., Chandler, 1972; Rothenberg, 1970; Selman, 1980). The result was a landslide of publications about perspective taking that were all "must reads". Fortunately, we are spared the often mind-numbing experience of sorting through this heap of materials by the fact that reviews are readily at hand (e.g., Chandler, 1978; Chandler & Boyes, 1982; Selman, 1971; Shantz, 1975; Urberg & Docherty, 1976), leaving us free to speculate about how this former jewel in developmental psychology's crown managed so quickly and completely to fall out of fashion.

The short answer to this seeming paradox, already hinted at earlier, is that, having tried to run off in every direction at once, the whole enterprise simply fell into a fit of incoherence, suffered an attack of incommensurability and died, if you will, a wastrel's death from over-indulgence in unhealthy category mistakes. That, more or less, is "how" it happened. The question of "why" is perhaps more subject to interpretation. If, as Gallup and Cameron (1992) and others (e.g., Dent-Read & Szokolszky, 1993) would have it, we are all somehow naturally inclined "to equate sight and understanding" (Gallup & Cameron, 1992, p. 97), and to "see" the workings of the eye and the mind as interchangeable, then it is perhaps not all that surprising that early contributors to the perspective-taking literature might have lapsed into a kind of syncretism that left them insufficiently mindful of a critical distinction: that which must be maintained between what it could possibly mean to "see" Piaget and Inhelder's three mountains display from a given angle of regard, and what is necessarily involved in "seeing" the world of meanings as they appear from the "perspective" of someone who occupies an epistemic or interpretive stance different from one's own. There was, to be fair, some talk within these circles about "perceptual," as opposed to "conceptual" role taking (e.g., Flavell et al., 1981b), but this was all viewed as more of a simple change of topic than a way of marking the fact that one was leaving one realm of conceptual discourse and entering another. As a result no one, or almost no one, seriously doubted that children who were perspectival in one of these "domains of application" were not also capable, at least in principle, of being equally perspectival somewhere else. It was understood, of course, that children assumed to be already in possession of the single and "unitary" ability to recognise the *existence* of points of view different from their own might, along the way, suffer through some situationally induced information-processing shortfall that could temporarily work to show them at their worst. As a way, then, of rationalising such cross-task variability while still clinging to a common catch-all or "wastebasket" (Pillow, 1995) notion of perspective taking, Flavell and his colleagues (e.g., Flavell, 1974, 1977; Flavell et al., 1968; Masangkay et al., 1974; Salatas & Flavell, 1976) and numerous others (e.g., Coie, Costanzo, & Farnhill, 1973; Mossler, Marvin, & Greenberg, 1976) all advanced variations on what came to be known as the "existence–need–inference–application model" (Pillow, 1995, p. 394). Viewed from this unitary competence perspective, any problem that children might experience in putting into practice what was assumed to be an already present and singular awareness of the "existence" of different points of view could be conveniently put down to what were discounted as merely "performance" or information-processing limitations.

Although seemingly bulletproof, the essential circularity of this line of argument became increasingly visible as evidence mounted that while certain perspective-taking abilities obviously came "on-line" in the early preschool years (e.g., Flavell, Shipstead, & Croft, 1978; Hughes & Donaldson, 1979; Liben, 1978; Mossler et al., 1976; Urberg & Docherty, 1976), others were known not to put in their first appearance until as late as middle childhood or even the adolescent years (Chandler, 1988; Chandler & Helm, 1984; Elkind, 1967; Feffer, 1959; Feffer & Gourevitch, 1960; Pillow, 1989, 1991, 1995; Roberts & Patterson, 1983; Selman, 1971; Selman & Byrne, 1974; Taylor, 1988a, b). Of course it remains possible that becoming perspectival actually is, as described, a singular and unitary accomplishment of the preschool years that is simply kept partially obscured, like some light under a bushel, until every conceivable trick of the information-processing trade is finally in place. As more and more lines of evidence kept cropping up, however, each showing new-found perspective-taking abilities emerging at essentially every age, the idea that all of these "performance" differences still masked a common, early-arriving competence became harder and harder to sell. In the end, all that was left was variability, unsecured by any bankable theory, and the whole perspective-taking enterprise went into receivership where, except for some minor dealings on the clinical margin, it currently remains.

Although paradigm crashes of the magnitude just described are obviously both the cause and effect of widespread conceptual bankruptcy, it is equally apparent that all of the loose equity stored in the fact that children do somehow regularly succeed in becoming better able to take the perspectives of others presented an investment opportunity that others were sure to take up. It should, therefore, come as no surprise that the remaining intellectual assets of the now defunct role- and perspective-taking enterprise were quickly bought up by new players in the market. As it was, the new moguls of this resurrected perspective-taking trade turned out to be a next generation of so-called "theory-theorists", to whose corporate structure and "theories of mind" marketing strategy I now turn.

PART THREE:
"THEORY-THEORY" AND THE THEORY-OF-MIND ENTERPRISE

Perhaps only because nature abhors a vacuum, but more likely for the reason that those involved in the study of the cognitive course find it difficult to avoid those perennial questions about the course of perspective-taking development, the vacancy created by the demise of the role-taking tradition was quickly filled. The new occupant was the so-called " theory-theory" (an account that, as James Russell, 1992, has pointed out, thinks of itself as so good "that they had to name it twice") and its first brainchild, the study of "children's developing theories of mind". Once sufficiently novel to have attracted onlookers merely on the strength of its odd way of referring to itself, this curio quality has long since worn thin and, in fact, there are accumulating reasons (to be brought out in the next section) to suspect that the whole theory-of-mind business may already have seen better times. Nevertheless because, beneath the surface of their apparent differences, the new theories-of-mind literature and the now moribund role- and perspective-taking enterprise are both fundamentally centred on the common subject of "representational diversity", we are perhaps honour-bound to deal equally with both. "Dealing", in this case, needs to get started by orienting the reader to what has ordinarily been meant by "developing theories of mind", and to track this approach's short history.

Getting definitional about the double-speak of theory-theory is made twice as difficult as it might otherwise be by the fact that most talk about children's developing theories of mind is talk in "a different voice", belonging to a separate language game that owes its distinctive semantic tradition more to recent matters afoot in the philosophy of mind and to current cognitive science aspirations, than to most of psychology's own past. Complicating matters still further is a symptom picture ordinarily associated only with severe oppositional disorders, but which, in this instance, might more generously be put down to the fact that, as Perner and Astington (1992, p. 146) put it, theory-theory views itself as resting on a solid "anti-Piagetian footing". As a result, there appears to be a somewhat studied effort on the part of many contributors to this literature to avoid terms like "perspective taking", which are thought to carry too much excess Piagetian baggage, and to mint in their place new terms and turns of phrase that, for many, do not trip lightly off the tongue. Still, all of this new-speak notwithstanding, the kernel ideas at work here are not, in the end, all that difficult. "Theory-theory", phrased perhaps less grandiloquently, essentially amounts to the "idea" that it is useful to try to understand people's behaviour as the consequence of their being in the grip of some organised set of beliefs, or "theory", about, say, the workings of mental life. Beyond this, it would seem, any more specific talk of "children's developing theories of mind" largely boils down to the singular, immaculately conceived, disjunctive, salutary, "one-miracle" proposition that, while children younger than 4 or 5 presumably suffer through some across-the-board "cognitive deficit" that has wholly blocked them from the possibility of any real insight into mental life, all older children are miraculously cured of their shortcoming as a result of having been strangely gifted with some new "theory of mind" that then stays with them, fundamentally unchanged, for the remainder of their days. If this rough caricature all comes as news to you, then what will really surprise you is what history has actually managed to do with this rather problematic and decisively anti-developmental set of ideas. Here is that surprising history in a nutshell.

Depending on who you ask, the candidate event taken to mark the beginning of the theory of mind enterprise is either Premack and Woodruff's germinal 1978 *Behavioral and Brain Sciences* paper "Does the chimpanzee have a theory-of-mind?" (which effectively coined the term) or Wimmer and Perner's (1983) now classic *Cognition* article "Beliefs about beliefs: …" (which outfitted it with its methodology). Measured from these recent beginnings, the speed and decisiveness with which the resulting theories-of-mind literature has moved from a place of total obscurity to cognitive development's absolute centre stage is nothing short of spectacular. During the late 1970s and early 1980s, as the study of role and perspective taking span out of control and crashed, only three papers dealing with children's theories of mind managed to find their way into the *Psychology Abstracts*. Then, as I have already hinted, the phoenix rose. In the short 15 or 20 years separating then and now, 12 edited or single-authored books have appeared on the subject, along with upwards of 200 published research studies. Again, a quick survey of the SRCD's programmes tells much the same story. During the period up to and including 1985, only two presentations having to do with theory-of-mind matters made it onto these programmes. By contrast, the last three meetings of this society have made a place for exactly 200 such papers. Something is obviously afoot here, and, whatever it is, it is made more interesting by the fact that the rise of the theory-of-mind literature and the fall of the perspective-taking enterprise are almost perfect mirror-images of one another.

My point is, roughly, that underneath it all, the new theories-of-mind literature deserves to be seen as an updated version of the discipline's ritual interest in all things perspectival—a familiar ritual played out this time in the sheep's clothing of contemporary cognitive science. As I will go on to show, this is lent support by the fact that both of these literatures seem equally guilty of having made what amount to the same category mistakes. However, before going on with an effort to justify such an accusation, it is first important to clarify as far as possible what this notion of children's theories of mind is really all about. Here, as before, we are spared the heavy obligation to précis this huge literature by the fact that reviews are already numerous (e.g., Chandler & Carpendale, 1998; Chandler & Sokol, 1999; Freeman, 1992; Lewis & Mitchell, 1994; Moses & Chandler, 1992; Russell, 1992). Still, the task of the moment demands, and I mean to supply, at least some quick and perhaps dangerously synoptic attempt to take the measure of all of this work.

A short course on theories of mind

First, it is generally assumed in theory-of-mind circles that, whatever children may actually do in practice, they are not born into the world with any appreciation of their own constructive or representational nature and, instead, spend the bulk of their preschool years largely ignorant of the fact that they and others are obliged to construct a vision in which beliefs about the world need not be the same thing as the world itself.

Second, it is assumed that children's first understanding of the fact that the mind actually invents its own mental environment is a late-arriving insight, reliably signalled by a dawning appreciation that an important gulf exists between what is true and what is taken to be true. Up to here at least, you might, if you had been nurtured on Piaget and Inhelder's theories, find yourself rather sympathetic to the way things appear to be going.

Third, following Davidson's (1984) admonition that the whole point of talk about beliefs is that they might be mistaken, it is regularly assumed by the typical theory-theorist that the first reliable evidence that children understand the representational character of mental life is provided by their emerging ability to appreciate that they and others can and do sometimes misrepresent reality by holding to, and acting upon, beliefs that are actually false.

Fourth, it is also broadly agreed that the best available evidence of the early appearance of such "false belief understanding" is provided by a small handful of "minimally complex" measurement strategies of the sort prefigured in Wimmer and Perner's (1983) classic "unexpected change" task, which provide a so-called "litmus test" (Wellman, 1990) of false belief understanding. In this task, subjects watch as a child and mother puppet are brought into a kitchen to deposit a chocolate bar in one of two available cabinets. Later, in the child puppet's (Maxi's) absence, the mother removes the chocolate from the one cabinet and places it in the other. In this and related ways available information is engineered such that Maxi is left in ignorance of truths clearly known to the subject. The key false-belief question then put to subjects is "Where will Maxi look for his chocolate when he returns?"

Fifth, it is assumed that, all other things being equal, 4- and 5-year-olds can be counted on to provide unimpeachable evidence of their early grasp of the possibility of false beliefs, and so deserve to be credited with a first and "fully representational" (Perner, 1991) theory of mind.

Sixth, and finally, it is proposed that preschool children, who are to be credited with an understanding of ignorance-based false beliefs, although sometimes less expert than their more practised elders, already possess the same interpretive (Perner, 1991) or constructive (Wellman, 1990) view of mental life subscribed to by ordinary adults.

As you might imagine, theory-theorists of various stripes happily subscribe to certain of these propositions, while taking serious exception to others. Although, for example, very few who are not otherwise in the grip of some radical eliminativist or nativistic theory would likely take issue with the ideas contained in propositions 1 and 2, more would be prepared to take special exception to the suggestion that so-called false belief understanding is necessarily the first or best marker of such emerging insights, or that now standard false belief measures are, as advertised, actually minimally complex measures of such abilities. More numerous still are those (and here I count myself as a charter member) who, while reasonably content with the idea that false belief understanding is an important watershed in the course of children's developing views of mental life, nevertheless hold out for the prospect that the earliest insights that are required to pass standard, ignorance-based "unexpected change" tests are not, by any stretch of the imagination, the final chapter in the ongoing story of children's maturing beliefs about beliefs.

The last of these critical possibilities, I will argue, is different from all the rest for the important reason that it alone fundamentally challenges the otherwise frankly non-developmental notion that children not only come abruptly to some first so-called theory-of-mind, but also that such first achievements are the be-all and end-all of what it means to subscribe to a mature conception of mental life. The reasons for entertaining such a more rounded view of the course of children's perspective-taking development are the subject of the fourth and final section of this chapter. Before turning to these concerns, however, it is perhaps best to say something synoptic about the current state of play within the larger theories-of-mind enterprise.

More trouble

Some of the many problems currently facing the theory-of-mind enterprise are of the relatively small, in-house sort, having to do with such questions as whether or not the line between having and not having a theory of mind has been drawn in exactly the right place (see, for example, Lewis & Mitchell's 1994 book, *Children's early understanding of mind: Origins and development*, for a sampling of such early-onset arguments). Others deal with potentially correctable shortcomings, such as the tendency of certain theory-theorists to be pugnaciously ahistorical or mischievously dismissive of evidence that seemingly runs against them. It would, of course, be altogether better if these colleagues were to imagine a history that stretched back further than the 1978 publication of Premack and Woodruff's classic paper, or if they were to abandon the trite idea that anyone and everyone (and especially Piaget and Inhelder) is automatically guilty of being a closet Cartesian, and so unworthy of serious consideration. However, simply being smug is not a capital offence, and so ought not to be any more fatal to theory-theorists than to anyone else.

What is fatal, in my view, is the seriously objectionable fact that, taken as a whole, the theories-of-mind literature is openly and unabashedly non-developmental. Of course, individual or whole scholarly enterprises are free, at least in principle, to adopt any sort of bad attitude they might like about the merits or demerits of viewing matters developmentally. What, in this instance, standard-issue theorists of mind are not free to do is turn a blind eye to a new and growing body of evidence which strongly suggests that the process of coming to a mature understanding of the perspectival character of mental life is not the "one-trick pony" it has commonly been portrayed as being. The fourth and final section to follow brings out arguments and lines of evidence intended to demonstrate that a more judicious reading of the available research literature would work to promote other than the "one-miracle" view of belief entitlement for which contemporary theorists of mind are infamous.

PART FOUR:
MAKING A DEVELOPMENTAL PROJECT OUT OF THE STUDY OF CHILDREN'S DEVELOPING THEORIES OF MIND

The foundational thought to which most contributors to the literature on children's theories of mind uniformly subscribe—and which in the end has cost the whole enterprise any real hopes of qualifying as a developmental theory in any strong sense—is the presumption that simple false belief understanding stands as an adequate demonstration of the presence of a fully "interpretive" or "constructive" theory of mind. If this were true (that is, if success on something like Wimmer & Perner's "Maxi" task did, as advertised, actually count as unambiguous proof of a fully interpretive theory of mind) then those who rest their case on such evidence would be right, and children's developmental progress towards an adult-like theory of mind would, as claimed, effectively come to an end during the preschool years. The problem with all such claims, however, is that they are nakedly false.

In order to make the case that I am right about this, and that a long list of notable colleagues who believe differently are simply mistaken, I mean to proceed on two fronts. The first of these is conceptual, and undertakes to persuade the reader that ignorance-based false belief understanding is formally distinct from, and in no way entails, an appreciation of the constructivistic fact that all knowledge is an interpretive achievement.

The second of these points of attack is more straightforwardly empirical, and works to demonstrate that merely appreciating that ignorance breeds mistaken assumptions is, as a matter of simple numerical fact, both earlier-arriving and otherwise different from the realisation that, even when playing with precisely the same informational deck, one individual can read a common set of facts in one way, while another observer can render precisely the same set of facts differently.

If both of these lines of argument are successful, then the reader will be convinced, as I am, that the standard conclusions, available throughout the theories-of-mind literature, are simply mistaken. While this would, of course, be bad news to anyone deeply committed to the truth of the common conclusions of this literature, it would have the positive consequence of reintroducing the possibility that a whole chunk of childhood (otherwise being sold down the river to those promoting a changeless, one-miracle view) could be re-opened for a more balanced examination. I now take up this two-step argument, beginning with what I believe are good reasons why standard measures of false belief understanding do not actually measure what they are purported to measure.

A conceptual re-analysis of standard measures of false belief understanding as windows onto an interpretive theory of mind

There are, as you might guess, longer and shorter versions of the argument that standard measures of false belief understanding do not provide any real evidence about when children first come to understand that different people can interpret the same thing differently. Although, due to considerations of space, this will be an argument on the very short side, attention needs to be directed to a short-list of key points.

First, it may seem counterintuitive that anyone looking at something like Wimmer and Perner's "unexpected change" measure (i.e., the "Maxi" task) with clear eyes could have possibly construed it as a reasonable measurement context within which to search for evidence of a truly "interpretive" understanding of the process of belief entitlement. However, such is the case. Gopnik and Wellman (1992), for example, explicitly argue that the ability to comprehend the falseness of false beliefs requires nothing less than the conceptual resources of an interpretive theory of mind. Similarly, as Wellman (1990, p. 244) puts it, the typical 4- or 5-year-old is already in possession of "an interpretive or constructive understanding of representations", and every preschooler sees mental contents as being constructed "actively by the person, on the basis of inference and as subject to biases, misinterpretations and active interpretation" (Wellman & Hickling, 1994, p. 1578). Making much the same point, Meltzoff and Gopnik (1993, p. 335) state that "By five years old, children seem to ... understand that a person's beliefs are about the world and are not just recordings of objects and events stamped upon the mind, but are active interpretations or construals of them from a given perspective." In much the same vein, Perner (1991, p. 275) argues that "around 4 years children begin to understand knowledge as representation, with all of its characteristics. One such characteristic is *interpretation*" (italics in original). Clearly, then, many major contributors to the theories-of-mind literature do actually promote and otherwise rely on the view that 4- and 5-year-olds already subscribe to the idea that knowledge is an interpretive achievement capable of being properly documented by success on standard measures of false belief understanding.

Although there is no way of knowing with certainty, the likely source of the common conviction that preschool children already hold an interpretive, and consequently very adult-like, view of mental life lies in the fact that there is some loose sense in which it seems permissible to say (and young children often do say) that both Maxi and his mother legitimately hold different beliefs concerning the whereabouts of "one and the same" chocolate bar.

What seems so decidedly wrong-headed about all such loose talk of an "interpretive" theory of mind is that, rather than allowing that both Maxi and his mother each have their own different rendering of what is really one and the same thing (as would be required of any persuasive demonstration of such a constructive outlook), standard "unexpected change" measures are explicitly engineered to create conditions in which one of the protagonists always responds to some larger compliment of the full array of facts, while the second (such as Maxi) is carefully manipulated to guarantee that they are operating with a different and explicitly less complete subset of the facts. In short, Maxi's situation is purpose-built to guarantee that he is playing with less than a full deck of information, and so it cannot reasonably be said that he and his mother merely have different interpretations of the same thing. False belief tests, then, are measures of an appreciation of the consequences of ignorance, and not measures of the presence or absence of some possible "interpretive" theory of mind.

Alternative routes to the possibility of an interpretive theory of mind

In what remains of this section, I outline in the most general of terms two related programmes of research that were meant to present young subjects with alternative means of demonstrating whatever real understanding they might have about the interpretive nature of the knowing process. In one of these (Carpendale & Chandler, 1996) 4- to 8-year-olds were provided with examples from that small world of stimulus objects that have the characteristic of affording two, and only two, equally legitimate interpretations of one and the same thing. One such example was Jastrow's (1900) classic "puzzle drawing" which seems to look like a rabbit but when thought of differently, also looks like a duck. Another is provided by various homophones such as "pair" and "pear", or "ring", as in jewellery or the sound of a bell. What our data show is that in a large sample of children, all of whom performed at ceiling on standard measures of false belief, only the older of our subjects (i.e., those of 7 or 8) gave clear evidence of understanding that different people might find different interpretive meaning in what amounted to the "same" thing.

In the second of these studies, done this time in collaboration with Chris Lalonde (Chandler & Lalonde, 1996), we chose instead stimulus materials that were especially vague and indeterminate—in the ways that Rorschach cards or cloud patterns are indistinct. This time 4- to 8-year-olds were not asked to offer up different interpretations of their own, but rather to evaluate the legitimacy of the efforts of confederates who reported understanding these stimuli in sharply different ways. As before, only the oldest of a group of young subjects, all of whom responded at ceiling on standard measures of false belief, were able to countenance the possibility that different persons were equally within their rights to discover different meanings of what was "objectively" the same thing.

The obvious implication of these two studies, and related work by other investigators (e.g., Pillow, 1995), is that false belief understanding is clearly not the be-all and end-all of children's epistemic development. That is, contrary to the standard conclusions of standard theorists of mind, the ontogenetic course by which young persons come to grasp the possibility of "representational diversity" would appear to have more than a single way-station. It is not my intention simply to be seen as agitating for some "*two*-miracle", as opposed to "*one*-miracle", view of what is involved in becoming fully perspectival. Rather, I suggest, there is considerable evidence, both for these and other age groups (e.g., Chandler, 1988; Chandler & Boyes, 1982; Clinchy & Mansfield, 1985; Kitchner & King, 1981; Kuhn, Pennington, & Leadbeater, 1983), all of which supports the conclusion that coming to a broad recognition that differently situated persons see the world in different ways is a process that occupies the whole of child development and beyond.

CONCLUSION

The strong conclusion to which I hope you will be led by all that has been presented here, is that the work Inhelder and Piaget completed in their original exploration of the development of children's spatial perspective-taking abilities is not best seen as the vague progenitor of some 50 years of often critical subsequent research. Nor do the facts of the matter easily support the conclusion, popular in some quarters, that their now dated claims were all in need of being excised through the application of this or that razor-sharp and thoroughly modern methodology. Less still, it would appear, were their efforts a false start that must be put behind us, in order to get with another more *au courant* cognitive science programme of the sort that often appears to be working to collapse the developmental course onto some imaginary point—some one-off miracle—without a past or a future. Instead, the evidence I have brought forward seems to suggest that, after half a century of false starts, we are now finally being carried back to a point where the child's protracted attempts to discover the possibilities of "representational diversity" begin to look embarrassingly like that similarly differentiated account of perspective-taking development originally worked out by Inhelder and Piaget in *The child's conception of space*.

REFERENCES

Baldwin, J.M. (1906). *Social and ethical interpretations of mental development*. New York: Macmillan.

Bickhard, M.H. (1992). Commentary. *Human Development, 35*, 182–192.

Borke, H. (1975). Piaget's mountain revisited: Changes in the egocentric landscape. *Developmental Psychology, 11*, 240–243.

Brainerd, C.J. (1996). Piaget: A centennial celebration. *Psychological Science, 7*, 191–195.

Bruner, J. (1990). *Acts of meaning*. Cambridge, MA: Harvard Press.

Burke, K. (1945). *A grammar of motives*. New York: Prentice Hall.

Carpendale, J.I., & Chandler, M.J. (1996). On the distinction between false belief understanding and subscribing to an interpretive theory of mind. *Child Development, 67*, 1686–1706.

Chandler, M. (1972). Egocentrism in normal and pathological childhood development. In F. Monks, W. Hartup, & J. DeWitt (Eds.), *Determinants of behavioural development* (pp. 569–576). New York: Academic Press.

Chandler, M.J. (1978) Social cognition: A selected review of current research. In H. Furth, W. Overton, & J. Gallagher (Eds.), *Knowledge and development: Yearbook of development epistemology* (pp. 93–147). New York: Plenum Press.

Chandler, M.J. (1988). Doubt and developing theories of mind. In J.W. Astington, P.L. Harris, & D.R. Olson (Eds.), *Developing theories of mind* (pp.387–413). New York: Cambridge University Press.

Chandler, M., & Boyes, M. (1982). Social-cognitive development. In B.B. Wolman (Ed.), *Handbook of developmental psychology* (pp. 387–402). Englewood Cliffs, NJ: Prentice-Hall.

Chandler, M.J., & Carpendale, J.I.M. (1998). Inching toward a mature theory of mind. In M. Ferrari & R. Sternberg (Eds.). *Self-awareness: Its nature and development* (pp. 148–190). New York: Guilford Press.

Chandler, M.J., & Helm, D. (1980). *Knowing the sort of help that is really needed*. Paper presented at the International Conference on the Development and Maintenance of Prosocial Behaviour, Warsaw, 29 June–3 July.

Chandler, M., & Lalonde, C. (1996). Shifting to an interpretive theory of mind: 5- to 7-year olds' changing conceptions of mental life. In A.J. Sameroff & M.M. Haith (Eds.), *The five to seven year shift: The age of reason and responsibility* (pp. 111–139). Chicago, IL: The University of Chicago Press.

Chandler, M.J., & Helm, D. (1984). Developmental changes in the contribution of shared experience to social role-taking competence. *International Journal of Behavioural Development, 7*, 1415–156.

Chandler, M., & Sokol, B. (1999). Representation once removed: Children's developing conceptions of representational life. In I. Sigel (Ed.), *Development of mental representation: Theories and application* (pp. 201–230). Mahwah, NJ: Lawrence Erlbaum Associates Inc.

Chapman, M. (in press). Constructivism and the problem of reality. *Journal of Applied Developmental Psychology.*

Clinchy, B., & Mansfield, A. (1985). *Justifications offered by children to support positions on issues of "fact" and "opinion"*. Paper presented at the 56th Annual Meeting of the Eastern Psychology Association, Boston.

Coie, J.D., Costanzo, P.R., & Farnill, D. (1973). Specific transitions in the development of spatial perspective-taking ability. *Developmental Psychology, 9*, 167–177.

Davidson, D. (1984). Thought and talk. In D. Davidson (Ed.), *Inquiries into truth and interpretation* (pp. 51–61). Oxford: Basil Blackwell.

Dent-Reed, C.H., & Szokolszky, A. (1993). Where do metaphors come from? *Metaphor and Symbolic Activity, 8*, 227–242.

Elkind, D. (1967). Egocentrism in adolescence. *Child Development, 38*, 1025–1034.

Elkind, D. (1985). Egocentrism redux. *Developmental Review, 5*, 218–226.

Feffer, M.H. (1959). The cognitive implications of role-taking behavior. *Journal of Personality, 27,* 152–168.

Feffer, M.H., & Gourevitch, V. (1960). Cognitive aspects of role-taking in children. *Journal of Personality, 28,* 383–396.

Fishbein, H.D., Lewis, S., & Keiffer, K. (1972). Children's understanding of spatial relations: Coordination of perspectives. *Developmental Psychology, 7*, 21–33.

Flavell, J. (1974). The development of inferences about others. In T. Mischel (Ed.), *Understanding other persons* (pp. 66–116). Oxford, UK: Blackwell, Basil, & Mott.

Flavell, J.H. (1977). The development and knowledge about visual perception. *Nebraska Symposium on Motivation, 25*, 43–76.

Flavell, J.H., Botkin, P.T., Fry, C.L., Wright, J.W., & Jarvis, P.E. (1968). *The development of role-taking and communication skills in children*. New York: John Wiley. (Reprinted by Robert E. Krieger Publishing Company, Huntington, NY, 1975)

Flavell, J.H., Everett, B.A., Croft, K., & Flavell, E.R. (1981a). Young children's knowledge about visual perception: Further evidence for the Level 1–Level 2 distinction. *Developmental Psychology, 17*, 99–103.

Flavell, J.H., Flavell, E.R., Green, F.L., & Wilcox, S.A. (1981b). The development of three spatial perspective-taking rules. *Child Development, 52*, 356–358.

Flavell, J.H., Shipstead, S.G., & Croft, K. (1978). Young children's knowledge about visual perception: Hiding objects from others. *Child Development, 49*, 1208–1211.

Freeman, M. (1992). Self as narrative: The place of life history in studying the life span. In T.M. Brinthaupt & R.P. Lipka (Eds.), *The self: Definitional and methodological issues* (pp. 15–43). Albany, NY: SUNY Press.

Gallup, G.G., & Cameron, P.A. (1992). Modality specific metaphors: Is our mental machinery "colored" by a visual bias? *Metaphor and Symbolic Activity, 7*, 93–98.

Gopnik, A., & Wellman, H.M. (1992). Why the child's theory of mind really is a theory. *Mind and Language, 7*, 145–171.

Gzesh, S.M., & Surber, C.F. (1985). Visual perspective-taking skills in children. *Child Development, 56*, 1204-1213.

Horan, P.F., & Rosser R.A. (1983). The function of the response mode in the coordination of perspectives. *Contemporary Educational Psychology, 8*, 347–354.

Hughes, M., & Donaldson, M. (1979). The use of hiding games for studying the coordination of viewpoints. *Educational Review, 31*, 133–140.

Huttenlocher, J., & Presson, C.C. (1973). Mental rotation and the perspective problem. *Cognitive Psychology, 4*, 277–299.

Huttenlocher, J., & Presson, C.C. (1979). The coding and transformation of spatial information. *Cognitive Psychology, 11*, 375–394.

Jacobsen, T.L., & Waters, H.S. (1985). Spatial perspective taking: Coordination of left–right and near–far spatial dimensions. *Journal of Experimental Child Psychology, 39*, 72–84.

Jastrow, J. (1900). *Fact and fable in psychology*. Boston: Houghton-Mifflin.

Kessen, W. (1996). American psychology just before Piaget. *Psychological Science, 7*, 196–199.

Kitchner, K.S., & King, P.M. (1981). Reflective judgement: Concepts of justification and their relationship to age and education. *Journal of Applied Developmental Psychology, 2*, 89–116.

Kuhn, D., Pennington, N., & Leadbeater, B. (1983). Adult thinking in developmental perspective. In P. Baltes & O. Brim, Jr. (Eds.), *Life-span development and behavior* (Vol. 5, pp. 157–195). New York: Academic Press.

Kurdek, L., & Rodgon, M. (1975). Perceptual, cognitive, and affective perspective taking in kindergarten through six-grade children. *Developmental Psychology, 11*, 643–650.

Laurendeau, M., & Pinard, A. (1970). *The development of the concept of space in the child*. New York: International Universities Press.

Lewis, C., & Mitchell, P. (Eds.). (1994). *Children's early understanding of mind: Origins and development*. Hove, UK: Lawrence Erlbaum Associates Ltd.

Liben, L.S. (1978). Perspective-taking skills in young children: Seeing the world through rose-colored glasses. *Developmental Psychology, 14*, 87–92.

Masangkay, Z.S., McCluskey, K.A., McIntyre, C.W., Sims-Knight, J., Vaughn, B.E., & Flavell, J.H. (1974). The early development of inferences about the visual percepts of others. *Child Development, 45*, 357–366.

Meltzoff, A., & Gopnik, A. (1993). The role of imitation in understanding persons and developing a theory of mind. In S. Baron-Cohen, H. Tager-Flusberg, & D.J. Cohen (Eds.), *Understanding other minds: Perspectives from autism* (pp. 335–366). Oxford: Clarendon Press.

Moses, L., & Chandler, M.J. (1992). Traveler's guide to children's theory of mind. *Psychological Inquiry, 1*, 286–301.

Mossler, D.G., Marvin, R.S., & Greenberg, M.T. (1976). Conceptual perspective taking in 2 to 6 year old children. *Developmental Psychology, 12*(1), 85–86.

Newcombe, N. (1989). The development of spatial perspective taking. In H.W. Reese (Ed.), *Advances in child development and behavior* (Vol. 22, pp. 203–247). San Diego, CA: Academic Press.

Nigl, A., & Fishbein, H. (1974). Perception and conception in coordination of perspectives. *Developmental Psychology, 10*, 858–866.

Perner, J. (1991). *Understanding the representational mind.* Cambridge, MA: MIT Press.

Perner, J., & Astington, J.W. (1992). The child's understanding of mental representation. In H. Beilin & P.B. Pufall (Eds.), *Piaget's theory: Prospects and possibilities* (pp. 141–160). Hillsdale, NJ: Lawrence Erlbaum Associates Inc.

Piaget, J. (1926). *The language and thought of the child.* New York: Harcourt Brace Jovanovich.

Piaget, J., & Inhelder, B. (1963). *The child's conception of space* (F.J. Langdon & J.L. Lunzer, Trans.). London: Routledge & Kegan Paul. (Original work published 1948)

Pillow, B.H. (1989). The development of beliefs about selective attention. *Merrill-Palmer Quarterly, 35*, 421–443.

Pillow, B.H. (1991). Children's understanding of biased social cognition. *Developmental Psychology, 27*, 539–551.

Pillow, B.H. (1995). Two trends in the development of conceptual perspective-taking: An elaboration of the passive-active hypothesis. *International Journal of Behavioral Development, 18*, 649–676.

Premack, D., & Woodruff, G. (1978). Does the chimpanzee have a theory of mind? *Behavioral and Brain Sciences, 1*, 515–526.

Roberts, R.J., & Patterson, C.J. (1983). Perspective-taking and referential communication: The question of correspondence reconsidered. *Child Development, 54*, 1005–1014.

Rotenberg, M. (1974). Conceptual and methodological notes on affective and cognitive role-taking (sympathy and empathy): An illustrative experiment with delinquent and nondelinquent boys. *Journal of Genetic Psychology, 125*, 177–185.

Rothenberg, B. (1970). Children's social sensitivity and the relationship to interpersonal competence, interpersonal comfort, and intellectual level. *Developmental Psychology, 2*, 335–350.

Russell, J. (1992). The theory theory: So good they named it twice? *Cognitive Development, 7*, 485–519.

Salatas, H., & Flavell, J.H. (1976). Behavioral and metamnemonic indicators of strategic behaviors under remember instructions in first grade. *Child Development, 47*, 81–89.

Selman, R. (1980). *The growth of interpersonal understanding.* New York: Academic Press.

Selman, R.L. (1971). Taking another's perspective: Role-taking development in early childhood. *Child Development, 42*, 1721–1734.

Selman, R.L., & Byrne, D.F. (1974). A structural developmental analysis of levels of role-taking in middle childhood. *Child Development, 45*, 803–806.

Shantz, C. (1975). The development of social cognition. In E. Hetherington (Ed.), *Review of child development research* (Vol. 5, pp. 257–323). Chicago: University of Chicago Press.

Shatz, M., & Gelman, R. (1973). The development of communication skills: Modification in the speech of young children as a function of listener. *Monographs of the Society for Research in Child Development, 38* (2, Serial No. 152), 1–37.

Silverman, I.W. (1994). Diagnosing the spatial perspective-taking competence of children: A training study approach. *Merrill-Palmer Quarterly, 40*, 253–271.

Taylor, M. (1988a). Conceptual perspective taking: Children's ability to distinguish what they know from what they see. *Child Development, 59*, 703–711.

Taylor, M. (1988b). The development of the seeing–knowing distinction. In J.W. Astington, P.L. Harris, & D.R. Olson (Eds.), *Developing theories of mind* (pp. 387–413). Cambridge: Cambridge University Press.

Urberg, K., & Docherty, E.M. (1976). The development of role-taking skills in young children. *Developmental Psychology, 12*, 198–203.

Wellman, H.M. (1990). *The child's theory of mind.* Cambridge, MA: MIT Press.

Wellman, H.M., & Hickling, A.K. (1994). The mind's "I": Children's conceptions of the mind as an active agent. *Child Development, 65*, 1564–1580.

Wimmer, H., & Perner, J. (1983). Beliefs about beliefs: Representation and constraining function of wrong beliefs in young children's understanding of deception. *Cognition, 13*, 103–128.

Yaniv, I., & Shatz, M. (1990). Heuristics of reasoning and analogy in children's visual perspective taking. *Child Development, 61*, 1491–1501.

CHAPTER FOUR

Building a theory of formal operational thinking: Inhelder's psychology meets Piaget's epistemology

Trevor G. Bond
School of Education, James Cook University,
Queensland, Australia

The stage of formal operational thinking has been a passion of mine for over two decades, although at times I feel like one of the few remaining rats that have not deserted the sinking ship. The research reported in this chapter is an attempt to throw light on the relative contributions of Inhelder and of Piaget to the formal operations stage of Piagetian theory. The widely accepted, and relatively unquestioned, view is of Piaget's dominant and Inhelder's subservient role. I am shamefaced to admit that even though I have had a number of opportunities to visit Geneva and to talk with Bärbel Inhelder about our mutual interest in formal operational thought, I had rather implicitly subscribed to the view that it was *le patron* who dominated this part of the Genevan intellectual landscape as strongly as he did the other parts. The lively and somewhat impassioned discussion that followed the presentation of the ideas in this chapter at the Cours Avancé of the Archives Jean Piaget in Geneva, in September 1998, made me realise that for more than a passing few of the participants, I had raised some issues of importance which went beyond my self-imposed boundaries on the research into and theorising of formal operational thought (see also, Smith, 1998).

In particular, I posed myself the question: How does one resolve the claim about the 1950s in Inhelder's 1989 autobiography "about how we had discovered a new stage: formal thought is not achieved before the age of fifteen or so!" (Inhelder, 1989, p. 223) with the generally known information that we have of the development of Piaget's theory? Moreover, how is the Inhelder claim of this 1950s discovery to be seen in light of a (French only) paper on formal thought by Piaget in 1922— one of his first empirical psychological reports?

While my research relies heavily on published resources, unpublished sources, and some personal accounts from Genevans of the 1940s, 1950s, and later, the argument, opinions, and conclusions should be attributed to me. I am sure that others have, and will, come to conclusions different from mine. Of course, it is the case that the powerful and changing contributions of the various members of the Genevan school can be only poorly interpreted from the printed records that still exist, but the disparity between the printed evidence on adolescent thinking and the received view is so great that the presentation of the following evidence is likely to cause some readers to think more deeply of Inhelder's role than they might have previously. Aside from any controversy it might raise, the more complete reporting of the Genevan work on formal operational thinking is a suitable end in itself for those who have, or have had, an abiding interest in the area.

THE CORE OF THE GENEVAN FORMAL OPERATIONAL *OEUVRE*

De la logique de l'enfant à la logique de l'adolescent (*LELA*, Inhelder & Piaget, 1955) is the core text of the Genevan formal operational *oeuvre* and was translated into English as *The growth of logical thinking from childhood to adolescence* (*GLT*, Inhelder & Piaget, 1958). The change of emphasis in the English title remains unfortunate: It focuses on the development of logical thinking *per se*, rather than how thinking changes from that based on "childhood" logic to that based on "adolescent" logic. The preface of that book (*GLT*, p. xxiii) reported a new style of synthesis of the research agendas of the two authors:

> In other words while one of us was engaged in an empirical study of the transition in thinking from childhood to adolescence, the other worked out the analytical tools needed to interpret the results. It was only after we had compared notes and were making final interpretations that we saw the striking convergence between the empirical and analytic results. This prompted us to collaborate again, but on a new basis. The result is the present work.

About a dozen chapters of the original hand-written manuscript for *LELA/GLT* have been housed in the Archives Jean Piaget in Geneva for over a decade, while another three chapters were added to the manuscript in 1998 when Inhelder's academic papers were collected together. All of the original manuscript that remains is in Piaget's own hand. The original published title was changed from that on the manuscript—*De la logique* concrète *de l'enfant à la logique* formelle *de l'adolescent* (*From the* concrete *logic of the child to the* formal *logic of the adolescent*, emphasis added). The order of the authors on the cover sheet was also changed to the well-known "Inhelder and Piaget" and a note, apparently added later to the preface in Piaget's hand, indicated that a book on Induction would "be the subject of a special work by the first author" (i.e., Bärbel Inhelder).

The strategy I adopt in this chapter is to trace the relative written contributions of Inhelder and Piaget to the theory of formal operational thought in (almost) chronological order. I presume to know only what remains of what was written, not the intention, motivation, or contributions of the authors. In particular, I do not want to claim that any of the works are the result of research conducted in splendid isolation; clearly, the very large portion of them could not be.

Two interesting papers of Piaget are particularly relevant in setting the scene for this research. The first is one of Piaget's earliest published papers with a psychological focus: *Essai sur la multiplication logique et les débuts de la pensée formelle chez l'enfant* (Essay on logical multiplication and the beginnings of formal thought in the child) (Piaget, 1922) and Piaget's address "Principal factors determining intellectual evolution from childhood to adult life" (Piaget, 1937) given on the occasion of the Harvard Tercentenary in 1936.

FORMAL THOUGHT: AN EARLY FOCUS OF PIAGETIAN RESEARCH

"You can think what you like about formal logic" is the provocative introductory sentence to Jean Piaget's 1922[1] paper, "Essay on logical multiplication and the beginnings of formal thought in the child". In this paper he not only immediately described certain views that would remain intact over more than half a century, but also safeguarded some bases of formal thought (sic) that would fall away with the 1950s focus on formal operational (sic) thought.

Piaget clearly defined formal thought as follows: "From this perspective and without any presupposition of logical order, I call formal reasoning that reasoning with which, from one or more propositions, the mind draws a conclusion to which it will stick with certainty without recourse to observation" (1922, p. 222). He particularly emphasised the nature of deductive premises in formal thought: "The psychological criterion of formal thought is then the fact of not discussing the given premises, not that one takes them as true, but because one takes them as given" (p. 223) and the logical relationship between concrete and formal thought: "But we have already had occasion to suggest that logical multiplication was a much more difficult operation for the child than logical addition and that child's intelligence has a tendency to substitute the latter operation where the former operation is essential" (p. 224).

Piaget's data-collection procedures were based on reasoning tests taken from the work of Cyril Burt. It is well known that Piaget worked with children in Paris using adapted versions of Burt's tests while he was under the direction of Simon at the Binet school for boys. "It is for this exact purpose that we have undertaken a study with a test of Burt's, when the analysis of the difficulties encountered showed that this question leads by an indirect route to that of formal reasoning in general" (p. 224). The general form of the tests is shown in the first example:

Test I. Here are three penknives, one at 10 francs, the other at 12 francs, and the third at 15 francs.

There are two of these knives which have two blades; these are those which cost 12 francs and 15 francs.

There are two of these same knives which have a cork-screw; these are those which cost 10 francs and 12 francs.

And yet, the one that I choose has two blades and a corkscrew. How much does it cost?

The results of the first of Burt's tests (given in four variations) were reported: "From the psychological point of view, the gropings of the child seeking to know if, being given a system of propositions like our test, the characters in play are compatible or not, are of great interest, because it is out of them that formal certainty is going to come" (p. 230). "Test II. If this animal has long ears ..." (p. 231ff). "When this test was given to 33 boys between the ages of 7 and 13 years, 17 of them solved it correctly ..."[2] (p. 231). "Test III. If I have more than ten francs ..." (p. 238ff). "When this test was given (with 2 variations) to 45 children between 7 and 13 years, only 10 of them could solve it ..."

Piaget concluded his paper by observing that "formal thought is derived from the reflection on verbal thought ..." (p. 243) and that "the verbal forms of hypothetical propositions are 'if ... then ...' or the alternatives 'either ... or ...' " (p. 252).

THE ABSENCE OF A FORMAL THOUGHT STAGE (1936)

Piaget was awarded a doctorate *honoris causis* in 1936 on the occasion of the Harvard Tercentenary. His presentation: "Principal factors determining intellectual evolution from childhood to adult life" which appeared (in English) in 1937 described the three (sic) developmental planes of sensorimotor activity, egocentric thought, and that of rational thought (based on the logic of relations, permanence of groups, and quantities) but made no particular mention of a formal stage!

This 1937 description of three planes is interesting in terms of Inhelder's later "discovery" claim in her autobiography. There, and in other places, Inhelder claims to have made significant contributions to that archetypical Genevan investigatory procedure, the *méthode clinique* or *critique*, and to the focus of the adolescent research project, as well as being responsible for its organisation and supervision. This is specifically confirmed in Piaget's (1959) report of the activities of the Institut des Sciences de l'Education. In the section titled Child Psychology (p. 312), he reported:

> Under the joint direction of B. Inhelder and J. Piaget the students of the Institute have been trained at interviewing children, at interpreting the results and at organising experimental work ... From 1948 to 1955, these systematic research projects have focused primarily on the inductive reasoning of the child from 5 to 15 years of age ... The first of these projects has resulted, after several years of effort by Mlle Inhelder and by her team of assistants in the publication of a collaborative book of eighteen chapters written by, amongst others, a large number of our past students.[3]

A CONTRAST: INHELDER ON ADOLESCENT THOUGHT

With that in mind it is not surprising that the published reports of Inhelder from 1948 onwards reveal a gradually growing exposition of the characteristics of adolescent thinking. In her presentation to the Fourth Summer Conference of Psychological Linguistics, Inhelder reported: "We are currently tackling the problem of the origin of inductive reasoning in the child. All inductive reasoning is supported sooner or later by formal logic" (Inhelder, 1948, p. 58). "… It is only from the age of 15, on average, that one observes in certain individuals the administration of rigorous proofs which consist of varying only one factor at a time, holding all others constant" (p. 60). "… The proof further consists of operating a suite of disjunctions on the five interdependent factors" (p. 60).

With reference to the magnetisation[4] task Inhelder claimed: "But it is only once again from about 14/15 years that the adolescent can, on the one hand, spontaneously discover the quantification of probabilities and, on the other, research systematically the cause of the invariant stopping point (of a roulette type wheel). Effectively, he then practices a series of operations of exclusive disjunction (either … or … or neither)" (1948, p. 61).

In an (apparently) unpublished draft of a symposium presentation *The experimental method of the child and the adolescent* (Inhelder, n.d.) where she aimed to demonstrate "the pedagogical aspect of the experimental method", Inhelder reported the three questions that were posed to the children faced with one of the induction tasks: "(1) How do you make the machine function? (2) What is the playing rule that you must give to a friend who would like to succeed at the first try without having the same tries as you? (3) Try to convince me that you are right in order that I would be obliged to believe you." Guided by these questions and a few unedited protocols, we might begin to discover what really took place to produce the *LELA/GLT* excerpts of those protocols (see also, Bond, 1994a).

At the Thirteenth International Congress of Psychology held in 1951 in Stockholm, Inhelder presented a paper entitled *Experimental reasoning of the adolescent* (Inhelder, 1952) in which she reported that "Our observations were carried out with 1500 subjects from 4 to 18 years of age, interviewed individually" (1952, p. 153). "… The structure of the organisation of the experiment is based on a group of formal and combinatorial operations. From 15 years of age the adolescent has recourse to methods of verification: he varies the factor at issue in play, one by one, holding all the others constant, he institutes a series of alternatives in the form of exclusive disjunctions, he makes combinations of factors, etc." (pp. 153–154).

It is interesting to note that a considerable number of the interim or annual reports written by Inhelder's *assistants* also identify the experimental strategy of posing alternatives in the form of exclusive disjunctions in the successful problem-solving strategies of the adolescents (e.g. that of Penard, n.d., mentioned later). At the close of that paper, Inhelder claimed that the development of mature inductive strategies is dependent in part on the cultural *milieu* and that it appears late in the child's development due to the prerequisite nature of the necessary concrete structures and accompanying transformation of cerebral structures. The general nature of Inhelder's work into experimental conduct of children, i.e., to understand the psychological stages of their inductive processes, was also reported to the XIe Congrès International de Psychotechnique in Paris in 1953 (Inhelder, 1954).

It is somewhat of a tragedy that Inhelder's 1954 paper on *The experimental approaches of the child and the adolescent* has remained so long untranslated for the English-speaking world. Indeed it reflects so well the particular skills of Inhelder and the immediate relevance of her work to education and psychology that one could easily imagine quite a different scenario if this paper had been published in a key English-language psychological journal at the same time as the French original had been. It appeared as "Les attitudes expérimentales de l'enfant et de l'adolescent" in the *Bulletin de Psychologie* in France, the year before *LELA* appeared in print.[5]

In outlining the general achievements of the Genevan school under the direction of Piaget, Inhelder noted that "... we are fully conscious of the fact that this picture contains two considerable gaps which concern, on the one hand, the functional aspect of thought, and adolescent reasoning, on the other" (Inhelder, 1954, Chapter 12 in this book, p. 193). In introducing the details of the tasks utilised in the investigation, Inhelder indicated the subjects were ignorant of both the task to be used and the laws to be discovered, "But it is clear that the solution to each problem implies an undeniable cultural and educational contribution" (Chapter 12, p. 195). So much for the overused criticism of the Genevan view of the child as the solitary learner.

The report contained descriptions and general outlines of differences in experimental planning and procedures between children and adolescents for the following 11 tasks: A: The equality of angles; B: The inclined plane; C: The conservation of motion; D: The balance; E: The trolley on an inclined plane; F: Communicating vessels; G: The hydraulic press; H: The projection of shadows; I: Flexibility; J: The pendulum; and K: Mixing liquids.[6] Those who were terminally put off by having to "mind the *P*s and *Q*s" of Piaget in *LELA/GLT* will be relieved to find that the results of the functional analyses comprise three pages while only one page is devoted to structural analysis.

The cross-sectional *functional analysis* revealed that "In each child's experimenting, one can distinguish the motives of action, an experimental strategy, an interpretation of the data and methods of verification. ... These four factors ... are not merely juxtaposed but always united" (Chapter 12, p. 202). In terms of longitudinal development, three principal stages can be distinguished by periods of profound transformation: (1) Imaginative techniques; (2) Concrete techniques; (3) Scientific techniques. In terms of the interpretation of the experiment, Inhelder reports that "It is between the ages of 8 and 10 years of age that the child is found to be closest to the facts. At an earlier age, he has a tendency to deform them; at a more advanced age he tends to go beyond them … The interpretation corresponds to translating the concrete data into abstract notions" (Chapter 12, p. 204).

One of the key questions for the *structural analysis* was to determine "… if the more highly evolved discoveries made by adolescents of 14–15 years with regard to our tasks, are supported by a core common structural nucleus, comparable to that which confers coherence on the concrete operations of the child, but, however, different from it. … everything happens as if there exists a sort of congruence between the available operations of the mental structures and the system of physical operations that the adolescent attempts to separate and understand" (pp. 206 & 207).

While the following conclusions from Inhelder's 1954 paper will come as no surprise to those who have read *LELA/GLT* carefully, and know of Inhelder's work as a school psychologist, it should be helpful to those who subscribe to the received view that the Genevan school regards intelligence as all, with cultural and educational context as irrelevant: "The conclusion from these facts is that the acquisition of experimental method is due to an interdependence of two groups of factors: the cultural climate and educational influences on the one hand, and the formation of a new psychological behaviour on the other. … Towards 14–15 years gifted adolescents seem then to possess the psychological dispositions necessary for the acquisition of the inductive experimental method—it's up to the school to create a climate favourable to their realisation!" (Chapter 12, p. 208).

At the risk of repetition of the evidence that Inhelder was intimately involved with the adolescent research, I should also note that her presentation at the 15th International Congress of Psychology in Montreal in 1954, "Patterns of inductive reasoning", published in *Acta Psychologica* in 1955, reported on the study of 1700 children and adolescents from 5 to 16 years and concluded that "[t]he inductive method involves a new mental structure, following precise laws such as the laws of the 'group' or 'lattice', which according to Cybernetics can be both of a mathematical and physiological nature" (Inhelder, 1955, pp. 217–218).

A STARK CONTRAST:
PIAGET ON FORMAL THOUGHT. c. 1950

By way of stark contrast to the wealth of relevant detail in Inhelder's reports in the late 1940s and early 1950s, it is interesting to read the text of Jean Piaget taken from the audio recording of a series of regular presentations that he made in the spring of 1951 on Radio Suisse Romande (French-speaking Swiss Radio) (Piaget, 1996).[7]

> Formal thought is the capacity to reason about simple propositions without having the need of objects to manipulate. While the peculiarity of concrete operations, about which we have already spoken is to bear, if not upon objects themselves, then at least upon the relationships (which they bear) between them or upon the classes which they (the objects) form one with the others. Formal thought then constitutes, what is

sometimes called, hypothetico-deductive thought, that is to say, deduction which does not bear upon classes or relations, but which bears upon simple hypotheses, that is to say upon verbal statements. ... A first hypothesis that we could make is simply about the role of language. Indeed, it is infinitely more difficult to reason about words or about verbal statements than about objects, and it is that which can explain the characteristic late development of formal thought. ... Here's another problem also taken from the tests of Burt. We say to the child: "I am going to think of an animal; you are going to find which one it is. If this animal has long ears, it will be a donkey or a mule. And if this animal has a bushy tail, it will be a mule or a horse. Ah well, the animal about which I am thinking has, both long ears and a bushy tail. Which one is it? ...

A second hypothesis that we can make is that formal thought constitutes a set of operations of the second degree, so to speak, that's to say operations upon other operations. For example, the notion of proportion is acquired only at the formal level: "one is to two, as two is to four". In the notion of proportion, we have, in effect, firstly the simple operations, the operation of relationship—"one over two" or just as well "two over four"; and following that, the establishment of the link between those relationships, that is to say, the relationships between the relationships. There, then, is a sort of operation of the second degree. A third hypothesis that we could make is that formal thought is combinatorial in nature. For example, the permutations of three objects ABC, make the permutations ABC, ACB, BCA, BAC etc. Well these combinatorial operations are also operations of the second degree. ...

Well, we can make an even more general solution, which consists of saying that formal thought is characterised by the logic of propositions, in the logical sense of the term, as opposed to the groupings of classes and of relations. The logic of propositions is indeed characterised by a series of new operations: implication, incompatibility, disjunction, reciprocal exclusion etc. And it just so happens that the logic of propositions presupposes all the preceding factors.—Firstly, it is a system of verbal statements and not a systems of objects like classes or like relations.— Secondly, it is a system of operations carried out on other operations, therefore, operations of the second degree; since they must be operations which bear necessarily on objects previously classified or seriated, they are operations of the second degree.— Thirdly, as everyone knows, the logic of propositions presupposes a combinatorial system, constitutes a combinatorial system, and is very much more complicated than those of the groupings of classes and of relations. We would say then that formal thought appears when the logic of propositions superimposes itself by abstraction on the grouping of classes and relations, and drawing from them what it must to constitute this new combinatorial system.

Whereas the Radio Suisse Romande series seems to rely on unchanged tasks and ideas published in 1922, augmented to some important extent with his logical ideas just previously expounded in *Traité de logique* (Piaget, 1949), Piaget's invited address to the University of Chicago on 3 April 1953 (but published much later in 1963) seems much better informed about the nature of the Genevan adolescent research. In particular, the focus is on the investigative strategy of requiring the child to work actively with Inhelder's specially constructed tasks, rather than rehearsing the Burt tests from his 1920s research (Piaget, 1963, p. 283).

Of late, our investigations have been conducted quite differently. We now try to start with some action that the child must perform. We introduce him into an experimental setting, present him with objects, and—after the problem has been stated—the child must do something, he must experiment. Having observed his actions and manipulation of objects we can then pose the verbal questions that constitute the interview. Note that this interview now pertains to a preceding action, and this seems to me to be a more fruitful and reliable method than the purely verbal enquiry.

  … Furthermore, while our earlier studies pertained to various classes of thought content, we later became increasingly more interested in the formal aspects of thought. These aspects transcend any single content category and provide the basis for the intellectual elaboration of any and all contents … [pp. 283–284]. I shall distinguish four stages in this development: … finally the stage of propositional operations with their formal characteristics which are attained in the pre-adolescent and adolescent stage [p. 285] … This is the period during which new logical operations appear: propositional operations, the logic of propositions, implication, and so forth [pp. 295–296].

Piaget considers why the logic of propositions co-occurs with the combinatorial operations (as shown in a poker chips problem), the operations of proportions (revealed in the balance problem), and the operations of probabilities (consideration of probable and possible events) "that have at first sight no particular relationship either among each other or to the logic of propositions. Here the concept of complex structures appears to me to be especially valuable. Let us take, for instance, the well known sixteen basic operations of the logic of propositions" (p. 297) … "I suggest that the structure of propositional operations is a complex structure which comprises both lattices and groups. Such a structure has many possibilities and implications. … They have two-fold interest: first by analogy with mathematical operations, which are, after all, operations of thought; and secondly, by analogy with the physiological structures, or, if you will, with the cybernetic models of hypothesised physiological structures" (p. 299).

In a paper on the "The stages of intellectual development in the child and the adolescent" presented to the 1955 symposium of The Association of French Language Scientific Psychology in Geneva (Piaget, 1956), Piaget describes aspects of the third and final stage of intellectual development: "III.—The period of formal operations [sic] Finally, comes the third and last period, that of formal operations. There, from 11–12 years of age from one part (first stage) with a plateau of equilibrium towards 13 or 14 years (second stage), we witness a mass of transformations which develop relatively rapidly at the time of their appearance and which are extremely diverse. It is, first and foremost, the beautiful studies of Mlle Inhelder on inductive reasoning and the experimental method of children and adolescents, which have allowed us to come to these conclusions …" (p. 40). … "And above all, what we see appear at the last level is the logic of propositions, the capacity to reason about statements, about hypotheses and no longer only about objects on the table (in front of them) or readily represented" (p. 41).

Interestingly, Piaget returns here to his 1922 and oft-repeated view of "the capacity to reason about statements, about hypotheses and no longer only about objects" although in Chicago he had acknowledged, "Of late … (w)e … present him with objects … he must experiment." The aforementioned description of the *méthode critique* technique given by Piaget hardly seems a faithful account of the procedures implemented by Inhelder and her team in the adolescent research.

A further interesting perspective on the development of the Genevans' ideas on formal operational thought can be accessed via the reports written by Inhelder's students and *assistants* (many of whom were former students) as each part of the investigative enterprise was completed. Mlle Claude Penard was one of those, producing a typed and annotated "Report of developmental research: Magnets task" (Penard, n.d.) In the late 1940s, she undertook a replication of the investigations conducted on the invisible magnetism task by Denis-Prinzhorn and others for the Chance book earlier in the decade. Of the dozen or so protocols that appear in Chapter 6 of *LELA/GLT*, only one is directly attributable to Denis-Prinzhorn (Mamb 8;3; *GLT*, p. 97). The vast majority of the remainder I can attribute, as a result of my personal research, to two-person teams from Inhelder, Bourquin, and Penard. While many protocols reveal Inhelder as the interviewer, the famed Gou protocol, (*GLT*, p. 100), along with those of Ful (*GLT*, p. 98), and San (*GLT*, p. 100) has Penard as the interviewer.

Given that Piaget was notorious among the research assistants for routinely ignoring their summary reports and conclusions by returning exclusively to the actual original protocols for writing his books, a comparison of the stage criteria used by Penard with those of Inhelder and Piaget in *LELA/GLT* several years later is potentially instructive. Penard concluded that "the processes of exclusion and verification differ according to age" (Penard, n.d., p. 4). "In the first stage (6–7 years) the child doesn't feel the need to verify its hypothesis … In the second stage (8–9 years) the child often abandons one hypothesis for another without excluding … (We observe) trial and error without method. (p. 5). At the third stage (from 9–10 years till 11–12 years) the child reasons according to the concrete contents. Concrete experience is the only means used to arrive at an exclusion or verification. At the fourth stage (over 12 years) verification and exclusion is effected by formal reasoning. The child reasons about the propositions emptied of all their concrete content … Another form of elimination appears, that of all factors except one … (p. 6). The question we ask ourselves is the following: why are the youngest children incapable of spontaneous exclusion (before 11–12 years) regardless of hypothesis, even when we provided them with all the concrete data? Why does the complexity of the hypotheses stop them, even though the concrete elements which would allow them the effect an exclusion are given in the task equipment?" (Penard, n.d., p. 9).

Reference to *LELA/GLT*—the core of the adolescence corpus—by Inhelder and Piaget (1955/1958) reveals the following characteristics of the developing cognitive stages. (Note that at the bottom of the first page of Chapter 6 of *LELA/GLT*, M. Denis-Prinzhorn is credited with the collaboration in the magnetism task. While I have no doubt that she was the assistant for this task when it was first used in the production of the book on Chance, the records that remain at the Archives Jean Piaget seem to confirm Penard's role in the *LELA/GLT* data collection, see Bond, 1994a.) The *LELA/GLT* stage descriptions are:

I. Preoperational Disjunctions and Exclusions as intuitive representations (*GLT*, pp. 94–95).
IIA. The Beginnings of Concrete Disjunctions and Exclusions (*GLT*, p. 96).
IIB. The Concrete Exclusion of Weight (based on lack of correspondence between classes and relations nor transitiveness) (*GLT*, pp. 100–101).
III. Propositional Operations or Exclusions (we are not exaggerating when we claim that it is possible for subjects at this level to work in turn with each of the sixteen binary combinations of propositional logic) (*GLT*, p. 104).

While the *LELA/GLT* book is an exposition on how thinking and problem-solving behaviour (as opposed to children) can be classified into stages based on Piaget's logico-mathematical modelling, and that sample was drawn to be illustrative of cognitive operations, not of a representative sample of children, a table from Reuchlin (1964, modified by Bond, 1994b) is still worthy of examination (Table 4.1). Reuchlin found a total of 192 segments of exemplar protocols (from $N > 1500$) in *LELA* and categorised them according to the age/stage allocation. From the table of distributions it seems that the interpretation of the age of the onset and the establishment of formal operations in *LELA/GLT* was rather optimistic— even with the original Genevan data.

TABLE 4.1

GLT subjects by age and stage (after Reuchlin, 1964)

Age	n	<III	IIIA	IIIB
7,0	8	8		
7,6	17	17		
8,0	13	13		
8,6	6	6		
9,0	11	11		
9,6	12	12		
10,0	13	13		
10,6	13	11	2	
11,0	7	4	3	
11,6	11	5	6	
12,0	8	1	7	
12,6	18	1	16	1
13,0	11		8	3
13,6	7		4	3
14,0	14		5	9
14,6	11		3	8
15,0	7			7
15,6	5			5
N	192			

INHELDER AND PIAGET: A NEW BASIS FOR COLLABORATION?

It would be foolish for me to claim that I have just taken the original sources and let the participants speak for themselves. The presentation that I made in Geneva, on which this chapter is based, is far different from the one I had planned to present. Although I had in my study a wealth of evidence garnered during three previous visits to the Archives Jean Piaget in Geneva to illustrate my planned talk, it was careful trawling of the treasury of historical material in the Piaget CD-ROM that prompted me to cast my pre-formed ideas aside. What I read put again into stark contrast key and somewhat conflicting ideas that I have carried with me for a number of years:

The first reflected the received view, especially among Anglophones, that, in spite of the disclaimer in *GLT*, Piaget was the "brains" behind the Genevan *oeuvre* in general and the adolescent research in particular; a belief apparently confirmed by the evidence that every word of the remaining *LELA* manuscript chapters was in Piaget's own handwriting, as well as the absence of a published book by Inhelder on Induction.

The second was Inhelder's autobiographical claim about her team's discovery of the new stage of formal thought and her role in Geneva around 1950; claims apparently supported by the 1954 *Bulletin de Psychologie* article (now translated for this collection, see Chapter 12) and copies of about 80 draft pages of the Induction manuscript that I had found in Geneva. My distinct impression is that Bärbel Inhelder held a special spot for the *LELA/GLT* books; she offered to search out the remainder of the Induction draft for me, saying that there was much more than I had uncovered. (The Induction draft assembled in 1998 comprises nearly 150 pages.)

To concentrate the concerns into one sharp question, I asked myself, "How could Inhelder discover a new stage of formal thought in the 1950s when Piaget wrote a paper on formal thought in 1922?" My conclusion is in two parts. First, and I think, incontrovertibly, Piaget and Inhelder were focusing on quite different topics: Piaget's self-limiting definition of formal thought in 1922 makes formal thought a far more restricted field than the one Inhelder focused on—inductive and experimental thinking in adolescents. Second, and somewhat more controversially —if I may judge from the somewhat heated discussion that followed in Geneva— all the written evidence leads me to assert that Piaget continued with this restricted view of formal thought for quite a while after Inhelder had developed a far more powerful conception of it, having gathered a surfeit of empirical evidence using tasks that make Piaget's continued return to Burt's reasoning tasks in the 1950s seem not very well informed.

The first protest that I must somehow field is the very obvious claim that the published output of a research team is, of necessity, a very poor summary of the ways in which the key members of a productive research team work. Attributing ideas and input on the basis of the written summary is indeed foolhardy—a warning oft-repeated to me in Geneva—even more so in the case of the Genevan school, and in particular of the vibrant, mobile, multi-faceted partnership of Piaget and Inhelder. Some of those warnings came from people who had worked as part of the team at some stage. My reply is that, if I take the time-honoured approach of Baconian induction by simple enumeration to all the written evidence that I have found, the table of comparisons looks something like this: One box shows Piaget's view of formal thought as generally restricted to reasoning about verbal statements of the sort found in the Burt puzzles; the second box shows Inhelder's view of the developmental acquisition of experimental methods of exclusion and confirmation including the *ceteris paribus* principle. This second box of evidence is very well developed in Inhelder's reports before any evidence of it appears in Piaget's writing.

Of course it is at this point that the second protest must be answered: My method could be held to be tendentious, and my conclusions to be the consequence of over-interpretation. My defence is that, apart from the exception noted shortly, I have referenced (almost?) all of the published information—and a deal of the unpublished documents—that I have uncovered relevant to the development of the theory of formal operations into the mid-1950s when *LELA* appeared. Admittedly, the organisation of the record in this paper—Piaget, then Inhelder, Piaget, and finally Inhelder and Piaget—is designed to set the contributions as contrasting, rather than as complementary. Quite frankly, I am astonished that the written evidence is so easily and neatly categorised. I am surprised to find Piaget's unequivocal attribution of the conduct of the "beautiful studies" to Inhelder in a number of places. As I uncovered each step in the process, I became more and more surprised at how the direction of my planned presentation for the Cours Avancé in Geneva was changing.

POST-GENEVA, 1998

Although the James Cook University copy of *The psychology of intelligence* (1947/1951) still has the record of my borrowing it in 1978, I managed to overlook the pages Piaget had written on formal operations there when preparing my talk for Geneva. When I was shown the French text after my Geneva presentation, I thought I had erred in a major way. So much so that I drafted all the text to this point before consulting both the English and French versions of the text. The book "contains the substance of the lectures … giv(en) … in 1942" and focuses on "Formal operations" in "Part Three—The Development of Thought".

Piaget's deliberations on formal operations revisit both the conceptions of "reasoning formally and with mere propositions" and (more unfortunately, I think) "The following neat example comes from one of Burt's tests: 'Edith is fairer than Susan; …'" (1947/1951, p. 149). Importantly however, he draws comparisons between the vertical separations (décalages, of course, in the original) which exist between concrete and formal operations and the horizontal separations (décalages) that are revealed between the various conservations of concrete stage. The fine distinction between the role of formal logic and that ascribed to formal operations in his developing theory seems to be coming to light: For the former, the role of formal logic: "We thus see why formal logic and mathematical deduction are still inaccessible to the child and seem to constitute a realm of its own—the realm of 'pure' thought which is independent of action" (p. 149) and for the role of formal operations: "But it is the function of the psychology of intelligence to set[8] the canon of formal operations in its true perspective and to show that it could not have any mental meaning were it not for the concrete operations that both pave the way for it and provide its content" (p. 150). This crucial (I had originally put "delightful") point is reiterated in *LELA/GLT*: "in other words, one must keep in mind that concrete structuring of the data is an indispensable prerequisite of the propositional structure" (*GLT*, p. 298) and is routinely overlooked in every simple-minded attack on the Genevan description of adolescent thinking. It seems that here (along with those from *Traité de logique*) we find some of the ideas that would be developed a decade later into LELA/GLT *only* with the collaboration of Inhelder and her invaluable input from the Induction investigations.

CONCLUSIONS

When I suggested to the editors of this collection that Inhelder's 1954 *Bulletin de Psychologie* article should be translated for Anglophones, I did so for a number of reasons. The paper very clearly shows the school psychologist Inhelder at work. While the popularity of Piaget's epistemology in English-speaking countries has been due, rather ironically, to its appeal to developmental and educational psychologists, it is Inhelder's psychological subject, rather that Piaget's epistemic subject, that is easily recognisable to those who work with children. Given that Inhelder's manuscript for the Induction book was not published, the 1954 paper is an even more important counter-balance to the dominantly logico-mathematical flavour and appearance of *LELA/GLT*. Interestingly, in an English-language version of a General Education course lecture (no. 24) titled, "The growth of logical thinking" (Inhelder, 1962), Inhelder gives more emphasis to the structural analysis of formal operational thought—in keeping with the emphasis we are used to in the joint Inhelder and Piaget text of *GLT*. Moreover, the 1954 paper helps readers of *LELA/GLT* to understand why the only Genevan book on adolescence focuses exclusively on problems of scientific method—Piaget apparently appropriated Inhelder's Induction project and data to a more general epistemological purpose.

While Piaget's devotion to epistemological questions is now quite clear and has been traced back at least as far as 1923—and even to his 1918 book *Recherche* (see Gruber & Vonèche, 1995, and commentary in Ducret, 1990; Smith, 1993; Vidal, 1994)—it is most clearly explicated in his 1950 trilogy, *Introduction to genetic epistemology* (Piaget, 1950). This regularly overlooked elaboration of Piaget's fundamental and overarching philosophical aims and orientations consists of three volumes (nearly 1000 densely written pages in all), devoted to Mathematical thought (Vol. 1), Physical thought (Vol. 2) and Biological, psychological and sociological thought (Vol. 3).[9] In the second volume Piaget attempts to describe how an objective science about physical reality is possible. The epistemological importance Piaget placed on the role of experimentation in the physical sciences can be ascertained, in part, by his attention to the role of Induction in the theory of scientific thought: "4. The Problems of Experimental Induction" in the section "Chance, Irreversibility and Induction" of *Introduction to genetic epistemology*, Vol. 2, pp. 165–223 (Piaget, 1950).

While acknowledging that many scientists and philosophers of science eschew the use of induction, holding to deduction as the hallmark of rational scientific thinking, Piaget adheres to Lalande's (1929) exposition on the complementarity of the two. Lalande insisted that induction is a *method*, not merely an incomplete or inferior form of deductive *reasoning*, and the impetus for important parts of the adolescence research is attributed directly and specifically to the philosophy of Lalande in a number of places (e.g., Inhelder, 1954; Piaget, 1950, pp. 191, see Chapter 12 in this book, p. 201). Piaget mentions one of the "connected vessels" tasks, *en passant*, but explicitly, and in detail, refers to the inclined plane task with the footnote: "This experiment forms part of a complete research project on the development of induction currently underway at our institute under the direction of B. Inhelder" (Piaget, 1950, p. 199).

So what then of the possibility of identifying and attributing the contribution of Bärbel Inhelder to our understanding of formal operational thinking, especially as it is realised in the core work of the field, *The growth of logical thinking from childhood to adolescence* (Inhelder & Piaget, 1955/1958)? Even the diagrams that illustrate the English translation (and subsequent translations), but which did not appear in the 1955 version of *LELA*, have Inhelder's planned *Induction* text as their source (*GLT*, p. xxiv)

The footnote to my translation of Bärbel's 1954 *Bulletin de Psychologie* paper (Chapter 12, p. 209) concludes: "While I am sure this paper does not present a theory of formal operational thinking … it does provide a systematic description of adolescent problem-solving behaviour which will appeal to secondary school teachers and others who work with adolescents." And it is at this exact point—the nexus between the systematic detailed description of events and the theorisation (or explanation) of them—that the tension in trying to untangle the relative contributions to a joint research enterprises resides. Poincaré (1902/1952) is attributed with: "Science is facts; just as houses are made of stones, so science is made of facts; but a pile of stones is not a house, and a collection of facts is not necessarily science." But one could hardly regard Inhelder's detailed descriptions of Induction in children and adolescents as a mere collection of facts.

It seems certain that Piaget's primary interest in philosophical/epistemological issues, informed in this case by the work of Lalande, provided the impetus for the research into the issues of chance, probability, and induction. Equally certain, it seems, is the insufficiency and inappropriateness of Piaget's conception of mature thinking as formal thought, as revealed in his prolonged attachment to Burt's tasks for over three decades from the early 1920s. The results of the Inhelder research into Induction was much more fruitful in this regard; even though the research project was not directed to the end of describing and theorising formal operational thinking as it would appear in *LELA/GLT*. *LELA/GLT* is the result of a remarkable confluence of circumstances, reflecting to differing extents, Piaget's interest in formal thought, his interest in logical modelling (*Traité de logique*, 1949), his epistemological interests (Piaget, 1950), and Inhelder's indispensable research on Induction. Until *LELA/GLT* was written, Inhelder's published work contained the more comprehensive descriptions and explanations of the features of adolescent thinking. With *LELA/GLT*, it was Piaget's contribution that conceptualised a theory of formal operational thinking; interesting, given the decades of criticism of the logico-mathematical modelling of formal operational thought.

In trying to conceptualise how a team effort might turn "a pile of stones" into "a house" according to Poincaré's distinction between facts and science, I am drawn to the description of the relationship between the famed Isaac Newton and the almost forgotten John Flamsteed, Astronomer Royal to Charles II of England. Flamsteed's detailed lunar observations were indispensable to the crucial aspect of Newton's theory of gravitation as it affected the moon. Newton (cited in White, 1997, p. 313) appealed in a letter to Flamsteed thus to obtain the lunar data:

> And for my part I am of opinion that for your observations to come abroad thus with a *theory which you ushered into the world* & which by their means has been made exact would be much more for their advantage & your reputation than to keep them private until you die or publish them without a theory to recommend them. For such a theory will be a demonstration of their exactness and make you readily acknowledged the most exact observer that has hitherto appeared in the world. But if you publish them without such a theory to recommend them, they will only be thrown into the heap of observations of former astronomers until somebody shall arise that by perfecting the theory of the moon shall discover your observations to be more exact than the rest.

Newton's biographer Michael White comments a little later (p. 315):

> Newton, on the other hand, saw Flamsteed as little more than a technician—a mere gatherer of data for Newton's free use. He regarded himself as the genius who translated raw observed facts into all-consuming theories capable of changing the way people thought ... It was Flamsteed's duty, so Newton believed, to offer up his findings willingly and unquestionably.

It is perfectly clear that the Piaget/Inhelder partnership was far different from the rather one-sided Newton/Flamsteed relationship; Inhelder was, by contrast, both well-informed about and an active partner in Piaget's theory-building enterprise. Indeed, Piaget has referred to it as a common *oeuvre*. But how did Inhelder's adolescence research become a book on *The growth of logical thinking*, instead of, rather than as well as, Inhelder's book on the development of experimental Induction?

ACKNOWLEDGEMENTS

I feel honoured to have been asked by the organising team of the 1998 Cours Avancé of the Archives Jean Piaget to make this contribution about formal operational thinking as a tribute to the memory of Bärbel Inhelder. While many colleagues have contributed over a long time to my appreciation and understanding of the Genevan *oeuvre*, I must thank Anastasia Tryphon, Jacques Vonèche, Leslie Smith, Jean-Jacques Ducret, and Bill Gray for their indispensible wisdom and patience during the preparation of this chapter. Alas, their advice was sometimes ignored: The remaining errors and inadequacies are all mine.

My thanks to the Piaget family for permission to quote from the text of the Radio Suisse Romande broadcast.

NOTES

1. The English translation of passages from the French for the purpose of this chapter were made by the present author.
2. A nice morsel of nomothetic detail from the 1922 Piaget!
3. *LELA/GLT* has 18 chapters with footnotes to each of the empirical chapters acknowledging the contribution of the *assistants*.
4. Reported in Chapter 6 of *GLT*: A metal bar on a roulette type wheel always stops when pointing to boxes containing hidden magnets. The boxes vary according to colour, weight, design, and location as well.
5. The editors of this current tribute volume agreed with my proposal that this paper was long overdue for translation and now for the first time an English-language version of the paper appears as Chapter 12.
6. The *GLT* tasks that are not included here include: 2. The law of floating bodies …; 6. The role of invisible magnetization …; 14. Centrifugal force …; and 15. Probable dispersions and correlations. The Hamilton Tower task which apparently formed part of the Induction suite of tasks is not mentioned in either source.
7. "*Set*" seems to carry the meaning of the French original (*replacer*) better than the "replace" of the 1951 English translation.
8. While published translations of these enormously difficult, but crucial, volumes exist in Spanish, Italian, and German—some for more than quarter of a century—no such English translations exist. Could this be due, at least in part, to Anglophones' attention to Piaget as psychologist, rather than as epistemologist/philosopher?

REFERENCES

Bond, T.G. (1994a, June). *Piaget's méthode clinique: There's more to it than we've been told*. Paper presented at the Jean Piaget Society Symposium, Chicago, IL.
Bond, T.G. (1994b). Epistemic subject versus quotidian subject: The adolescence research of Inhelder and Piaget. *Education Section Review, 18*, 9–14.
Ducret, J.-J. (1990). *Jean Piaget: Biographie et parcours intellectuel* [Jean Piaget: Biography and intellectual itinerary]. Neuchâtel: Delachaux et Niestlé.

Gruber, H.E., & Vonèche, J.J. (Eds.). (1995). *The essential Piaget: An interpretative reference and guide*. Northvale, NJ: Aronson.

Inhelder, B. (1948). Contribution à l'étude de la formalisation spontanée chez l'enfant [Contribution to the study of spontaneous formalisation in the child]. *Synthèse, VII*(1–2), 58–62.

Inhelder, B. (1952). Le raisonnement expérimental de l'adolescent [Experimental reasoning of the adolescent]. In D. Katz. (Ed.), *Proceedings and papers of the 13th International Congress of Psychology* (pp. 153–154). Stockholm: Bröderna Lagerström.

Inhelder, B. (1953). La conduite expérimentale de l'enfant [Experimental conduct in children]. In R. Zazzo (Ed.), *XIe Congrès International de Psychotechnique, Section Psychologie de l'Education* (pp. 1–3). Paris: s.n.

Inhelder, B. (1954). Les attitudes expérimentales de l'enfant et de l'adolescent [The experimental approaches of the child and the adolescent]. *Bulletin de Psychologie, 7*(5), 272–282.

Inhelder, B. (1955). Patterns of inductive reasoning. *Acta Psychologica, 11*, 217–218.

Inhelder, B. (1962). *Social sciences 8. The growth of logical thinking*. General Education course lecture, No. 24 (9 January 1962). Unpublished lecture notes, Geneva.

Inhelder, B. (1989). Autobiography. In G. Lindzey (Ed.), *A history of psychology in autobiography, Vol. 8* (pp. 208–243). Stanford, CA: Stanford University Press.

Inhelder, B. (n.d.). *La méthode experimentale chez l'enfant et l'adolescent* [Experimental method in the child and adolescent]. Unpublished presentation notes, Geneva.

Inhelder, B., & Piaget, J., (1958). *The growth of logical thinking from childhood to adolescence* (A. Parsons & S. Milgram, Trans.). London: Routledge & Kegan Paul. (Original work published 1955)

Lalande, A. (1929). *Les théories de l'induction et de l'experimentation* [Theories of induction and experimentation]. Paris: Boivin.

Penard, C. (n.d.). *Rapport sur une recherche en génétique: Expérience des aimants* [Report of developmental research: Magnets task]. Unpublished research report, Geneva.

Piaget, J. (1922). Essai sur la multiplication logique et les débuts de la pensée formelle chez l'enfant [An essay on logical multiplication and the beginnings of formal thought in the child]. *Journal de Psychologie Normale et Pathologique, 19*, 222–261.

Piaget, J. (1937). *Principal factors determining intellectual evolution from childhood to adult life*. Paper presented at the Harvard tercentenary conference of arts and sciences. Cambridge, MA: Harvard University Press.

Piaget, J. (1949). *Traité de logique: Essai de logistique opératoire* [Treatise on logic: An essay on operatory logic]. Paris: A. Colin.

Piaget, J. (1950). *Introduction à l'épistémologie génétique: Vol. 2. La pensée physique* [Introduction in genetic epistemology: Vol. 2. Physical thought. (No English translation exists)]. Paris: Presses Universitaires de France.

Piaget, J. (1951). *The psychology of intelligence*. London: Routledge & Kegan Paul. (Original work published 1947)

Piaget, J. (1956). Les stades du développement intellectuel de l'enfant et de l'adolescent [The stages of intellectual development in the child and the adolescent]. In P. Osterrieth, J. Piaget et al. (Eds.), *Le problème des stades en psychologie de l'enfant: symposium de l'Association de Psychologie Scientifique de Langue Française* (pp. 33–42). Paris: Presses Universitaires de France.

Piaget, J. (1959). L'Institut des sciences de l'éducation (Institut J.-J. Rousseau) de 1912 à 1956 [The Institute of educational sciences (Institute J.-J. Rousseau) from 1912 to 1956]. In *Histoire de l'Université de Genève. Annexes: Historique des facultés et des instituts* (pp. 307-316). Genève: Librairie de l'Université, Georg.

Piaget, J. (1963). The attainment of invariants and reversible operations in the development of thinking. [A lecture delivered at the University of Chicago on 3 April, 1953] *Social Research*, *30*, 283–299.

Piaget, J. (1996). Stade des opérations formelles [The stage of formal operations. (Recorded from broadcast on Radio Suisse Romande, 1951)]. In *Piaget: Cheminements dans l'oeuvre sientifique, Causerie 6* [CD-ROM]. Genève: Delachaux et Niestlé.

Poincaré, H. (1952). *Science and hypothesis*. New York: Dover. (Original work published 1902)

Reuchlin, M. (1964). L'intelligence: Conception génétique opératoire et conception factorielle [Intelligence: A genetic oparatory conception and a factorial conception]. *Revue Suisse de Psychologie Pure et Appliquée*, *23*(2), 113–134.

Smith, L. (1993). *Necessary knowledge: Piagetian perspectives on constructivism*. Hove, UK: Lawrence Erlbaum Associates Ltd.

Smith, L. (1998). Learning and the development of knowledge. *Archives de Psychologie*, *66*, 201–219.

Vidal, F. (1994). *Piaget before Piaget*. Cambridge, MA: Harvard University Press.

White, M. (1997). *Isaac Newton: The last sorcerer*. London: Fourth Estate.

CHAPTER FIVE

The impact of social structure on development: An analysis of individual differences in cognition

Wolfgang Edelstein
Max Planck Institute for Human Development, Berlin, Germany

Eberhard Schröder
University of Potsdam, Germany

SOME THEORETICAL CONSIDERATIONS

Introduction

In this chapter we present a set of data from a longitudinal study entitled "Individual development and social structure". This study represents an attempt to combine Piaget's developmental universalism with a sociologically enlightened theory of socialisation, that is sensitive to time, place, and the individual's constructive ability. In this introductory part, we develop, as briefly as possible, a rationale for extending Piaget's theory to the development of individual differences. Then we shall briefly delineate the sources of variability internal and external to the cognitive action that influence the subjects' developmental performance. After this theoretical introduction we shall present the design of the longitudinal study. Repeated assessment of the individual is basic to the reconstruction of the course of development (cognitive and otherwise), including developmental variations in growth, and a condition of the possibility of attributing variability to sources internal to the cognitive process as well as to sources external to it, relative to situation, personality, and socio-cultural structure. The presentation will be limited to a set of data that relate to class effects in cognitive development, a paradigmatic case of the relationship between structural development and socially induced variations in the study. Eberhard Schröder and Wolfgang Edelstein's analysis of the development of syllogistic reasoning in Chapter 6 of this book will complement the present account of external effects on cognitive development by a case study of internal constraints, covering the variability generated by content and context.

Both accounts should be viewed together as a study designed to reconstruct both direct and indirect (moderator) effects, over time, of internal and external constraints on developmental outcomes and developmental processes in the area of cognition.

Finally we shall discuss the findings in view of a Piagetian theory of cognitive socialisation. This is the term we give to the process by which constructive individuals evolve across facilitative or constraining experiences on their pathway towards a more or less restricted equilibrium.

To sum up, the present chapter and the one following it derive from the same study, project "Individual development and social structure", a longitudinal study of development from childhood to early adulthood conducted in Iceland. The two chapters adopt a complementary stance. Whereas the present chapter focuses on the socialisation of individual differences in cognitive development, as it impacts on developmental performance, Chapter 6 highlights the development of individual differences as they moderate the developmental dynamic. The present chapter, in consequence, adopts a more sociological view, stressing inter-individual variations in developmental outcomes. The next chapter, by contrast, stressing a genetic point of view, focuses on intra-individual differences and changes over time characterised by the changing influence of the moderators themselves.

SOME HISTORY

It has been a major focus of interest in our studies to understand the intersection of two forces operating on the human mind: universalism and particularism. One represents the regularities of thought operating on the diversities of experience. Conversely, the other reflects the constraints that the particularities of experience derived from culture and social conditions impose upon the universals of the mind and their development. It is one of the mysteries of sociality how socially generated constraints affect individual human behaviour, including mental capacities and operations, even to their most intimate core and expression. Simultaneously it is one of science's great challenges to discover and unveil the universal and essential unities of the mind's operations beyond the variabilities of its situated performance.

The presentation we offer here is a tribute to this double-tiered enterprise. We wish to demonstrate, using Piaget's universalistic theory, the *variability* of the very operations that constitute the topics of this theory. Incidentally, this endeavour shows that the theory is easily extended beyond its inherited focus on epistemological universals to domains it has ignored or rejected, as Piaget and Inhelder openly declared in their closing remarks to the Green, Ford, and Flamer conference report (Inhelder & Piaget, 1971). It is easily extended, this means, to the analysis, reconstruction, and explanation of variability in development. A theory that highlights the causal and functional role of social construction and interaction in the activity and the development of mental operations forfeits a substantive part of its reach and explanatory power if it leaves unattended the variability of developmental growth patterns, and the role that contextual constraints and social conditions play in the emergence and unfolding of individual differences. This has been the focus of our extended longitudinal study conducted in Iceland for some 20 years under the more or less programmatic title "Individual development and social structure".

In 1989, Bärbel Inhelder wrote in the *Bulletin de Psychologie*: There has been a change of focus from the epistemological to the situated individual psychological subject. … there is a renewed interest in the relations between representations and meanings of actions, as procedural aspects of behavior and the individual's interpretive network are closely connected" (p. 466, our translation). We share this point of departure, with the proviso that it is not merely the situated individual, but the social subject whom we purport to approach through the lens of Piaget's theory.

Let us first devote a few words to this programmatic approach to the theory. In an address dating from 1966 and published in the "*Homage*" of the Université de Genève on the occasion of Piaget's 80th birthday in 1976, and again in *Campus*, Geneva's university magazine, on the occasion of his centenary in 1996, Piaget vindicates for his psychological studies the descriptive stance appropriate to a natural science of species behaviour, focused on the epistemic behaviour of humans, a naturalistic description of mind. Piaget's claim, however, is explicitly formulated on the background of the affirmed existence of another, more generally appreciated and more conventional psychology of individual differences (presumably including the "American question" of technologies to change them). Piaget's epistemological programme visibly emerges in contrast to an accepted mainstream psychology and claims a right of place in it.

Today, in a much more variegated mainstream, but for the ignorance and prejudice of the protagonists, Piaget's theory could quite easily place itself among the recognised provinces of the psychological territory: evolutionary psychology, decision theory, rationality theory, etc., all have laid out their claims. But we still miss, both in the mainstream of differential psychology, and in the universalist constructivism of Piaget, a *social science* of the mind's constructive action, a programme using Piaget's descriptive and explanatory apparatus to reconstruct individuals' pathways and patterns of (more or less) equilibrated cognitive experience. Individual pathways are constrained by the interaction between developmental universals and the particularities of experience generated by refractory world objects and conflictual interactions which are assimilated by meaning-making structures that change with the very assimilation. The study of individual pathways could activate Inhelder's heritage.

We lack space here to describe in any detail the types and modalities of encounters that constitute the qualities of individual development. Elsewhere the first author has described how the transition to modern social organisation transformed the developmental trajectories of children (Edelstein, 1983). We have described the impact of positively or negatively cathected objects on cognition (Edelstein, 1992), the influence of attachment to the caretaker on the development of exploration and search from a secure base (Edelstein, 1996), and the differential provision and pattern of experience based on the child's position in the system of social inequality (Edelstein, Keller, & Schröder, 1990). Further studies have been undertaken to investigate the effect of various personality disorders on developmental performance (Jacobsen, Edelstein, & Hofmann, 1994; Hofmann, 1991 for depression; Jacobsen & Hofmann, 1997 for insecurity of attachment; Schellhas, 1993 for anxiety).

Internal constraints

Within the traditional psychometric framework of differential experimental psychology, Hofmann (1982) has listed a number of performance factors that produce variability in cognitive performance. In this view, performance is the product of tests using Piagetian tasks as test devices. The variance-inducing factors are taken to represent so many reasons for the structural invalidity of Piaget's theory. In line with Lourenço and Machado's (1996) brilliant refutation of this performance view, we take these factors to represent specific constraints on competence which produce variability within structural development. In fact, these performance factors, far from proving Piaget's theory invalid, represent *internal constraints* on cognitive action, more or less resistant experiential input for the construction of schemes. They impose functional constraints on assimilation and thus potentially bias the equilibration process towards overassimilation. They may systematically limit generalisation.

Eberhard Schröder (1989) used Hofmann's list to construct a systematic account of the structural variants of operational tasks. We use this account to identify sources of variation in performance (See Table 5.1.) Internal constraints due to variations in task construction, procedures, sensory modalities, and performance modes affect the very act of cognition, and, viewed as a programme of systematic exploration, lead to *thick description* of development, mapping the intrinsic developmental dynamic of cognitive growth and the pattern of horizontal décalages it entails. Décalages, then, cease to be an arbitrary phenomenon, and description and explanation finally coincide. Failure to push for an in-depth theoretical description of the phenomenon of décalage and to explore the field structure of cognitive development following Inhelder and Piaget's pioneering achievements has been detrimental to the growth of the theory, including application to clinical and educational phenomena. Moreover, it has contributed to the separation of the theory from the mainstream. Each of the experimental variants has been taken to represent an anomaly that cast doubt on the validity of the programme. But each of these variants should have been an element in an explanatory account of the dynamic of development, a function relating experience via assimilation to the operational structure of the mind.

External conditions

Whereas "internal constraints" account for the set of variations that are due to task variables, procedural forms, and sensory modalities—i.e., parameters of world objects that affect the act of cognition—there are clearly other types of constraints that also affect the production of performance. We have chosen to label these constraints "external", in deference to the fact that they represent parameters of the cogniser outside the locus of cognition proper. They are institutionalised "out there" in the world, in the personality system or in the social matrix. Of these, the former reflect aspects of the system of cognitive socialisation, while the latter represent influences deriving from the system of socio-economic, socio-cultural, or socio-ecological inequality in which the former are embedded. Taking a Piagetian view, external conditions cannot be taken to represent so many "independent variables" separated from the subject. They must be incorporated into constructivist theory as factors that influence the nature, representation, and modalities of experience from which cognition arises (Edelstein & Hoppe-Graff, 1993; Seiler, 1991). So far, we lack theoretical accounts of cognitive socialisation in terms of Piagetian theory. On the most molecular level, the functionalist account of schema activity given by Cellérier (1987) holds promise for a connection between theories of socialisation and equilibration. On the more molar level of personality, accounts of deficits or disorders, such as insecurity of attachment, depression, or anxiety may represent conditions of deprivation, an impoverishment of exploration, invention, and construction (Cicchetti, 1996; Edelstein, 1996; Noam, Chandler, & Lalonde, 1995; Schellhas, 1993).

Finally, in the macro-system of social structures, accounts of social class or socio-ecological environment may indicate deprivation (or enrichment) of experience of social interaction, communication, or the challenge of objects in the lifeworld that impact directly or indirectly on the opportunity for construction and growth-related cognitive action (Figure 5.1) (see e.g., Bronfenbrenner & Crouter, 1983; Deutsch, 1973; Kohn, 1969).

Studying individual differences through the lens of Piaget's theory, project "Individual development and social structure" is an endeavour to map these factors onto the design of a quasi-experimental study or else to represent them theoretically through the set of independent variables included in the research. Accounting for variations in world objects and epistemologically relevant parameters of the knower does not appear as a very revolutionary enterprise once the real psychological subjects are given the attention they merit even from the epistemological perspective.

DESIGNING THE EMPIRICAL STUDIES

Weinert and Helmke have recently (1997) pointed out that most information about development has originated in cross-sectional studies that aggregate data within

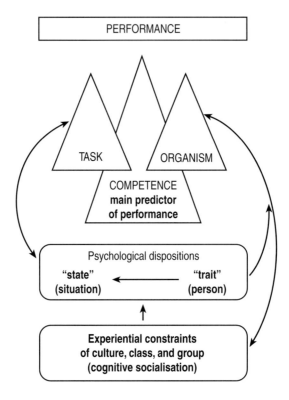

Figure 5.1.   Factors determining performance (Edelstein, 1996, p. 99).

age groups to age means while interpreting mean differences as equating intra-individual change. However, if we are to disentangle the universal thrust of development and the vicissitudes of individual change including the process dynamic driving it, the first requirement is to disaggregate the group data and map intra-individual change across ages through repeated measures of the same individuals longitudinally. In order to accomplish a fair view of development we need to include a sufficiently broad array of tasks, with a sufficient set of within-task variations to represent intrinsic constraints. We would benefit from factorially controlled designs representing developmentally relevant parameters of the social and personal variations of the knower's conditions. Analysis of variance with repeated measures appears to open up a royal road to the reconstruction of developmental pathways: with interactions between developmental time and task constraints representing décalage, or intra-individual differences in intra-individual change. In the case of social factors, interactions represent inter-individual differences in intra-individual change (e.g., different growth rates in different groups). These are, of course, relevant instances of theoretical concern. The more interesting interactions, however, go beyond these cases and represent the interface between the former and the latter: Specific contexts of cognition, or world objects, interact with the dynamic of growth in particular groups. Thus, a verbal task modality may enhance performance in middle-class subjects; or restrict the performance of lower-class subjects on an abstract task. A social science stance in genetic epistemology implies awareness of the dynamic of development in the complex settings of cognitive socialisation. This requires a methodology enabling the researcher to observe a set of ordered multiple interactions over time to map the course of development and age-specific patterns of factors influencing development along the path.

Figure 5.2 summarises the theoretical rationale of a study focused on cognitive socialisation in development in accordance with the arguments just outlined. The theoretical relationships represented in Figure 5.2 appear almost self-explanatory; nevertheless, a few comments may be in order. Three major strands of development are taken to represent the developing person, logical cognition, socio-moral cognition, and personality or emotional development. Together they form the developmental context for each of the single dimensions that, depending on person, situation, or social condition, or on developmental phase, stage, or style (Noam, 1985) represent developmental determinants for each other. Some of these determinants are represented in the design (family as the primary source of socialisation; social class as the system of opportunities for developmentally relevant experience; the school as an instance of cognitive socialisation). Some are organised into the sampling design of the study. They include major sources of variation hypothesised to affect development differentially: social class as a proxy for the opportunity system for developmentally relevant experience; gender and competence assessed at the onset of schooling as proxies for the quality of the previous socialisation of cognition.

In the context of a large-scale study on social inequality in intelligence and school achievement in Iceland (Björnsson, Edelstein, & Kreppner, 1977) a measure of occupational social class in Iceland was developed on the basis of work

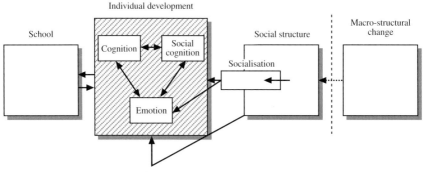

Figure 5.2.   Theoretical design.

characteristics, education, and financial benefits to the person. Six social classes were identified: (1) unskilled manual workers; (2) skilled workers and artisans; (3) low-educated service employees; (4) teachers and technicians; (5) entrepreneurial and managerial; (6) academic and professional. The measure represents both a hierarchy (which can be dichotomised into lower- and upper-class levels), and a multinominal measure accounting for the qualitative differences between lifeworlds and systems of practices indicated by class affiliation.

Sample

In the first week of school, teachers of the 26 first grades of all schools in the city of Reykjavik were asked to nominate three pupils from each of three groups in their respective classes: the most competent, the average, and the least competent third. Subsequently the middle third was dropped. The two others were pooled across schools. Interviews with teachers disclosed that their classifications of the children into the three groups or levels of competence took into account children's ability to communicate with teacher, ability to handle spatial arrays, and ability to abide by rules for classroom behaviour. After identifying each child's family's social class a random sample of 120 children was drawn from the two pools of high- and low-competence children and the six social classes to fill the 24 slots of the design constituted by competence level (2), gender (2), and social class (6) with five children to each cell (see Figure 5.3).

In addition, the entire birth cohorts of three small communities were included in the sample to represent non-urban subjects from socio-historically divergent origins (farming, fishing, industrial service). The point of the sampling design is the following: It enables the researcher to account for (actually to ignore) prior differences and focus on situated change between 7 and 17 in contrasting groups based on various combinations of competence and social class. Thus, to take an example, it is possible to contrast trajectories of high- and low-competence children from lower- or upper-class origins, in other words: to study class-related variation in the course of development while keeping initial competence constant.

To complete the picture, Table 5.1 shows the array of tasks used to assess concrete and formal thought across these measurement occasions extending from childhood (age 7) through adolescence (age 17, and beyond for a number of variables outside the scope of this chapter).

To sum up this section: A quasi-experimental longitudinal design was used to identify the effects of social class, gender, and initial competence on developmental outcomes and developmental processes in cognition at various time points in the developmental trajectory. The analysis thus purports to assess inter-individual variation in cognitive development as represented by a set of age-adequate Piagetian tasks of concrete and formal thought.

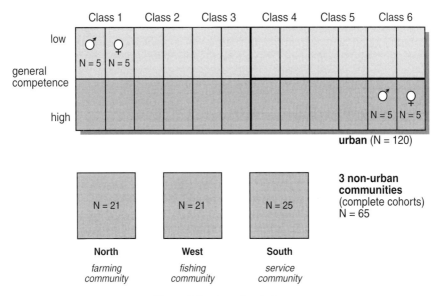

Figure 5.3.   Sampling design.

TABLE 5.1

Measurement design of the cognitive tasks

Concepts	Number of different tasks at ages						Source of variation
	7	8	9	12	15	17	
Concrete operations							
Conservation	12×2	12×2					content, performance
Experimental class inclusion	4×2	4×2	4×2				presentation, performance
Verbal class inclusion	13×2	13×2	13×2	3×2			content, performance
Log. multiplication	4×2	4×2	4×2				presentation, performance
Early formal operations							
Multiple compensation			5×2	4×2	5×2	6×2	content, performance
Syllogistic reasoning			9×4	3×4	3×4	3×4	contextualisation, content, form
Pendulum task			1	1			procedure
Isolation of variables			3	3			contextualisation, content
Mature formal operations							
Proportions					2	2	procedure
Combinations					1	1	procedure
Correlation					1	1	procedure

Numbers in table refer to numbers of tasks by sources of variation.

RESULTS

Our purpose, in this section, is to analyse class effects on Piagetian measures of cognitive development under the assumption that the social classes represent different opportunity structures or regimes of experience relevant to cognitive growth. Class effects may in fact be direct or indirect: The class-specific opportunities may affect cognitive development by making experience available in different quantities, or social class may mediate between lifeworld effects and the structure of cognitive development. In this chapter, in a first attack on social class as a possible repository of influence on cognitive development, we choose to analyse direct effects and ignore indirect or moderator effects although interactions with other influential conditions are, in fact, plausible. Indirect effects will be the topic of Chapter 6.

In the following, we shall demonstrate the pattern of class effects on Piagetian measures of cognitive competence in the six social classes in the two ability groups across five measurement points between ages 7 and 15 years. To exemplify the pattern we begin this demonstration with the results of an analysis of variance of the conservation tasks from Goldschmid and Bentler's Conservation kit (1968) at age 7, with the dimension of social class, either as a continuum of six expressions or as a dichotomous variable (lower vs upper class), as the between-subjects factor.

Tables 5.2 and 5.3 show two separate analyses of *judgements* and *justifications* of these judgements in a set of 13 conservation tasks in the low-competence (1) and high-competence (2) groups, first across the six social classes (Table 5.2), and then in the dichotomous version of the social class continuum (with the lower SES range encompassing classes 1–3, and the upper SES range encompassing classes 4–6) (Table 5.3). The effects of competence level are overriding, whereas the class effects reach statistical significance for both competence levels only in the dichotomous version. The high-competence children reach ceiling, and thus leave less variance for the expression of group differences. The low-competence children are far from fully conserving, and evidence clear class-related differences. This pattern sets the stage for the expression of social inequality in cognitive development.

TABLE 5.2

Mean values of conservation at age 7 by teacher-rated competence and social class

| | Social class | | | | | | Competence | |
	1	2	3	4	5	6	Low (1–3)	High (4–6)
Low competence								
Judgement	5.58	7.06	6.00	9.00	8.30	7.83	6.21	8.38
Justification	4.42	5.06	3.71	6.80	6.30	5.67	4.40	6.26
High competence								
Judgement	11.17	11.36	11.00	11.40	11.27	11.36	11.18	11.34
Justification	10.67	11.09	10.36	10.90	10.27	9.82	10.77	10.33

TABLE 5.3

Analyses of variance of conservation performance by teacher-rated competence and social class

	I ANOVAs using full scale of social class		II ANOVAs using dichotomous measure of social class	
Main effect	F 12.05	p < .000	F 39.62	p < .000
Competence (low)	F 58.64	p < .000	F 68.89	p < .000
Social class (1–6)	F 1.48	ns		
Social class (low/high)			F 10.35	p < .002
Main effect	F 39.62	p < .000	F 42.23	p < .000
Competence (high)	F 68.89	p < .000	F 79.93	p < .000
Social class (1–6)	F 10.35	p < .002		
Social class (low/high)			F 4.53	p < .05

Let us next turn to the overall pattern of social class effects on developmental outcomes in cognition measured in various groups at various time points along the developmental trajectory from childhood to late adolescence (see Table 5.4). Each "*" represents the results of an analysis of variance with significant post hoc contrasts of social class effects. Separate analyses were conducted for judgements and justifications in each task (within concrete thought: conservation, class inclusion, verbal classification, logical multiplication; within formal thought: multiple compensation, syllogistic reasoning, the pendulum task, and isolation of variables) for both competence levels. The non-significant results (represented by "–") in the low-competence group at ages 7 and 9 are due to floor effects. This is also true for the justification part of the logical multiplication task, the volume task, the pendulum task, and the isolation of variables task. (The pattern is more complex for the syllogisms and for formal operations in general.) The pattern can be described in terms of variance: the low-competence group, in a variety of tasks, does not provide the variance needed for class effects to emerge. In contradistinction, non-significant differences between social classes in the high-competence group are due to ceiling effects—although, in fact, this statement simplifies matters somewhat. As can be seen from Table 5.4, class effects are both frequent and meaningful. But it is important to note that the absence of significant differences provides a no less meaningful pattern: it pictures the progression from next to no competence in performing a task to fully generalised competence at different points of time for different groups depending on task.

The pattern may disclose floor effects due to relative difficulty, or ceiling effects due to fully equilibrated competence; and these may obtain, at different ages, in different groups. Floor effects and ceiling effects, in fact, may demonstrate quite different things: On the one hand they represent the temporal dynamic of development in face of task demands. Thus, while competent performances gradually spread from top to bottom competence in the judgements, these remain visibly ahead of performance in the reflexive exercise of justification or explanation

TABLE 5.4
Social class effects in cognitive development at ages 7–15, results of analyses of variance: Cognitive tasks by social class, stratified by competence level

Age	Conservation		Classification		Verbal classification		Logical multiplication		Multiple compensation		Syllogistic reasoning			Pendulum	Isolation of variables		
	A	*B*	*A*	*B*	*A*	*B*	*A*	*B*	*A*	*B*	*1*	*2*	*3*		*1*	*2*	*3*
Low teacher-rated competence																	
7	*	—	—		*	*	*	—									
8	*	*	*	*	*	*	*	—									
9			*	*	*	—	*	—									
12									—	—	*	*	*	—	*	—	—
15									—	—	—	—	—	—	—	—	—
High teacher-rated competence																	
7	—	—	*	*	*	*	*	—									
8	—	—	—	—	*	*	*	*									
9	—	—	—	—	*	*	—	*	*	—	*	—	—	*	*	*	*
12									—	—	—	*	*	*	*	*	—
15									—	—	*	*	*	—	*	—	—

A Judgement, B Justification.
* *p* < .05; — n.s.
Syllogistic reasoning 1: = experience-oriented, Syllogistic reasoning 2: = counter-intuitive, Syllogistic reasoning 3: = abstract.

where, at the time, floor effects still prevail. This represents décalage *within* task, a separate class of décalage phenomena besides the better known décalages *between* tasks of identical logical structure. A third kind of décalage is mirrored by patterns of differences between competence groups, representing delay of operational competence due to social causes. The causes themselves remain hidden among the structures of epistemic opportunities provided by the various social groups. Fourth (but this requires close scrutiny and local knowledge of the class structure) specific patterns of competence within social classes tell tales of structural tensions and opportunities related to upwards or downwards mobility in relation to cognitive merit. Thus, in the earlier example, inspection of the statistical contrasts reveals the entrepreneurial group (class 5), which is the most socially mobile of all groups, to contain notable contradictions between teacher-assessed lower competence at age 7 and later proof of high developmental competence achieved. The household heads in this group frequently originate in the blue-collar workers group (class 1) with a large proportion of low-competence subjects. At the same time this group is propelled by intense aspirations, which make members more similar to the high-ranking academic and professional group. Conversely, members of the lower service class evidence several instances of initial high teacher rating of individual competence turning out to perform at low developmental levels. Such microanalyses tell a story about the regime of epistemic opportunities available for development in the respective groups (see Björnsson et al., 1977 and Grundmann, 1998 for a more thorough treatment of class-based cognitive milieu effects).

EPILOGUE

There is little research on class effects on cognitive competence in the Piagetian tradition. Among the few examples are a study of object constancy (Golden & Birns, 1968) and a study of classification (de Lacey, 1970, 1971). This lack of interest has been insistently criticised (Broughton, 1981; Buck-Morss, 1975) and viewed as proof of the ideological bias of Piaget's theory. True, Piaget made but a few rather general remarks about "social factors"—mostly cultural influences that affect décalage, or differences between lifestyles or degrees of urbanisation that influence intellectual growth and affect achievement of advanced competence (see Inhelder & Piaget, 1955/1958; Piaget, 1970/1972, 1975/1977). In the eight volumes of Modgil and Modgil's (1976) compilation of Piagetian research, variations of cognitive performance in function of social class are not mentioned. In Gruber and Vonèche's (1977) *The Essential Piaget* even the term fails to appear.

A Piagetian appraisal of cultural differences has, in fact, been carried further than has the debate about effects of social structural differences. Piaget's universalism provided a challenge to anthropology's relativist heritage (see Hallpike, 1979). The controversy has generated an impressive body of research that mostly supported the universalist position, basically replicating Piaget's findings throughout tribal cultures around the world (see Dasen, 1977). By the same token, however, the debate tended to limit the question of validity to the basic Kantian concepts and to concrete operations. But cultural differences mostly concern representations rather than functions, whereas social differences predominantly concern function, so that only very few Piagetian studies of cultures approach their subject in a manner that is useful for the cognitive study of societies and their functional differences in view of development. The closest we get to a functional analysis are "tests of milieu effects" on Piagetian tasks (Goodnow, 1962; Hollos, 1974; Hollos & Cowan, 1973). Both Goodnow and Hollos come close to functional analysis of social structural differences, Goodnow by comparing educationally deprived with educationally privileged milieus in Hong Kong, thus holding the culture constant. Similarly, Hollos holds culture constant by comparing two widely different social ecologies in Norway, a thinly populated community and an ordinary town. Whereas Goodnow's hypotheses focus on cognitive functioning in two functionally different but culturally similar groups, Hollos, in deference to Piaget's social constructivist theory, centres on the structure of interaction as a functional prerequisite of the development of basic logical and social cognitive structures. She assumes a dearth of exposure to interaction in the thinly populated areas and engages in "thick description" of the differences between communities, including measures of role-taking activity. In a sense, these two studies, which painstakingly describe the milieus they compare, serve as forerunner exemplars to project "Individual development and social structure" from which we have reported in this chapter.

The present study attempts to advance beyond theirs on several counts: It takes social structure seriously, and adopts a theoretical stance towards class formation and its consequences for cognitive socialisation. This stance includes a view of class-related patterns of opportunity for experience and constructive action in conjunction with family-related models of enhancing exploration, interaction, and cooperation. Further, the study identifies different sources of variation seen to contribute differentially to intra-individual and inter-individual differences, and to both, directly and indirectly, in conjunction and as moderators of developmental change. The present report highlighted direct effects of social class (considered as an ecology of experience) on developmental outcomes in different areas of cognition at different time points in the developmental trajectory. Although these effects appear small it should be borne in mind that due to a design that maximally equalises the competence of subjects originating in the different social classes at the outset of the study, the cognitive inequalities between classes have emerged during the course of the study as products of the ongoing process of class-related differentiation. Thus, although outcome effects are smaller than the moderator effects reported in Chapter 6 that affect the very course of the developmental process, they are nevertheless meaningful, both because their pattern discloses important aspects of the temporal dynamic of differential growth, and because the differences themselves become moderators of school learning and school success (Edelstein, 1996): Inequalities of cognitive outcomes, alongside differences in cognitive growth rates, contribute to the differences in the cognitively patterned opportunity structure of schooling that ascertain the persistence of class in educational performance.

But in spite of a legitimate insistence on outcomes providing the grist of social analyses of inequality, the main object of developmental analysis is change. Designing a representative yet quasi-experimental and multivariate longitudinal study including a set of context conditions for development, we focus on individual *change* and intra- as well as inter-individual differences in individual change in significant dimensions rather than on average performance in aggregates. This will be the focus of the next chapter. Instead of tucking individual differences in competence away in the under-analysed category of décalage, we centre our concerns on their emergence and the causes for their increase. To ignore these, in fact, amounts to ignoring a question of great epistemological importance: whether, and how, individuals differ in their opportunities to make meaning of experience, to represent the world to themselves and to others, and to operate on it with cognitive means. These are, it seems to me, truly Piagetian questions. But they may have been closer to Bärbel Inhelder's heart.

REFERENCES

Björnsson, S., Edelstein, W., & Kreppner, K. (1977). Explorations in social inequality: Stratification dynamics in social and individual development in Iceland. In *Studien und Berichte 38*. Berlin: Max Planck Institute for Human Development.

Bronfenbrenner, U., & Crouter, A. (1983). The evolution of environmental models in developmental research. In P.H. Mussen (Seeries Ed.), & W. Kessen (Vol. Ed.). *Handbook of child psychology Vol. I. History, theory, and methods*, (pp. 357–414). New York: Wiley.

Broughton, J.M. (1981). Piaget's structural developmental psychology. IV. Knowledge without a self and without history. *Human Development, 24*, 320–346.

Buck-Morss, S. (1975). Socio-economic bias in Piaget's theory and its implications for cross-cultural studies. *Human Development, 18*, 35–49.

Cellérier, G. (1987). Structures and functions. In B. Inhelder, D. de Caprona, & A. Cornu-Wells (Eds.), *Piaget today* (pp. 15–36). Hillsdale, NJ: Lawrence Erlbaum Associates Inc.

Cicchetti, D. (1996). Child maltreatment: Implications for developmental theory and research. *Human Development, 39*, 18–39.

Dasen, P. (Ed.). (1977). *Piagetian psychology: Cross-cultural contributions.* New York: Gardner Press.

De Lacey, P.R. (1970). A cross-cultural study of classification ability in Australia. *Journal of Cross-Cultural Psychology, 1*, 293–304.

De Lacey, P.R. (1971). Classification ability and verbal intelligence among high-contact aboriginal and low socioeconomic white Australian children. *Journal of Cross-Cultural Psychology, 2*, 393–396.

Deutsch, C.P. (1973). Social class and child development. In B.M. Caldwell & H.N. Ricciuti (Eds.), *Review of child development research* (Vol. 3, pp. 233–282). Chicago: University of Chicago Press.

Edelstein, W. (1983). Cultural constraints on development and the vicissitudes of progress. In F.S. Kessel & A.W. Siegel (Eds.), *The child and other cultural inventions* (pp. 48–81). New York: Praeger.

Edelstein, W. (1992). Sozialer Konstruktivismus [Social constructivism]. In Center for Development and Socialization (Ed.), *Sozialer Konstruktivismus* (pp. 5–12). Berlin: Max Planck Institute for Human Development.

Edelstein, W. (1996). The social construction of cognitive development. In G. Noam & K. Fischer (Eds.), *Development and vulnerability in close relationships* (pp. 91–112). Mahwah, NJ: Lawrence Erlbaum Associates Inc.

Edelstein, W., & Hoppe-Graff, S. (Eds.). (1993). *Die Konstruktion kognitiver Strukturen* [The construction of cognitive structures]. Bern: Huber.

Edelstein, W., Keller, M., & Schröder, E. (1990). Child development and social structure: Individual differences in development. In P.B. Baltes, D.L. Featherman, & R.M. Lerner (Eds.), *Life-span development and behavior* (Vol. 10, pp. 152–185). Hillsdale, NJ: Lawrence Erlbaum Associates Inc.

Golden, M., & Birns, B. (1968). Social class and cognitive development in infancy. *Merrill-Palmer Quarterly, 14*, 139–149.

Goldschmid, M.L., & Bentler, P.M. (1968). *Manual: Concept assessment kit—conservation.* San Diego, CA: Educational & Industrial Testing Service.

Goodnow, J.J. (1962). A test of milieu differences with some of Piaget's tasks. *Psychological Monographs, 76* (Whole No. 36).

Gruber, H.E., & Vonèche, J.J. (Eds.). (1977). *The essential Piaget.* New York: Basic Books.

Grundmann, M. (1998). *Norm und Konstruktion* [Norm and construction]. Opladen: Westdeutscher Verlag.

Hallpike, C.R. (1979). *The foundations of primitive thought.* Oxford: Clarendon Press.

Hofmann, R.J. (1982). Potential sources of structural invalidity in Piagetian and Neo-Piagetian assessment. In S. Modgil & C. Modgil (Eds.), *Jean Piaget: Consensus and controversy* (pp. 233–239). London: Holt, Rinehart & Winston.

Hofmann, V. (1991). *Die Entwicklung depressiver Reaktionen in Kindheit und Jugend. Eine entwicklungspathologische Längsschnittuntersuchung* [The development of depressive reactions in childhood and adolescence: A developmental pathological longitudinal study]. Berlin: Sigma.

Hollos, M. (1974). *Growing up in Flathill.* Oslo: Universitetsforlaget.

Hollos, M., & Cowan, P.A. (1973). Social isolation and cognitive development: Logical operations and role-taking abilities in three Norwegian social settings. *Child Development, 44*, 630–641.

Inhelder, B. (1989). Du sujet épistémique au sujet psychologique [From the epistemic to the psychological subject]. *Bulletin de Psychologie, 42*, 466–467.

Inhelder, B., & Piaget, J. (1958). *The growth of logical thinking from childhood to adolescence.* New York: Basic Books. (Original work published 1955)

Inhelder, B., & Piaget, J. (1971). Closing remarks. In D.R. Green, M.P. Ford, & G.B. Flamer (Eds.), *Measurement and Piaget.* New York: McGraw-Hill.

Jacobsen, T., Edelstein, W., & Hofmann, V. (1994). A longitudinal study of the relation between representations of attachment in childhood and cognitive functioning in childhood and adolescence. *Developmental Psychology, 30*, 112–124.

Jacobsen, T., & Hofmann, V. (1997). Children's attachment representations: Longitudinal relations to school behavior and academic competency in middle childhood and adolescence. *Developmental Psychology, 33*, 703–710.

Kohn, M.L. (1969). *Class and conformity: A study in values*. Homewood, IL: The Dorsey Press.

Lourenço, O., & Machado, A. (1996). In defense of Piaget's theory: A reply to 10 common criticisms. *Psychological Review, 103*, 143–164.

Modgil, S., & Modgil, C. (1976). *Piagetian research* (Vols 1–8). Windsor, UK: NFER.

Noam, G.G. (1985). Stage, phase, and style: The developmental dynamics of the self. In M. Berkowitz & F. Oser (Eds.), *Moral education: Theory and application* (pp. 269–296). Hillsdale, NJ: Lawrence Erlbaum Associates Inc.

Noam, G.G., Chandler, M., & Lalonde, C. (1995). Clinical-developmental psychology: Constructivism and social cognition in the study of psychological dysfunctions. In D. Cicchetti & D. Cohen (Eds.), *Developmental psychopathology: Vol. 1. Theory and methods* (pp. 424–464). New York: Wiley.

Piaget, J. (1972). Intellectual evolution from adolescence to adulthood. *Human Development, 15*, 1–12. (Original work published 1970)

Piaget, J. (1976). Qu'est-ce que la psychologie? [What is psychology?]. In Université de Genève (Ed.), *À Jean Piaget à l'occasion de son 80e anniversaire*. Genève: Université de Genève. [Reprinted in *Campus*, magazine de l'Université de Genève, July–Sept. 1996, pp. 26–29.]

Piaget, J. (1977). *The development of thought: Equilibration of cognitive structures*. New York: Viking Press. (Original work published 1975)

Schellhas, B. (1993). *Die Entwicklung der Ängstlichkeit in Kindheit und Jugend. Befunde einer Längsschnittstudie über die Bedeutung der Ängstlichkeit für die Entwicklung der Kognition und des Schulerfolgs* [The development of anxiety in childhood and adolescence: Results of a longitudinal study on the significance of anxiety in the development of cognition and school achievement]. Berlin: E. Sigma.

Schröder, E. (1989). *Vom konkreten zum formalen Denken* [From concrete to formal thought]. Bern: Huber.

Seiler, T.B. (1991). Entwicklung und Sozialisation: Eine strukturgenetische Sichtweise [Development and socialization: A structure-genetic view]. In K. Hurrelmann & D. Ulich (Eds.), *Neues Handbuch der Sozialisationsforschung* (p. 99–119). Weinheim: Beltz.

Weinert, F.E., & Helmke, A. (Eds.). (1997). *Entwicklung im Grundschulalter* [Development in primary school children]. Weinheim: Psychologie Verlags Union.

CHAPTER SIX

The impact of developmental change and social constraints on cognition: The example of syllogistic reasoning

Eberhard Schröder
University of Potsdam, Germany

Wolfgang Edelstein
Max Planck Institute for Human Development, Berlin, Germany

In this chapter we deal with processes in cognitive development and the unfolding emergence of individual differences. The empirical focus is on the influence of developmental change and of social constraints on development. What is the role of the interaction between cognitive development and social conditions in this process? We reconstruct the development of individual differences in the context of a structural theory of development (Case & Edelstein, 1993; Edelstein & Hoppe-Graff, 1993). Conditions of development will be distinguished according to the criterion of their internality vs externality to cognitive development (Schröder & Edelstein, 1991; Seiler, 1991). Internal constraints relate to the process of formation of cognitive structures; they generate differences in the actual genesis of the concepts deriving from the tasks and the subject's behaviour relative to the task, i.e., from characteristics inherent in the data-collection situation itself. By contrast, external conditions derive from the social lifeworld of the developing subjects. This framework is to enable us to investigate adequately the differential, divergent, and changing effects of socialisation on cognitive development.

We illustrate the procedure adopted using the example of the development of syllogistic reasoning for ages 9–17. First, we analyse the internal conditions of development, then we demonstrate the mediating and changing influence of social constraints on cognitive development.

Whereas research on the impact of socialisation on cognitive development seeks to establish differences between groups exposed to different socialisation practices, the empirical analysis of interactions between development and socialisation in a constructivist perspective is more complex. The constructivist model of the development of competence does not merely account for the outcome of development but includes the process of the formation of structures and the dynamic of this structuration (Fetz, 1988; Schröder, 1992; Seiler, 1991). Therefore, in view of universal processes, the internal conditions must be analysed first; in a second step, then, social conditions are shown to be effective in the ongoing process of development. Third, in order to establish how social factors influence the process of development, it must be asked whether some developmental advantage or disadvantage, functioning independent of its original causes, may be continued or even strengthened in spite of a merely passing effectiveness or the discontinuation of the external conditions responsible for the (dis)advantage.

A constructivist orientation in research on cognitive development is bent on reconstructing the changing and contingent effects of external conditions on the internal constraints or, rather, on studying their interactions. Once the processes of cognitive structuration follow a logic of their own (as postulated in the framework of a constructivist model of development), it must be shown that external conditions do not influence the processes directly but indirectly, and mediated through the inner dynamic of development. To take an example that we shall dwell on in greater length later: Social class will generate differences in the development of syllogistic reasoning only for those children who are already at a structural disadvantage, having previously developed under the sway of these differences in their cognitive socialisation.

STRUCTURATION AND CONTEXTS OF DEVELOPMENT

We now turn to the dynamic and the conditions of cognitive self-organisation. First the concept of structuration must be defined. This will serve to clarify that the formation of cognitive structures may be viewed, in the context of constructivist developmental theories, as an independent and externally uninfluenced process of self-organisation. Processes of structure formation take place in a circular or spiral form. At all levels of cognitive interaction, relationships between subject and object are reciprocal. Knowledge is constructed in as much as the organism recognises and produces objects of knowledge by its own actions and activities. Conversely, the organism recognises itself only in as much as it engages in relationships with recognised objects, which constitutes the main characteristic of cognitive self-organisation. Knowledge never derives from characteristics of objects, but from the interaction between the knower and the known. Structuration thus represents a circular reciprocal relationship between subject and object. Objects, and the attributes of objects, are meaningful for the constructive subject only in as much as these are assimilated to existing schemata. The construction of meaning is therefore necessarily an ever-changing process, as existing schemata are confronted again and again with new experiences. This is the process that generates the dynamic of cognitive systems. When, through generalising application, a schema has been formed, differentiation of assimilable characteristics of the object follows. The emerging schemata are then modified through accommodation, only to be schematised again through generalising assimilation.

The study of conditions of development thus presupposes the analysis of the interaction between the formation of structures and the contexts of development (see Table 6.1). But contexts are both—internal constraints on development and conditions of socialisation. It is therefore essential to examine whether and to what extent processes of structuration and self-organisation are, on the one hand, independent of the conditions and the contexts of their application but, on the other hand, necessarily enter into interaction with them. Thus they represent complementary parts of the same interactive process. The question arises whether internal processes of cognitive interaction follow a structural logic, or whether these processes are determined by their contexts of application. Once this has been clarified it must be ascertained where and how the considerable inter- and intra-individual differences in cognitive development originate.

TABLE 6.1

Conditions of cognitive development

Developmental constraints on cognition

Internal constraints (genetic constraints on cognitive development)
- Procedural schema
- Presentation of task
- Form of task
- Contextuation, domains, and contents of task

Antecedent constraints (developmental prerequisites)
- Individual resources and competences that derive from antecedent development

External resources and competences that derive from antecedent development

Social constraints
- Social class
- Gender socialisation

Lifeworld and ecological constraints
- Social ecology (urban, rural)

To ascertain adequate empirical investigation of the conditions of individual construction in the course of cognitive development, we distinguish factors of influence on individual development depending on their position in the process of cognitive interaction, as either inherently part of it, or antecedent to it, or as a moderator variable acting on it from outside (Schröder, 1992). We have already stated that the construction process always represents structuration on the basis of previously generated schemata. Thus any cognitive structure includes its ontogenetic history of past constructions. Therefore the internal conditions need to be distinguished into genetic and antecedent ones. By contrast, social conditions represent sociocultural moderators of epistemic interactions. They influence the opportunity structure and the availability of developmentally relevant experience (Goodnow, 1990) and thus enhance or delay the formation of cognitive structures.

INTERNAL AND EXTERNAL CONSTRAINTS
OF COGNITIVE DEVELOPMENT

As mentioned in Chapter 5, Hofmann (1982) has proposed a taxonomy of potential sources of structural invalidity in Piagetian and neo-Piagetian measurement models. In spite of the fact that the taxonomy was proposed in the context of a critique of Piaget's theory, it may serve as a point of departure for the distinction of various performance factors that contribute to the development of cognitive operations and influence the formation of cognitive structures. On the basis of Hofmann's taxonomy, Schröder (1989) proposed a model of potential sources of variation in cognitive development.

The model distinguishes two factors (see Table 6.2). The first factor relates to the task and highlights differences relative to the nature of the stimulus, the procedure in processing the task, and the response modalities. The second factor relates to the epistemic subject (organism) and refers to aspects of mental representation and conceptualisation of thought. These sources of variation will be termed internal factors and distinguished from external influences, such as different lifeworlds.

TABLE 6.2
Internal constraints on cognitive development

Presentation of task	*Representation by organism*
Media of presentation: • substantial • pictorial • symbolic–verbal • phonetic	Sensory perception: • visual • tactile • kinaesthetic • auditory
Modes of presentation: • covered • uncovered	Mental representation: • encoding • chunking • capacity for processing information • attentional capacity
Constellation of variables (complexity)	
Attributes of reference systems: • open vs closed gestalt • defined vs undefined	*Conceptualisation (contexts)* Dimensions and domains: • attributes of objects • attributes of the signified
Procedure	
Reproductive interiorised: (S→O→R)	Contextualisation in the lifeworld: • experiential–counterintuitive–abstract • experiential knowledge • culture, class, society
Exploratory manipulative constructive: (S→(O↔S')→R)	
Performance (Type of response) Recognition Pictorial reproduction Construction Behaviour and explanation Judgement and justification	Reference to self Reference to objects • interest–motivation • affective cathexis Structures of knowledge: • expertise

Later, we shall demonstrate strong effects of both types of conditions on the formation of structure in syllogistic reasoning. In the study reported here, we administered longitudinally a variety of syllogisms to children and adolescents aged 9–17 years. We intended to study separately the following internal conditions: (a) form of proposition (modus ponens, negation of antecedent, affirmation of consequent, modus tollens); (b) contextualisation of task (experiential, counterintuitive, and abstract).

Whereas internal constraints on development relate to the cognitive interaction between the cognitive subject and the object of knowledge, external constraints may be taken to constitute mediators or moderators of the cognitive interaction. They influence the availability of epistemic experiences and objects of knowledge, thus enhancing or delaying the development of cognitive structures. But this does not lead to different forms of cognitive competencies.

Whereas in the context of psychometric studies internal constraints on development count as measurement error, external conditions of cognitive socialisation are the object of the analysis of individual differences, or of socialisation research. The historical division of research fields is reflected by Piaget's theory, which has frequently been criticised for granting little attention to socialising influences on individual development (Broughton, 1981; Buck-Morss, 1975; Edelstein, 1983; Schröder & Edelstein, 1991).

Piaget was indeed scarcely concerned with cognitive socialisation. He was less interested in the study of psychological and social conditions than in the epistemic and biological basis of the growth of cognitive competencies (Inhelder & Piaget, 1971; see Bullinger & Chatillon, 1983; Chapman, 1988). However, this does not exclude the possibility that Piaget's theory may benefit from potential extensions into the field of socialisation research (Edelstein, 1996; Grundmann, 1997).

A number of misconceptions, weaknesses, and contradictions in Piaget's theory derive from the fact that Piaget and the Genevan school ignored individual differences in development. Rarely were studies in the Genevan tradition devoted to influences of cultural, socio-ecological, or socialising conditions of individual development (de Ribaupierre, Rieben, & Lautrey, 1985; Edelstein, Keller, & Schröder, 1990; Longeot, 1978; Schröder, 1993). But Piaget (1965) himself assumed that social interaction with peers influences cognitive development positively (see Youniss, 1980) and stimulates the formation of cognitive structures. Interaction—as a means of exploration, negotiation, and mutual coordination—depends on experience and knowledge. The opportunity structure grounded in these cognitively relevant experiences affects the course of cognitive growth in significant ways: It contributes to individual differences between children who grow up in different milieus of cognitive socialisation (Goodnow, 1990). Thus external conditions of development represent opportunities for or restrictions of cognitive interaction, and enhance or delay cognitive growth.

In the empirical study described here, the family's social class and the child's gender are used as indicators for opportunity structures of cognitive socialisation.

Children's competence level at the inception of the study was used as a measure of previously constituted individual differences. This stratification attribute was taken to represent a mediator variable affecting the selection and perception of cognitive experience in family and school.

GENERALISATION AND CONSOLIDATION IN COGNITIVE DEVELOPMENT

The analysis of internal constraints on development leads to a differentiated picture of the emergence and acquisition of cognitive competencies. External constraints or conditions of cognitive socialisation intervene or moderate this structuration process in cognitive development and the availability of knowledge-related experience, and thus may promote or delay the developmental dynamic in the application of assimilatory schemata. In the case of blocking the inner dynamic of development, cognitive schemata could not be applied to different objects of knowing and therefore the process of stucturation and consolidation of structure may not come to an end (Piaget, 1977). On this reading, intra-individual differences between tasks within the individual reflect a more or less delayed application of cognitive schemata to new domains of experience. In other words, some subjects have failed to adequately generalise the application of cognitive structures. By contrast, as such structures become more broadly generalised and consolidated there are fewer restrictions on their domain of application. If contextual or performance factors have a substantive impact on cognitive development, it may be assumed that the cognitive structure is not yet consolidated or generalised to different domains of knowledge. The cognitive system therefore remains bound to particular domains of experience. If intra-individual differences decrease over time or no longer occur, the cognitive structure has been applied to different domains of application resulting in a generalised schema that may be characterised now as consolidated. As in Piaget's (1977) theory of equilibration, diversification and generalisation in the application of cognitive schemes constitute a necessary condition for the consolidation of the structure. Decreasing impact of contextual constraints on development and invariabilisation of the structure (decrease of variation within the individual) are therefore necessary in the acquisition of cognitive competencies (Schröder, 1989, 1993; Schröder & Edelstein, 1991). Thus, the development of cognitive competence corresponds to the progress that has been made in the consolidation of the structure. Mature, consolidated competencies will be acquired relatively late in development, because such generalised structures require that a series of constraints be overcome. In contrast, particular domain-specific abilities can be expressed earlier, as they represent only one developmental step in the acquisition sequence leading to a consolidated structure.

Whereas intrinsic conditions affect intra-individual differences between tasks, external conditions affect inter-individual differences in the formation of cognitive structures. The structure of opportunities will provide individuals with different amounts and qualities of epistemic experience, thereby either advancing or delaying the process of structuration. Thus, the timing of consolidation will vary as a function of socio-cultural factors, a fact that Piaget himself has acknowledged, proposing differential developmental courses in the emergence of formal thought (Piaget, 1972).

A LONGITUDINAL STUDY OF SOCIAL CONDITIONS IN DEVELOPMENT

In order to examine the development of children's deductive reasoning strategies, a number of syllogistic propositions were administered to the urban and non-urban samples at ages 9, 12, and 15, and to the urban sample again at age 17 (see Chapter 5 for the sampling and measurement design of the study and Edelstein et al., 1990; Schröder, Bödeker, & Edelstein, 2000). Three syllogistic tasks were chosen for the present analyses. The syllogistic statements contained different propositions and were applied to different contexts (Figure 6.1). The first proposition referred to an experiential context available to all school children. The second was based on a counterintuitive statement beyond concrete experience. The third included abstractly symbolised content. For each syllogistic task the four basic forms of syllogistic arguments were presented: modus ponens, negation of antecedent, affirmation of consequent, and modus tollens. The response outcomes of the syllogistic deductions were "yes", "maybe", or "no". Subjects were asked to judge the arguments and then to justify their judgements. The following analyses are based on the justifications of the judgements. As the complete set of tasks was not administered to the rural sample at age 9, only data of the 12- and 15-year-olds will be used for the rural sample.

The dynamic of internal constraints of development

As there were large differences between the four forms of arguments, and as modus ponens and modus tollens were solved adequately by nearly all children from age 9 onwards, the following analysis uses only the two other forms of arguments, i.e., negation of antecedent and affirmation of consequent.

First we present two analyses of stability and change in development under internal constraints. Figure 6.2 represents the question of change in intra-individual differences between the different forms of contextualisation. As can be seen for the urban sample, differences decrease from age 9 to age 17. In the rural sample the decrease in variability is stronger still: No differences between contexts are found at age 15. These results indicate that the differences between the three contexts decrease over time while the development of the concept is progressing, with the application of syllogistic reasoning becoming increasingly generalised across contexts. The decrease in context variability can be interpreted as evidence for the progressive consolidation of the cognitive system.

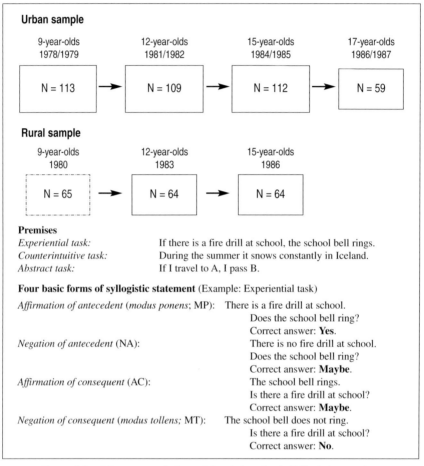

Figure 6.1.   Measurement design and description of task: Syllogistic reasoning.

As shown in Figure 6.3, intra-individual differences between the two forms of argument depend systematically on the contextuation of the task. While in the case of the experiential task the affirmation of consequent is easier than the negation of antecedent, in the counterintuitive task the reverse is true. Contrary to these large differences, no intra-individual differences between forms were found in the abstract task. In the case of an experiential task, an affirmative presupposition, even of the consequent sentence, is much easier to perform than the negation of the antecedent. Therefore the cognitive operation of negating a syllogistic sentence seems to be structurally different from the operation of inversion of antecedent and consequent propositions. In the case of the counterintuitive task this relationship between form and context is reversed. Here negation is easier than inversion, as

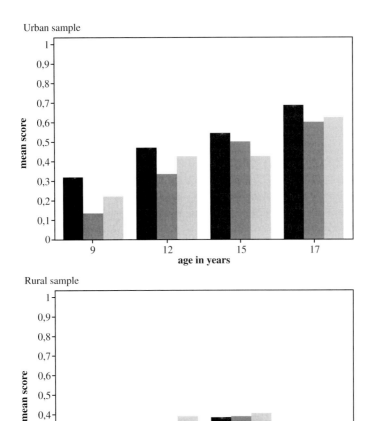

Figure 6.2.   Differences between contexts over time.

the counterintuitive premise may be interpreted as an experiential or meaningful proposition once the antecedent is negated.

In the abstract task no differences were found between forms. Presumably subjects solve abstract syllogisms by applying a formal rule that does not differentiate between the two forms of task. By contrast, in the case of contextualised tasks the previously acquired knowledge about the context and the form of the syllogism interact systematically.

Urban sample

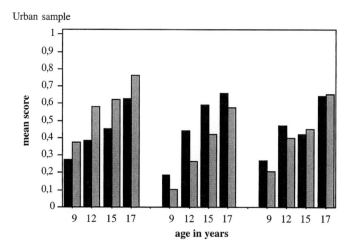

Rural sample

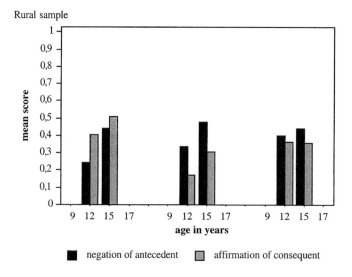

■ negation of antecedent   ▨ affirmation of consequent

Figure 6.3.   Interaction of form and context over time.

Differences between forms for each context remain stable across time. Therefore, in the interface between form and context, invariability and stability prevail. Whereas contextualised and decontextualised tasks are processed in different ways, the context-specificity of the processes remains stable over time.

The stable relationship between form and context indicates an invariant cognitive process in the development of syllogistic reasoning. This is the invariability of form depending on the abstractness of the domain of application.

The impact of developmental differences on later development

Now we turn to the question of stability and change in inter-individual differences, i.e., the external conditions of deductive reasoning as represented by the design factors, teacher-rated developmental competence level, social class, social ecology, and gender.

The competence level at the onset of schooling as an indicator of developmental outcomes of family socialisation explains the largest part of the individual differences found in the development of syllogistic reasoning. The influence of developmental prerequisites is threefold, as can be seen in Figure 6.4: (1) There are large differences between advanced and delayed children at age 9; advanced children attain a level about two times higher than slow developers. (2) Differences between the two groups increase over time. Whereas at age 9 there is an absolute difference of about .15, at age 17 the difference reaches .50. This means that highly developed adolescents use three times more correct syllogistic deductions than is the case for the slow developers. (3) Changes and rate of progression differ greatly between slow and advanced subjects. Whereas low-competence children show slight progression between ages 9 and 12 and stagnation between ages 12, 15, and 17, highly developed children progress rapidly between 9, 12, 15, and 17 years.

The same patterns of developmental change were found in the rural sample. While slow rural adolescents stagnate between ages 12 and 15, highly developed adolescents progress greatly between these years. The same amount of developmental change was found for the highly developed subjects in the rural sample.

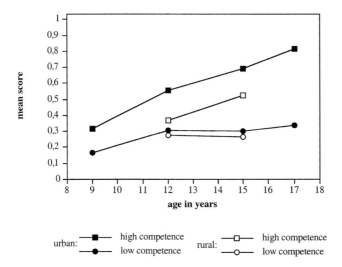

Figure 6.4.   Change in individual differences between competence levels.

Although one might have expected that the influence of the teacher-rated competence, evolving before children enter school, would decrease in the course of development, we have shown this influence to increase greatly even across a time span of 10 years. Individual differences due to developmental prerequisites were not compensated for (nor even slightly decreased by) schooling. As shown in the example of syllogistic reasoning, schooling and institutionalised processes of socialisation do not seem to fit the needs and necessities of progress in cognitive development. The developmental trajectory and the institutionalised life course of the individual diverge more and more. The slow developers do not progress, while children with good developmental prerequisites have the highest progression rates in cognitive development at the time when they enter school. If school were designed to help compensate for developmental deficits stemming from the cognitive socialisation of the child, this should boost the cognitive development of the slow developers.

Social class as moderator of the effects of developmental differences

Contrary to the developmental prerequisites at the onset of schooling, gender and social lifeworld do not directly affect the development of syllogistic reasoning. Individual differences due to gender and social lifeworld of the children were found only in conjunction with competence level and depending on the contextuation of the tasks and developmental age.

Figure 6.5 shows the developmental courses of slow and advanced developers from the lower and the middle classes separately for contextualised and abstract tasks. High-competence children progress independently of their social origin and the contextualisation of the task; for them, no differences were found between social classes and/or between contextualisations of task. By contrast, the trajectories of slow developers differ with respect to both the social origin of the children and the contextualisation of the task. Whereas slow middle-class children show slight progression, slow lower-class children stagnate between ages 9 and 17. Further, late developers differentiate with respect to the contextualisation of the tasks. Experiential and contextualised tasks were performed better than abstract and decontextualised tasks. When looking separately at the changes between ages 9 and 12 and between ages 12 and 17 in function of the contextualisation of the task, lower-class children evidenced regression in adolescence when solving abstract tasks. When solving contextualised tasks no regression was found, but stagnation obtained between ages 12 and 17.

These results demonstrate a process of selective differentiation in cognitive development. Constraints on the individual resources of the children in conjunction with a more deprived social lifeworld lead to additional developmental disadvantages if, when entering adolescence, abstract tasks have to be solved that necessitate the application of hypothetico-deductive strategies. Abstract tasks do

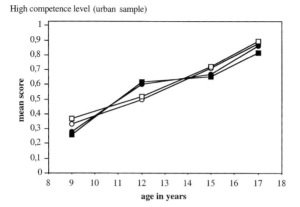

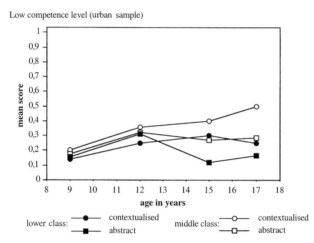

Figure 6.5.   Individual differences between social classes by competence level.

not represent interesting and motivating tasks for these adolescents. Only contextualised tasks were perceived as relevant. Presumably these adolescents do not dissociate form and content of the task, an achievement that is assumed to underly the emergence of formal thought. The argumentation of these adolescents remains bound to specific contents and domains of experience. No dissociation from specific contexts in terms of logical abstraction emerges.

The emergence of gender differences in the effects of developmental differences

In order to analyse how gender moderates the emergence of individual differences between low- and high-competence children, in Figure 6.6 the developmental

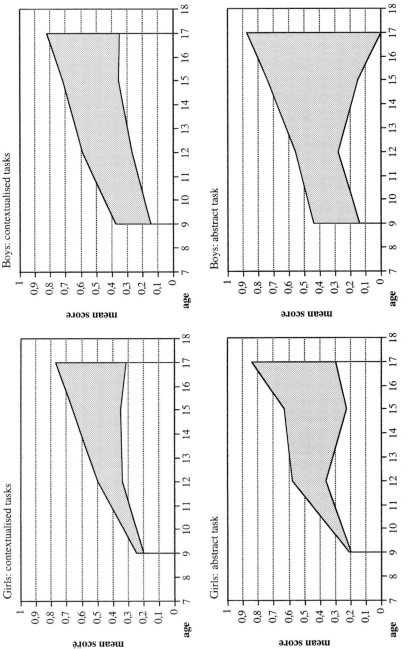

Figure 6.6. Change in individual differences between competence levels by gender.

116

courses of these groups are charted separately for girls and boys in contextualised and abstract tasks. The upper line in the graphs represent the developmental courses of the high-competence children and the lower line that of the low-competence children.

While large individual differences between low- and high-competence boys were found from ages 9 to 17 in both contextualised and abstract tasks, individual differences between low- and high-competence girls did not emerge before age 15. Furthermore, there were marked differences in the increase of individual variation between low- and high-competence subjects. The large increase of inter-individual variation of boys in adolescence when solving an abstract task may be due to the fact that abstract tasks play an important rule in the emergence of formal thought in adolescence. Thus the contextualisation of the task and the emergence of hypothetico-deductive thought appear to interact. Looking at the developmental trajectories of low- and high-competence girls one also finds an increase of differences in adolescence, but compared to the increase of the boys it is quite gradual and not strengthened again in adolescence. Although there are no differences between the developmental trajectories of girls and boys at any measurement occasion, inter-individual differences between low- and high-competence girls at ages 15 and 17 reach about the same magnitude as those of boys only in contextualised tasks. In the abstract task, however, the variation in the trajectories of boys is about three times larger than the inter-individual differences between low- and high-competence girls.

Thus, individual differences in teacher-rated competence impact only on the cognitive development of boys. The developmental trajectories of girls are not affected by these differences even 5 years later or more. The emergence of individual differences in the girls' courses of development between ages 15 to 17 does not, therefore, represent "remote" or delayed effects of preschool socialisation, as a corresponding increase is also found in boys' trajectories. Whereas in the case of the trajectories of the boys a constant influence of family and preschool socialisation is reinforced by the impact of schooling and the emergence of formal operations in adolescence, the developmental courses of girls merely show the gradually increasing impact of schooling as well as developmental change in adolescence.

One reason for the differential and selective power of the cognitive socialisation of boys at the onset of schooling may be that the physical and cognitive world of preschool boys, as well as the expectations of their parents and peers, seem to fit the specific topics and tasks taught in schools. The cognitive development of school- girls in both contextualised and abstract tasks is independent of developmental prerequisites; that is, individual differences in cognitive resources at the onset of schooling do not further affect individual differences in cognition during the school years. Thus, expectations of parents and peers as well as the cognitive world of preschool girls appear to be less linked to specific tasks and domains of action. Therefore, the emergence of inter-individual differences in girls in late adolescence can only be traced back, on the one hand, to school socialisation as a novel field of experience, and, on the other hand, to developmental changes in cognition that have to do with the emergence of formal thought. For boys, however, additional constraints in development and especially in the emergence of individual differences have to be taken into account. These are the individual resources at the onset of schooling. The large impact of individual resources on later cognitive development of boys leads to a process of selective differentiation in development. While advanced developers at the onset of schooling progress and make constant gains from ages 7 to 17, low-competence boys show only moderate advances in childhood, and stagnate or even regress in development in adolescence.

The relation between formation of structure and context of development

With regard to intrinsic constraints, the analyses of change in intra-individual differences showed that there is a decrease of differences between task contexts and an invariant interaction between form of proposition and contextualisation of task, which is stable over time. With regard to external constraints, the analyses of the emergence of inter-individual differences have shown that differences in developmental competence at the onset of school have the strongest impact on later development. This result may appear to be tautological, but it confirms the assumption that differences in cognitive development can be traced back to antecedent constructions in the ontogenesis of the subject. The social and ecological lifeworld as well as gender differences on cognitive socialisation also represent important constraints on development, but their influences are much smaller and above all mediated by developmental resources and by the contextualisation of the tasks.

The analysis of the emergence of inter-individual differences in cognition necessarily leads to the question of optimal conditions in development. Concerning differences in the cognitive socialisation of girls and boys, the study has shown that school socialisation does not compensate for disadvantages in individual resources, but, especially in the case of boys applying abstract tasks in adolescence, schooling leads to a developmental process of selective differentiation that reinforces dramatically the impact of previously acquired differences in individual resources. Somewhat better opportunities to compensate developmental disadvantages were shown to be available in the developmental courses of the girls. Their cognitive interactions seem to be relatively independent of individual resources and less linked to specific contexts of development.

These results demonstrate the continuing and moderating effect of socialisation on the impact of developmental differences in the formation of cognitive structures. Social conditions have only minor direct effects on the development of syllogistic reasoning. Broadening the scope of the analysis of external constraints by including further factors mediating the interactive process of structure formation, such as the differential and changing impact of developmental differences in the example of syllogistic reasoning, we obtain a clear picture of the interaction between structure formation and contexts of development that shows the recursive characteristic of the developmental processes examined. The influence of developmental differences on later development as an outcome of previous developmental processes hardly been analysed so far, presumably because only very few long-ranging longitudinal studies exist in this field. Non-constructivist approaches in developmental research generally do not respond to such empirical questions, as non-constructivist approaches view child development mostly as a result or an outcome of a more or less complex inter-relationship between different contextual factors. These studies do not focus attention on the function of the genetic and socialisatory history in the formation of cognitive competencies. Taking into consideration the changing dynamic of internal conditions on development and the differential and changing moderating impact of socialisation over time is, therefore, a specific characteristic of the constructivist approach in the empirical analysis of cognitive socialisation. The goal of a constructivist approach is to account for the impact of social experience mediated by the formation process in the development of cognition.

REFERENCES

Broughton, J.M. (1981). Piaget's structural developmental psychology: IV. Knowledge without a self and history. *Human Development*, *24*, 320–346.

Buck-Morss, S. (1975). Socio-economic bias in Piaget's theory and its implications for cross-cultural studies. *Human Development*, *18*, 35–49.

Bullinger, A., & Chatillon, J.-F. (1983). Recent theory and research of the Genevan school. In P.H. Mussen (Ed.), *Handbook of child psychology. Vol. 3: Cognitive development* (pp. 231–262). New York: Wiley.

Case, R., & Edelstein, W. (1993). Introduction: Structural approaches to individual differences. In R. Case & W. Edelstein (Eds.), *The new structuralism in cognitive development: Theory and research on individual pathways* (pp. 1–10). Basel: Karger.

Chapman, M. (1988). *Constructive evolution: Origins and development of Piaget's thought.* Cambridge: Cambridge University Press.

de Ribaupierre, A., Rieben, L., & Lautrey, J. (1985). Horizontal décalages and individual differences in the development of concrete operations. In V. Shulman, L. Restaino-Baumann, & L. Butler (Eds.), *The future of Piagetian theory: The Neo-Piagetians* (pp. 175–197). New York: Plenum Press.

Edelstein, W. (1983). Cultural constraints on development and the vicissitudes of progress. In F.S. Kessel & A.W. Siegel (Eds.), *The child and other cultural inventions: Psychology and society* (pp. 48–81). New York: Praeger.

Edelstein, W. (1996). The social construction of cognitive development. In G. Noam & K. Fischer (Eds.), *Development and vulnerabilities in close relationships* (pp. 91–112). Mahwah, NJ: Lawrence Erlbaum Associates Inc.

Edelstein, W., & Hoppe-Graff, S. (Eds.). (1993). *Die Konstruktion kognitiver Strukturen: Perspektiven einer konstruktivistischen Entwicklungspsychologie* [The construction of cognitive structures: Perspectives of a constructivist developmental psychology]. Bern: Huber.

Edelstein, W., Keller, M., & Schröder, E. (1990). Child development and social structure: A longitudinal study of individual differences. In P.B. Baltes, D.L. Featherman, & R.M. Lerner (Eds.), *Life-span development and behavior* (Vol. 10, pp. 152–185). Hillsdale, NJ: Lawrence Erlbaum Associates Inc.

Fetz, R.L. (1988). *Struktur und Genese. Jean Piagets Transformation der Philosophie* [Structure and genesis: Jean Piaget's transformation of philosophy]. Bern: Paul Haupt.

Goodnow, J.J. (1990). The socialization of cognition: What's involved. In J. Stigler, R. Shweder, & J.G. Miller (Eds.), *Cultural psychology* (pp. 259–286). Cambridge: Cambridge University Press.

Grundmann, M. (1997). Vergesellschaftung und Individuation. Sozialisationstheoretische Überlegungen im Anschluß an Alfred Schütz und Jean Piaget [Socialization and individuation: Theoretical considerations following Alfred Schütze and Jean Piaget]. *Schweizerische Zeitschrift für Soziologie, 23*, 83–115.

Hofmann, R.J. (1982). Potential sources of structural invalidity in Piagetian and Neo-Piagetian assessment. In S. Modgil & C. Modgil (Eds.), *Jean Piaget: Consensus and controversy* (pp. 233–239). London: Holt, Rinehart & Winston.

Inhelder, B., & Piaget, J. (1971). Closing remarks. In D.R. Green, M.P. Ford, & G.B. Flamer (Eds.), *Measurement and Piaget* (pp. 210–213). New York: McGraw-Hill.

Longeot, F. (1978). *Les stades opératoires de Piaget et les facteurs de l'intelligence.* Grenoble: Presses Universitaires de Grenoble.

Piaget, J. (1965). *The moral judgment of the child.* New York: Free Press. (Original work published 1932; first English publication, London: Routledge & Kegan Paul, 1932)

Piaget, J. (1972). Intellectual evolution from adolescence to adulthood. *Human Development, 15*, 1–12.

Piaget, J. (1977). *The development of thought: Equilibration of cognitive structures.* New York: Viking Press. (Original work published in French in 1975)

Schröder, E. (1989). *Vom konkreten zum formalen Denken: Individuelle Entwicklungsverläufe von der Kindheit bis zum Jugendalter* [From concrete to formal thought: Individual courses of development from childhood to adolescence]. Bern: Huber.

Schröder, E. (1992). Strukturbildung und Kontexte der kognitiven Entwicklung. Bedingungen und Prozesse der kognitiven Selbstorganisation [Formation of structures and contexts of cognitive development: Conditions and processes of cognitive self-organization]. In W. Edelstein (Ed.), *Sozialer Konstruktivismus* [Social constructivism]. (Contributions of the Center for Development and Socialization, 40/ES) Berlin: Max Planck Institute for Human Development.

Schröder, E. (1993). Individuelle Konstruktion und kognitive Entwicklung: Eine Analyse der Veränderung intra-individueller Unterschiede [Individual construction and cognitive development: An analysis of change in intra-individual differences]. In W. Edelstein & S. Hoppe-Graff (Eds.), *Die Konstruktion kognitiver Strukturen: Perspektiven einer konstruktivistischen Entwicklungspsychologie* (pp. 139–155). Bern: Huber.

Schröder, E., & Edelstein, W. (1991). Intrinsic and external constraints on the development of cognitive competencies. In M. Chandler & M. Chapman (Eds.), *Criteria for competence: Controversy in the conceptualization and assessment of children's abilities* (pp. 131–152). Hillsdale, NJ: Lawrence Erlbaum Associates Inc.

Schröder, E., Bödeker, K., & Edelstein, W. (2000). *The development of syllogistic reasoning: A manual including measurement procedures and descriptive analyses*. Berlin: Max Planck Institute for Human Development.

Seiler, T.B. (1991). Entwicklung und Sozialisation: Eine strukturgenetische Sichtweise [Development and socialization: A structure-genetic view]. In K. Hurrelmann & D. Ulich (Eds.), *Neues Handbuch der Sozialisationsforschung* (pp. 99–119). Weinheim: Beltz.

Youniss, J. (1980). *Parents and peers in social development: A Sullivan-Piaget perspective*. Chicago: University of Chicago Press.

CHAPTER SEVEN

Mental imagery: From Inhelder's ideas to neuro-cognitive models

Jacques Vonèche
Archives Jean Piaget, University of Geneva, Switzerland

THE GENEVA SCHOOL AND MENTAL IMAGERY

The position of the Geneva School on mental imagery is well known. Mental imagery is located half-way between perception and reasoning. This means that, for Piaget and Inhelder, a sensory component exists in mental imagery, but imagery is not a mere continuation of perception in a less vivid form, because there is a motor component too. This motor component is essential for Piaget and Inhelder. Developmentally speaking, it originates in "deferred imitation", one of the five markers, for Piaget and Inhelder, of the emergence of the so-called symbolic or semiotic function along with language, (symbolic) play, dreams, and drawings.

The Genevan hypothesis is as follows: Through imitation, schemes of correspondence are established between certain sensory events and the kinesthetic sensations accompanying motor activity. Thus, mental imagery develops out of imitation as the result of a progressive interiorisation of action. Evidence for this was provided by Piaget's two younger children, Laurent and Lucienne, who were observed to mimic the opening and closing of a matchbox with their mouths or hands.[1]

Furthermore, Piaget was convinced that visual imagery itself could not originate in sensory perception only, as the very eye-movements were viewed by him as a sort of imitation of the object looked at! Motoric competence is, thus, crucial in the formation of mental imagery for Piaget. Therefore, the relationship between mental imagery and action is clear and evident to him. But, because thinking comes from action, the relationship between mental imagery and mental operations is also clear and evident. It is clearer and more evident even than the relationship between perception and mental imagery.

As we have already seen, images differ from perception in at least three ways: (1) Image is not a weaker perception (we cannot read under the "light" shed by the image of a lamp); (2) there are unlimited perceptions of any object but one or few images of it; (3) developmentally, perception is inborn, imagery develops later.

However, images are also somewhat similar to perception in a sense that Piaget and Inhelder call figurative. They are a form of knowledge focusing on the external figural aspect of an event in a static manner closely tied to a particular accommodation, thus a more or less accurate "copy" of reality. We can "see" the Parthenon in mental imagery but we cannot count its columns, one by one, as in direct perception.

Thus imagery is as particular as perception but it is conversely as symbolic as language. In other words mental imagery bears the same relationship to objects as that of language to concepts. Language and mental imagery are both signifiers, but the former is general and conceptual, where as the second is figural and individual.

This theory is common to Piaget and Inhelder. However there is a difference between them about the exact role of mental imagery. For Piaget, there was a primacy of operations upon imagery whereas, for Inhelder, mental imagery was the support of thought: "The act of symbolically translating successive events into simultaneous spatial images does not only fix the information from which the judgment is elaborated but also serves as a continuous support for the elaboration itself" (Inhelder, 1965, p. 17). As Inhelder points out in her conclusion of the same paper: "The successive structures of operative thought, as Piaget has shown, may be accelerated by many external factors; their mode of construction, however, does not seem to be modified by such factors. ... The development of symbolic imagery, we believe, depends to a large extent on external contributions. It is as if, in the initial phases, symbolic imagery bore the imprint of motor-imitation schemes from which it stems" (1965, p. 18).

What is important to underline here is the passage "as Piaget has shown", demonstrating the distance between Inhelder and Piaget on this point as well as on the point of the role of mental imagery. Nevertheless, they both agree that the encoding and decoding systems evolve over time and with age on the basis of operative development. In other words, what is claimed by Piaget and Inhelder is that mental imagery is not a copy of perceptual reality but its symbolic representation: Mental imagery is not residual perception but active imitation of the model by the sensory-motoric organs of the observer, and, as such, depends on the stage of mental development reached by the child.

Piaget and Inhelder involve two ranges of observations in support of their viewpoint: (1) peripheral electromyographic activity during mental imagery; and (2) eye-movements in mental representation similar to those observed in actual perception—hence Piaget's bold assumption that eye-movements are imitations of the shape of objects equivalent to electromyographic discharges. Thus mental imagery is a creative motoric construction on the basis of sensory experience and as such is fundamentally different from sensory perception, in so far as it depends heavily on the schemata of assimilation and accommodation, and not on immediate field-effects as does sensory perception. When these schemata evolve, so does mental imagery.

OTHER PERSPECTIVES

Such a view apparently coincides with the "imagist" position of today's cognitive psychology (Denis, 1979, 1989; Kosslyn, 1980, 1983, 1994; Shepard & Cooper, 1982; Shepard & Meltzer, 1971) and is the opposite of the "propositionalist" perspective according to which mental imagery is a mere epiphenomenon. In fact, the "imagists" have shown that some specific retinotopic areas of the occipital cortex are activated during mental imagery. These areas are the same as those fired during actual perception. Piaget and Inhelder anticipated such a convergence.

However, as a matter of fact, this convergence is more apparent than real, as the operations generated inside the visual buffer imagined by cognitive psychologists (Dean, 1990) are not the result of children's coordinations of actions structuring the event to be represented or figured out according to certain categories of understanding such as seriation, class inclusion, etc. On the contrary, the "operations" of the cognitivists are more like a processing system of the information given in a given task (Kosslyn, 1983; Shepard & Meltzer, 1971). We are dealing here, not with Piagetian operations, but with psychological metaphors such as visual "buffer" or attention "window", supposed to represent what takes place in the cortex during mental imagery. Thus, for the cognitivists, the distinction is between two parallel encoding systems: one for spatial properties, and one for object properties corresponding to different sites and paths in the brain as demonstrated by careful analyses of the pathologies of brain-damaged patients.

These analyses provide Kosslyn (1994) with a distinction between two sorts of transformations: "encoded movement", corresponding to the reproduction of a previously perceived event, and "added movement", corresponding to a mental simulation of displacements and transformations without previous perception. The second sort of movement is very similar to Piaget's and Inhelder's conceptions on the subject.

Moreover some experiments, especially one by Berthoz and Petit (1996), showed that the visual cortex is activated by mental imagery in a way very similar to its activation by perception. Thus Berthoz (1993) suggested that one should not differentiate perception and action, as "perception is simulated action" (p. 16).

Once again, such an approach had been anticipated by Piaget and Inhelder. But when one focuses more carefully on the cognitive psychology of mental imagery one is forced to observe that most "developmental" studies of mental imagery fail to be true to Piaget and Inhelder in their approach and that they fuse aspects that were clearly distinct in the Genevan approach.

A case in point is given by the research of Lejeune (1995) into mental rotation through space. Unlike others (Corballis, 1982; Kail, 1985), Lejeune does not consider mental rotation as an automatic process. Starting from Shepard and Meltzer's (1971) pioneering study of tri-dimensional rotation, showing that subjects were using an analogue transformation process to reorientate the disoriented stimulus before carrying the comparison between identical stimuli except for orientation, Lejeune does observe children under the age of 8, which is considered by most researchers (Dean, 1990) as the age at which mental rotation is mature. Kosslyn et al. (1990) showed that young children are relatively poor at rotating objects in images, although they are relatively good at maintaining images in memory for a short while (circa 3 seconds). Consequently, Lejeune studied the correlation between mental rotation and visuo-spatial short-term memory span by submitting subjects of different ages (5, 8, young adults, and old people) to two sets of tasks: mental rotation and memory span. He observed a fairly good positive correlation between the two sets of tasks from a developmental point of view. Such a finding seems rather trivial: If one cannot keep in mind something, how could one operate on it? In addition, a close analysis of the study raises many more questions. First of all, all the studies mentioned (including the author's own study) take for granted the very existence of mental representation or mental imagery. Moreover, mental rotation is also considered as self-evident. More puzzling still, object recognition, visual information maintenance in short-term memory, and rotating visual images seem to be considered as one and the same thing. This seems to be the case for all the studies made by cognitive psychologists (Shepard & Cooper, 1982; Shepard & Meltzer, 1971). They fail to understand that stimulus orientation recognition is quite different from rotating an object mentally "in one's own head" as Genevan children put it. In the first instance, the necessary equipment is quite limited; one needs only a mapping system, and it has been known for a long time that such an equipment is readily available to babies only a few months old. In the second case, one needs to *conserve*, in one way or another, some physical properties of an object such as size, shape, etc. and *transform* others like orientation, for instance, while anticipating the results of these conservations and transformations. This activity supposes, at least, some form of permanence of the object. Mere recognition does not allow any grounded conclusion about the observer's sensitivity to perspective, rotation, or point of view. What could be a good test of these capacities would be a series of objects that are locally different but conceptually equivalent. Shepard's shapes have no other identity than computational: placing cubes, counting them, specifying their angles, and so forth. On the contrary, visual imagery supposes displacements of contours in forms other than merely computational, as ancient experiments on eidetic imagery have shown. In rotating an object "in one's own head" one is representing intermediary steps of the rotation between the final and the initial states. What is visualised (or "motorised" in motoric imagery) is a construction of reality and its representation. This is quite different from comparing states with one another, especially as, in many instances, one of the two possible final states is the mirror-image of the other. This is unfortunate because, most of the time, children do not differentiate mirror-images from their original. Consequently, when they say they are the same, it is by lack of differentiation between states, rather than by awareness of a rotation of the same and only object.

CONCLUSION

Instead of deepening the investigation into mental imagery by testing Inhelder's and Piaget's hypotheses, neuro-cognitive psychologists have set a new paradigm which is quite different from the Piagetian one, and also a clear return to the ancient empirical hypothesis. Consequently, cognitivistic psychologists have neither verified nor falsified the Genevan constructivistic theory. They have simply missed the point, which is that mental imagery is constructed on the basis of sensory elements according to rules of invariance built along children's mental development and thus changing with it at every new stage of ontogenesis.

NOTE

1. In Piaget (1936/1952), *The origin of intelligence in children*, observation 180 of Lucienne, and in Piaget (1945/1962), *Play, dreams and imitation*, observation 58 of Laurent.

REFERENCES

Berthoz, A. (1993). *Leçon inaugurale* [Inaugural lecture]. Paris, Collège de France.
Berthoz, A., & Petit, L. (1996). Les mouvements du regard: Une affaire de saccade [Eye movements: A question of saccade]. *La Recherche, 289*, 58–65.
Corballis, M.C. (1982). Mental rotation: Anatomy of a paradigm. In M. Potegal (Ed.), *Spatial abilities: Developmental and physiological foundations*. New York: Academic Press.
Dean, A.I. (1990). The development of mental imagery: A comparison of Piagetian and cognitive psychological perspectives. *Annals of Child Development, 7*, 105–144.
Denis, M. (1979). *Les images mentales* [Mental imagery]. Paris: Presses Universitaires de France.
Denis, M. (1989). *Image et cognition* [Image and cognition]. Paris: Presses Universitaires de France.
Inhelder, B. (1965). Operational thought and symbolic imagery. *Monographs of the Society for Research in Child Development, 2*, 4–18.
Kail, R.V. (1985). Development of mental rotation: A speed–accuracy study. *Journal of Experimental Child Psychology, 40*, 181–92.
Kosslyn, S.M. (1980). *Image and mind*. Cambridge: Cambridge University Press.
Kosslyn, S.M. (1983). *Ghosts in the mind's machine*. New York: W.W. Norton.
Kosslyn S.M. (1994). *Image and brain: The resolution of the imagery debate*. Cambridge, MA: MIT Press.
Kosslyn, S.M., Margolis, J.A., Barrett, A.M., Goldknopf, E.J., & Daly, P.F. (1990). Age differences in imagery abilities. *Child Development, 61*, 995–1010.
Lejeune, M. (1995). Mental rotation and maintenance of visuo-spatial information. In *Journée annuelle de la Société belge de psychologie*. Louvain-la-Neuve: Société belge de psychologie.
Piaget, J. (1952). *The origin of intelligence in children* (M. Cook, Trans.). New York: International University Press. (Original work published 1936)

Piaget, J. (1962). *Play, dreams and imitation* (C. Cattegno & F.M. Hodson, Trans.). New York: W.W. Norton. (Original work published 1945)

Shepard, R.N., & Cooper, L.A. (1982). *Mental images and their transformations.* Cambridge, MA: MIT Press.

Shepard, R.N., & Meltzer, J. (1971). Mental rotation of three-dimensional objects. *Science, 171,* 701–703.

CHAPTER EIGHT

Learning in Geneva: The contribution by Bärbel Inhelder and her colleagues

Peter Bryant
University of Oxford, UK

A SURPRISING INITIATIVE

Developmental psychologists rarely see developmental changes as they happen. They usually have to infer the changes that interest them from the differences that they find between children—sometimes the same children—at different ages. The changes that go with age usually take place well away from the laboratory and far from the eyes of the curious researcher. Naturally, developmental psychologists often yearn for a direct look at the phenomena, which they think and talk and write about so much and see so little of.

This has always been one of the main motivations behind intervention studies and microgenetic studies of development. Psychologists want to make the changes happen in the laboratory, where they are on hand to see them take place. Intervention studies and microgenetic studies on children have the merit that the researchers often see the actual changes that interest them happening under their own noses.

The training study has another advantage too, for this kind of study is an essential weapon in research on the causes of change. Hypotheses about the causes of change need training studies. If you believe that some factor determines a particular developmental change and you can embody this factor as a condition in an experiment, then you surely must put it into a training study and demonstrate that your factor does have the effect that you say it has. Of course, this is a frankly reductionist argument, but, frankly, reductionist causal hypotheses do exist and some of them are about developmental changes that interest the Genevan school a very great deal.

For quite a long time, nonetheless, the Genevans kept well away from the training study, even though the method was adopted with enthusiasm and sometimes apparent success elsewhere. One can see the Genevan point. It is desperately hard to embody disequilibrium or reflective abstraction as an experimental procedure in an intervention study. How does one provoke, how does one even measure, such abstractions? Furthermore, many of the training studies that were done in other places had a different agenda, and one that was inimical to the Genevan spirit. Inhelder, Sinclair, and Bovet (1974) revealingly commented that "A great deal of the current learning research in the United States is based on an empiricist type of epistemology. Surprisingly enough, some extensions of this theory are also found in contemporary French psychology" (p. 11). In many cases the main aim of such studies was not to test developmental theory, but to find ways of speeding up development. Piaget and his colleagues preferred to think about the nature rather than the speed of development, and quite right too.

So it was something of a surprise when Bärbel Inhelder and her colleagues, Mimi Sinclair and Magali Bovet, launched an ambitious series of intervention studies in the mid-1960s and eventually published the results of this formidable programme in 1974 (Inhelder et al., 1974). The book's opening sentence acknowledges its inherent oddity. "It may be surprising that Genevan developmental psychologists have seen fit to add yet another book on learning to the large number already published, particularly since Jean Piaget and his colleagues have frequently emphasised the subject's own activity rather than his reactions to environmental stimuli as being important for the acquisition of knowledge" (p. 1). Yet soon enough in this book the driving forces behind the project become clear enough. The authors of it express two main aims.

One was to look at developmental changes as they happen. "It is difficult to apprehend the essentially cross-sectional studies of mechanisms of equilibration by means of cross-sectional studies of children of different age groups. In learning studies, a child's successive cognitive acquisitions in a given experimental setting can be followed over a certain period of time, and transition processes can therefore be observed more closely" (p. 17). The other aim was to study the importance of two possible environmental factors in development. These were linguistic and socio-cultural influences, and the avowed intention of the authors was to see whether the part that these play in development "may … be governed by equilibratory mechanisms" (p. 17).

The tension between the two aims

There is a certain tension between these two very different aims. The fact is that they make quite different demands as far as the design of empirical research is concerned. All that one needs to do in order to satisfy the first aim is to arrange a set of reasonably close, on-the-spot, encounters with children as they change from one intellectual level to another. What makes these changes happen is not tremendously important if all you want to do is to observe them happening.

However, what makes such changes happen is precisely the issue when we come to the second of the two aims, and this aim produces an entirely different set of requirements for the person designing the relevant research study. Suppose that we want to show, for example, that a certain linguistic factor leads to a particular developmental change. We must, of course, give some of the children (the experimental group) taking part in the study concentrated doses of that aspect of language in as meaningful and natural a way as possible, and then study whether this leads to the expected development. But simply to find that this group of children does make the relevant developmental progress is not nearly enough.

The trouble is that there are bound to be other possible explanations for any subsequent developmental change. The most obvious is the possibility that the children made the change without the help of the experimenter's intervention. The most banal version of this kind of worry is that the children are older at the post-test than they were at the pre-test, and might have got to the next level anyway without any help from anyone else. Another possibility is that some other variable than the one that interests the experimenter may be at work. Pure interventions—pure in the sense of being confined to the factor that the experimenter thinks important—are out of the question. Along with the added measure of this factor will come (1) extra attention from adults, (2) extra chances for verbal interactions with these same adults, and (3) extra experience with the physical props that are an inevitable part of the experimenter's armoury. We have to ensure that these are not the factors that make the difference, and this requires at least one control group of children, who must be given all the added experiences that the children in the experimental group receive apart from the one whose effects the experimenter wishes to study.

This worthy, but rather tedious, point was already well worked out at the time that Inhelder, Sinclair, and Bovet began their momentous series of studies. In fact, they implicitly recognised the need for adequate research designs in training studies when they acknowledged the achievements of others who had done such studies. "A careful distinction must be made between empiricist methodology, which is heuristically useful, and its postulates which in many respects do not seem to stand up to critical analysis" (1974, p. 11). The "heuristic" usefulness of the empiricists' enterprise lay in their careful use of different groups to tease out the effects of particular variables. They knew about control groups.

THE EXPERIMENTS

I have mentioned one book so far, but for a full account of the remarkable set of intervention studies carried out by Inhelder, Sinclair, and Bovet one actually needs to read two books. As well as the Inhelder, Sinclair, and Bovet (1974) volume, there is the earlier book by Sinclair herself (Sinclair-de-Zwart, 1967) which tells of her studies on intervention in relation to the acquisition of language. This second book is less well known, partly, I think, because one of the main intervention studies in it is also given a chapter in the Inhelder, Sinclair, and Bovet book. I suspect that people have concluded that this twice-reported study is all one needs to know about

Sinclair's training studies. But that view, as we shall see, is entirely incorrect, for in another of her studies Sinclair produced a remarkable result, which actually militates against some of the conclusions eventually reached in the later joint book by the three authors.

Let us, for the moment, stick with the later and far better known book. It describes eight studies on intervention and children's learning of the central Piagetian concepts; one-to-one correspondence, conservation of continuous and discontinuous quantities, and class inclusion. The first study was about the conservation of continuous quantity, and in the pre- and post-tests the children were given liquid and clay conservation problems. The aim of the experiment was to find the "type of situation that is particularly favourable for progress" (Inhelder et al., 1974, p. 39), and also to look at the effects of the children's initial capabilities. To that end the experimenters divided the children into non-conservers and intermediate conservers (children who solved conservation problems sometimes but not at other times) on the basis of their performance in the pre-tests. They put both groups through a training regime and, let it not be missed, they also added a control group of intermediate conservers who went through the pre- and post-tests but were given no training in between.

The intervention itself was designed to produce a conflict between the child's expectations about the results of a transformation before it happened and what the child eventually saw had happened after the transformation occurred. The experimental display was of three pairs of containers, arranged vertically, so that the liquid in each of the containers in the top pair could, by the turn of a tap, be jettisoned into the container below and so on. The containers in the top row had the same dimensions as each other, but in the pair below one container was a great deal narrower than the other, which meant that if the liquid was at the same level in the top pair, it would not be so when the liquid was poured into the containers below. The child was asked to predict what would be the relative levels of the liquid when it was let through into the lower-level containers, and it is easy to see that children at the non-conserving and the intermediate stages would often anticipate the wrong outcome. These children would predict one outcome and then witness another.

Inhelder et al. reported that the intervention did indeed have a striking effect, but that the children's initial (pre-test) intellectual levels determined whether they were helped or not by the experiences that they went through with the banked bottles. None of the non-conservers qualified as conservers in the post-test. In contrast, very nearly all of the children at the intermediate level improved significantly, and over half became full-fledged conservers.

What is the reason for the impact of the children's initial levels of understanding? The authors argue that the experience of making a prediction, and then seeing that prediction so clearly confounded, forced the children to notice features that they would normally ignore. This led to improvement in the case of the intermediate children because they already had the inferential mechanisms to work out the significance of these hitherto neglected aspects of their environment. The non-conservers, on the other hand, also became aware of these new features but could not "put them to use" (p. 59). Indeed the illuminating protocols that the authors give us illustrate this particular difference between the two groups. Both could dwell on the relevant features of the situation, but the more advanced group eventually made sense of these features whereas the less advanced children struggled but in the end failed to do so.

So much for the experimental group. The control group's performance was described more economically by Inhelder et al. In a single sentence they tell us that these children made no progress at all from pre-test to post-test. So, it is reasonable to conclude that the children in the experimental group, whose understanding improved between the pre- and the post-tests, did turn in a better performance because of the intervening experiences that the experimenters imposed on them.

However, the control was in many ways a thoroughly unsatisfactory one. It was an unseen control group: The experimenters had nothing to do with the children in this group between pre-test and post-test. This means that there were many differences in the treatment of the two groups. The authors assumed that the relevant difference was that the children in the experimental group were forced to reconsider the significance of various aspects of the environment that are associated with quantity, whereas of course the control group children were not. However, the children in the experimental group also received more attention than the control group children did, they had more experience of witnessing liquid transformations, and they had more conversations with the experimenters. One cannot, therefore, assume that it was specifically the experience of making a prediction, and then being forced to consider why that prediction turned out not to be right, that caused the change in so many of the experimental group children's approach to the conservation problems.

Viewed as a description of learning and developmental change this study was a tour de force. The experimenters' method of promoting change was excellent, their observations of the children's comments during the training were enthralling, their demonstration of the importance of the children's initial level of functioning in the pre-test was entirely convincing. However, when one considers the experiment as an attempt to show, through intervention, what causes children to develop, it is easy to see many ambiguities. The tension, mentioned earlier, between the experimenters' two very different aims becomes very clear, for they are much better with the first aim (acute observation of transition) than with the second (discovering the causes of developmental change). Their observations of the way in which children change, and improve, their thoughts about conservation are persuasive: Their conclusions about the causes of these changes are not at all convincing.

Most of the subsequent studies in the Inhelder, Sinclair, and Bovet book pursued the possibility of the importance of the child's initial level of performance, and they repeatedly confirmed the importance of these starting levels. The consistency of this result was undoubtedly the single most important contribution of this volume. But it had a close rival, for one of the other chapters in the book reported a completely different and most interesting kind of result. This chapter described a study, which was originally presented in Sinclair's own book, on the effects, or rather the lack of effects, of verbal training on children's ability to solve the conservation problem.

Verbal training and operativity

The verbal training study started with an observation, which is of great interest in its own right. Sinclair established a close relation between children's performance in conservation problems and the linguistic terms that they adopt in order to describe quantity. The quantitative terms that most interested her were "scalar terms" which deal with more than one dimension ("this one is long and thin: that one is short and fat") and "vectorial terms" like "bigger" or "more". Sinclair observed that non-conservers tend to avoid such terms, using instead descriptions like "the big one" and "a lot". Conserving children, by contrast, used differentiated and comparative terms happily and accurately.

The relation between, on the one hand, the children's level of success in the conservation problem and, on the other hand, the linguistic terms that the children adopted in order to describe quantity, was slightly stronger in the case of comparative terms than of differentiated terms. This is something of a puzzle, as it seems reasonable to expect a close relationship between conservation and the ability to describe the different relevant dimensions (e.g. height and width) in the conservation problem, where changes in such dimensions play such an important part.

At any rate, there are two quite different possible explanations for the strong connection that Sinclair found between children's linguistic activities on the one hand and their cognitive performance on the other. One possible hypothesis—the linguistic hypothesis—is that children eventually become conservers as a direct result of their learning to use comparative terms. The other possible hypothesis—the cognitive hypothesis—is that it is the other way round. Children eventually master the meaning of comparative terms because they now understand the complex of quantitative relations involved in conservation. As it is one of the canons of the Genevan theory that linguistic development is paced by cognitive development, Sinclair naturally favoured the second of these two hypotheses. But her research strategy was unusual. She decided to test the hypothesis that she did not believe in, rather than the Genevan hypothesis.

She gave children pre- and post-tests in conservation, and in between the two tests taught them to use differentiated and comparative terms. It is easy to see that her prediction was a negative one. The cognitive hypothesis leads to the null hypothesis. If this hypothesis is right, verbal training should have no effect on the children's cognitive structures.

Sinclair gave this training to 31 children, 28 of whom were non-conservers at the beginning of the experiment. Two of the remaining children were conservers and one was an intermediate conserver at the time of the pre-test. There does not seem to have been a control group in this study, probably because no improvement was expected anyway.

The negative prediction, it turned out, was the right one. There was very little improvement in this experiment. Most of the children (18/28) who began as non-conservers ended as non-conservers. Some progressed to the intermediate stage, but only 3 out of 28 became conservers.

Because of the absence of a control group, we cannot be sure whether or not the small improvements that did take place were a direct result of the verbal training. For her part Sinclair was more interested in the general lack of progress, and argued that it meant that linguistic development is not an important cause of cognitive change.

There are at least two problems with this interpretation. One is that the study concentrated on non-conservers, and yet other experiments which I have already described established that these children did not progress even after interventions that, according to Genevan theory, are the most likely to be successful. Indeed, as we have seen, in these other experiments the lack of improvement in the non-conservers, when contrasted with the progress made by children at the intermediate stage, is taken as support for the Piagetian ideas about learning and development. Why then should their failure to improve after verbal training be seen as a deadly blow to linguistic determinism?

This leads us to the second problem, which is the problem of the null hypothesis. It is usually a bad mistake to predict a negative result and then, having found it, to conclude that this negative result supports your hypothesis. In this case there was at least one other possible reason for the no-change result. The intervention, for example, might have been unnatural, by which I mean that the children might indeed have improved linguistically but not in a way that represents the way children normally learn how to use the linguistic expressions in question.

It is not as though Sinclair was forced into this uncomfortable corner because the negative prediction was the only one that it was practicable to test. On the contrary, her own hypothesis—the cognitive hypothesis—produced a definite positive prediction. She could have predicted that intervention that improves children's performance in the conservation task should as a direct consequence also hasten their learning of how to use those linguistic expressions that tell conservers and non-conservers apart. The ideal design would have been to have two experimental groups (and probably two control groups as well), one of which was trained to use the linguistic terms and then post-tested on conservation, and the other trained on conservation and post-tested on their use of linguistic terms.

This experiment of Sinclair's is well known, despite its ambiguities, and yet another of her experiments (Sinclair-de-Zwart, 1967: Section II: chaps. 1 and 2), despite its remarkable results, is hardly known at all. This second experiment was a study of the relation between seriation and children's use of linguistic terms, and it started and continued in much the same way as the conservation study that I have just described. Sinclair began by establishing a strong and impressive relation between children's success in ordering sticks of different lengths into an ordered series on the one hand, and their use of comparative terms on the other hand. Then she gave 23 children a training programme in the use of comparative terms, and she finally post-tested them both on the linguistic variables and on seriation.

In this experiment Sinclair's results were startlingly different from those of the earlier study with conservation. Her acid test of seriation was the ordering of the sticks in both directions—from smallest to largest and vice versa. None of the 23 children could manage this in the pre-test; but as many as 12 of them could do it in the post-test. Another 5 of the children managed to complete a series in one direction only in the post-test, even though they were quite unable to do so in the pre-test. Thus 17 out of 23 children showed substantial improvement in the seriation task after verbal training. This was a substantial positive result, although the apparent absence of a control group weakened it slightly. Nevertheless it was a difficult result for the cognitive hypothesis, and therefore for Sinclair, to explain.

What can account for this improvement? Sinclair's own argument is that she may have unwittingly trained the children in seriation as well as in the use of more sophisticated linguistic terms. This idea should be taken seriously. She did introduce ordinal series when she was encouraging children to use comparative terms. The trouble is that we cannot say, because Sinclair did not introduce an appropriate control group (trained with the same series, but not taught about comparative terms).

There is, of course, another possible explanation for these results. It is that the children's linguistic experiences might have prompted the improvement in seriation. Sinclair, as we have noted, was not sympathetic to this idea, but it certainly cannot be ruled out in this case. How would it work?

One point to note is that in any ordinal series all the quantities except for the endpoints have opposite relations to each of their neighbours. Each is smaller than one neighbour, and larger than the other. This bi-directionality of relations is, according to Piagetian theory, precisely the problem that children have with any ordinal series. It is possible that the considerable experience the children were given of calling the same quantity both "smaller" in one comparison and "larger" in the other helped them to get over their difficulty in understanding that a quantity can be simultaneously smaller than one thing and larger than the other. The linguistic hypothesis might well be the right one.

A REPLICATION AND A TEST OF THE LINGUISTIC HYPOTHESIS

Recently we carried out a replication of Sinclair's result and at the same time a test of the linguistic hypothesis (Bryant & Fyfe, in press). The question that we asked was whether the experience of calling the same quantity "larger" on some occasions and "smaller" on others does have an effect on children's understanding of ordinal series. We worked with 5- and 6-year-old children, all of whom either failed in a seriation pre-test to form an ordered series of ten sticks or were unable to insert an eleventh stick in the right place in a series that they had just formed.

We formed these children into three groups, and each group went through different training regimes in three separate sessions. All of them were introduced to various series of sticks and pieces of clay of different sizes during the sessions, and all of them formed them into ordinal series, sometimes with the help of the adult experimenter. Two of the groups were encouraged to use comparative terms to describe the relation between neighbouring quantities in each of the series, once they were formed. One of these two groups (the bi-directional group) was taught to use comparatives in both directions. We prompted them to describe the same stick, in a single sentence, as smaller than one neighbour and larger than the other ("the red stick is shorter than the blue one, and longer than the green stick").

The second group (the uni-directional group) was also taught to use comparative terms, but always just in one direction. So half of them made each comparison by using comparative terms for the larger quantity ("the blue stick is longer than the red one and the red one is longer than the green one") while the other half made their comparisons in the opposite direction ("the green stick is shorter than the red one and the red one is shorter than the blue one"). The third group was a control group. The children in this group, like the children in the other groups, were given experience in forming ordinal series, but this was all that they were given. They were not prompted verbally in any way: they were given no encouragement to use comparative terms to describe relations within the series.

The results of this experiment can be told quite simply. There were 20 children in each of the three groups, and they were closely matched in terms of their performance in the pre-test. In this pre-test, seven children in each group regularly succeeded in forming ordinal series. However, in the pre-test none of these successful children was able with any consistency to insert an additional quantity in its right place somewhere in the middle of each series after it had been formed. The remaining children (13 in each group) did not manage to form ordinal series on their own and were unable to insert additional items in their correct place in any of the series.

In the post-test the performance of the bi-directional group improved significantly. Three of the seven children, who had successfully formed ordinal series in the pre-test without being able to insert the additional items in their correct place, now began to place these extra items correctly in most series. Of the 13 children who had been unable to form ordinal series successfully in the pre-test, 7 now were able to do so, and one of these even managed to insert additional quantities in their correct places in most of the new series.

In the other two groups (the uni-directional and control groups) there was some improvement but it was much less marked, and there was no difference between these two groups. None of the children in either group succeeded in inserting the additional quantity in a consistent manner in the post-test. Three children in the bi-directional group, who had not been able to form ordinal series on their own, and four such children in the control group, now began to do so.

These results suggest that language plays an important and rather a specific role in children's growing ability to understand and form ordinal series. It seems that Sinclair's little known discovery of a formidable effect of verbal training is reliable and important. Concentrated experience of using comparative terms certainly does help children to form series and to understand ordinal relations, provided that the children are encouraged to apply opposite comparative terms to the same quantities ("smaller than blue, and larger than green").

In one way these conclusions fit well with Genevan theory: In another they do not. The experiment certainly supports the idea, a central one in Piagetian theory, that the main obstacle in the way of children trying to form ordinal series is their difficulty in understanding that the same quantity can bear different relations to different neighbours. However, the conclusion that children's experience with the use of linguistic terms helps children to recognise and deal with these bi-directional relations is not a congenial one for Genevans.

CONCLUSIONS

The enterprise, so bravely launched by Inhelder, Sinclair, and Bovet, was certainly worth its while. They set out to observe developmental changes directly, and they succeeded in doing so. The protocols that they give us of the children's growing insight into conservation and class inclusion problems stand among the best and most illuminating in the Genevan collection of protocols. The fact that the intervention in several of the studies was apparently successful is also highly impressive.

However, their successful interventions raise some awkward questions. The absence of control groups in some of the studies, and an unsatisfactory control group in the best-known of the Inhelder, Sinclair, and Bovet studies, make it impossible to draw firm conclusions, positive or negative, about the causes of developmental change.

Yet, in the end, the most interesting contribution made by the experiments of these three formidable psychologists is to our thoughts about the causal question, and here the message is a mixed one. Despite some weaknesses in the design of their studies, it looks as though Inhelder, Sinclair, and Bovet really did find an effective way of improving young children's performance in the conservation task. The technique of confronting children with the failures of their own predictions is a useful and exciting addition to our knowledge of how to change and improve children's solutions to this basic problem. The remarkable improvement in seriation after verbal intervention that Sinclair demonstrated (an improvement that, as our subsequent work showed, withstands the introduction of some necessary controls) is an equally important and provocative result, even though it does not fit well with

Piagetian theory. Many of the implications of these imaginative and unusual studies still have to be worked out. They will continue to affect developmental psychology for some time to come.

REFERENCES

Bryant, P., & Fyfe, M. (in press). The role of opposite terms in verbal training: An experiment on seriation. *Cognitive Development.*

Inhelder, B., Sinclair, H., & Bovet M. (1974*). Learning and the development of cognition.* London: Routledge & Kegan Paul.

Sinclair-de-Zwart, H. (1967). *Acquisition du langage et développement de la pensee: Sous-systèmes linguisitiques et opérations concrètes* [Language acquisition and development of thought: Linguistic sub-systems and concrete operations]. Paris: Dunod.

CHAPTER NINE

Scheme theory as a key to the learning paradox

Ernst von Glasersfeld
University of Massachusetts, USA

INTRODUCTION

Unlike other contributors to this book, I have not had the benefit of a Genevan education or of doing research under the guidance of either Bärbel Inhelder or Piaget. But I have had the good fortune of a few extended conversations with Bärbel Inhelder in Geneva and when she visited the United States. Still, I am in no position to judge how large a part, or what particulars, of the Genetic Psychology invented in Geneva can be considered Inhelder's personal contribution. To me, the whole is very much a joint venture—and when people work, talk, and think together as intensively and for so long as did Inhelder and Piaget, the question of individual authorship tends to lose importance.

Besides, I am uneasy about the separation of psychology and epistemology. Every researcher—man or woman, psychologist, physicist, or mathematician—is a manifestation of the *sujet épistémique*, and it has been one of the characteristics of the twentieth century that the researchers in these three disciplines can no longer afford to forget this.

All psychology, empirical no less than theoretical, requires an epistemological position, and the topic I have chosen is a good example of this.

The notion of a learning paradox was introduced in contemporary literature as a late and not always acknowledged reflection of Plato's theory of innate ideal forms. Piaget never tired of reiterating his opposition to that theory and to any form of preformation in the realm of cognition. The model of the scheme provided him with the source of sensorimotor know-how from which reflective abstraction could derive level after level of "operative" abstract ideas.

In the first chapter of *Le cheminement des découvertes de l'enfant*, Bärbel Inhelder and de Caprona make the distinction between "a general architecture of knowledge" that consists of "the structures of the *epistemic subject*" and, on the other hand, "the vast domain of conducts that rely on a variety of cognitive schemes that are more heuristic" (Inhelder & de Caprona, 1992, p. 20). A few pages later they ask, "is the scheme a structural unit or a functional one?" (p.29). This is a difficult question, but they supply an answer (p. 33) that I find thoroughly convincing:

> Structures are the permanent connective patterns of the cognitive system. They engender its possibilities, that is, its openness, and they also determine what is necessary in it, its closure. ... For us, they have above all the sense of a dynamic pattern.

I hope that this definition will be found to cover the scheme theory that I am using to resolve the learning paradox and which I shall explain in the pages that follow.

PREFORMATION: A RUSE TO AVOID RESEARCH

Anyone who has read some of Plato's dialogues will have noticed that Socrates appears there not only as a wily character, but sometimes also as contradicting himself. In one place he says: "I know that I know nothing", in another he describes himself as a midwife, because he helps a young boy to give birth to an important piece of knowledge.

It is, of course, a matter of context. When Socates said: "I know nothing", he referred to the kind of knowledge that philosophers have tried to capture in the many centuries since then—objective knowledge of a world as it might be before we experience it. Socrates was in fact re-phrasing what Xenophanes and Protagoras had said before him. He could not have meant that he did not know Athens. After many miles of peripatetic philosophising all day long, he never had trouble finding his way home. Indeed, Socrates knew a lot of practical things, among which, at the end, was the fact that the drink of hemlock would kill him.

In contrast, the knowledge he leads a boy to bring forth in Plato's *Meno* had to do with the square root of 2 and therefore was not merely know-how. It belonged to the domain that the Platonic School considered to be one of eternal, absolute truths. It was one of those truths that, as he said, "you find in yourself" in the sense that you *remember* it. According to Plato's theory, this kind of knowledge is innate but inaccessible to us until we call it forth from the hidden treasury of the soul. Clearly, however, Socrates himself had remembered it long ago. He knew it perfectly well when, step by step, he led the boy to recall it. One could say that it was a little disingenuous for him to say that he knew nothing, but I would not hold this against him. Much like the Zen masters, Socrates liked to shock his listeners into thinking. And by saying that one simply *remembered* the "true" ideas, he could skirt the problem of how we come to learn them.

Put bluntly, the "learning paradox" is the paradox of how one might know something one does not yet know. In times and places where science has not been weaned from metaphysics, Plato's theory of metempsychosis (the transmigration of souls) may have seemed a satisfactory resolution. But the notion that the gods instilled all "real" knowledge into the first human beings and that it is transmitted with their souls from generation to generation seemed too fanciful to most modern philosophers. Yet Chomsky succeeded in launching an analogous theory, replacing the gods with the principle of genetic determination. According to the new version, abstract knowledge is supposed to lie dormant in the human genome, waiting to be triggered by experiential stimuli. How such knowledge came to evolve in the first place remains no less mysterious than divine providence. Therefore, the question of how an individual might come to possess it, once more intrigues a good many people.

THE SOURCE OF THE PARADOX

In 1985, Carl Bereiter published a paper with the title "Towards a solution of the learning paradox". It became famous and served as the basis for countless discussions, but it did not lead to a solution. In my view, this was due to the fact that Bereiter unquestioningly accepted the problem as it had been formulated by Fodor 10 years earlier, at the unfortunate meeting of Piaget and Chomsky at Royaumont in 1975. I call this meeting unfortunate, because the 25 authorities who took part in it—all experts in cognition and communication—managed to talk past each other in a manner that was both spectacular and tragic.

The learning paradox was presented by Fodor (1980, pp. 148–149) as follows:

> … it is never possible to learn a richer logic on the basis of a weaker logic, if what you mean by learning is hypothesis formation and confirmation. … There literally isn't such a thing as the notion of learning a conceptual system richer than the one that one already has; we simply have no idea of what it would be like to get from a conceptually impoverished to a conceptually richer system by anything like a process of learning.

Fodor claimed—and Bereiter followed him—that hypothesis formation is an *inductive* process. This is a technical expression of the widespread view that researchers who create new knowledge spend considerable time collecting "data", and that the examination of these data then induces the hypotheses they set up. This induction, Fodor asserts, is only possible if the logical structure of the hypothesis was in some form already present in the researcher. Les Steffe has politely but effectively argued against this contention by presenting a number of careful microanalyses of children's generation of novel conceptual structures in the context of counting and elementary arithmetic (Steffe, 1991, pp. 26–44).

As a radical constructivist I could take a much cruder and more "radical" path and begin by saying that, far from being given, what is called "data" can be seen as the result of the experiencer's own construction. From that perspective, conceptual learning begins at the very outset of the child's cognitive career, at least at birth, but probably already in the womb. And instead of remembering innate "true" ideas, the child has the innate tendency to search for "Rhythms, Regulations, and Groupings" (Piaget, 1947, title of Conclusion) and to test its constructs for their viability in actual experience. But I will not pursue this line of argument here.

Instead, I shall try to show, first, that forming hypotheses does not have to be an inductive process; and second, that every induction (and generalisation) requires a conceptual jump that is not *given* by the data but constitutes a small but genuinely creative act on the part of the observer.

THE NOTION OF "ABDUCTION"

The logic of creative acts has been studied and clarified by Charles Peirce, who coined the term "abduction". He added it as a third kind of inference to the traditional logical patterns of induction and deduction. In induction, thought moves from a plurality of experienced cases to a rule. In deduction, it moves from a rule to a case at hand. In abduction, a hypothetical rule is generated from a single case. Peirce (1931–35, 5.189) described this novel pattern as follows:

- The surprising fact C is observed
- But if A were true, C would be a matter of course
- Hence, there is reason to suspect that A is true

In Peirce's formulation, "A" stands for a hypothetical rule invented on the spur of the moment. To become viable as explanation and for making predictions, this new rule must then be tested in the course of further experience—a kind of induction in reverse. If it turns out to be false, other abductions have to be made, until one is found that fits the experiential facts. In principle, this is not unlike natural selection in the theory of evolution. The big question, then, is: *How are such hypothetical rules invented?*

At the end of his initial presentation at Royaumont, Chomsky referred to "the principles, now unknown, that underlie what Peirce called 'abduction' ... I see no reason to doubt that here, too, there are highly specific innate capacities that determine the growth of cognitive structures, ..." (Chomsky, 1980, p. 52). Saying that he sees no reason to doubt such highly specific innate capacities, implies that he starts by assuming them. This is where we disagree. Assuming a capacity to be innate is a quick way to avoid further investigation. No one doubts that any theory of cognition has to assume some innate capacities, but the *less specific* these capacities are, the more powerful the theory will be.

The first computers that were able to carry out complex mathematical operations had some "innate",—i.e., built-in—capacities. They were three extremely general ones: recording binary digits, reading binary digits, and comparing them. I prefer to start theory construction with such simple assumptions and not to add more specific ones unless I get hopelessly stuck.

In abduction, where it is a case of inventing hypothetical rules, it has been suggested that analogy may be one possibility. This seems to me a reasonable suggestion. Let me give an example.

How did people come to have the notion that the sun goes *round* the earth? I do not think that this is much of a mystery. It may have happened long before the invention of the wheel, when we were still living in caves. In that non-technological world, there were not many rotational motions to be seen—eddies in streams, perhaps, and a whirlwind here and there. But the cave dwellers' children sometimes rushed out in the morning and played among the trees. One who felt particularly lively would pick up a dead branch and swing it round and round, as chimpanzees occasionally do in their famous "rain dance". And when this happened, any observer could see the end of the branch coming up at one side, moving in a semicircle, and disappearing in the high grass on the other side. Every day, the sun appears in the east, moves up in the sky, and disappears in the west, setting at a point opposite to where it rose. To see this movement as a rotation requires the conception of an analogy. What has to be assumed *innate*, therefore, is no more than the capacity to remember experience, reflect on it, and to make comparisons.

THE GENERALISING ABDUCTION

There may be other ways of intuiting a rule on the strength of a single observation, but I would suggest that the conception of analogy can explain a great many such intuitions (especially in the acquisition of language). *Which* aspects of the experiences are to be compared and found to be analogous, is not *given*—it is a conceptual step of generalisation.

This brings me to a point where I may diverge from Peirce. He said that both abduction and induction differed from deduction because neither of them could produce logical certainty. And he also held abduction to be "entirely different" from induction, because the second involves probability, whereas the first does not. Yet he also held that generalisation could be the outcome of an abduction that is then tested inductively (Fann, 1970, p. 34). I want to go a step further and suggest that every inductive inference contains an implicit abduction.

Take the notorious example of an inductive generalisation: "All swans are white". How would you come to make it? The obvious answer seems to be that you look at a certain number of swans, notice that they are all white, and conclude that probably all swans you are going to see in the future will also be white. Why did you pick whiteness as the generalisable property? There are many others you could have chosen. The first swan you actually saw had a head and two feet, a long neck, a dark beak, a nicked tail feather, and many other properties that you might have looked for in the swans that followed. But you chose colour as a candidate for a common feature. This choice, I would say, was a kind of abduction, because at some point along your swan-experiences you must have decided to check whether all of them were white.

AN INTERPRETATION OF SCHEME THEORY

You may be wondering what all this might have to do with scheme theory. I was reinforced in making the connection by Inhelder's remark that schemes can be procedural "in that they employ procedures of invention and discovery, heuristics that assure innovation" (Inhelder & de Caprona, 1992, p. 42). This fitted perfectly with my conception of the scheme.

As I see it, a sensorimotor scheme consists of three elements. There is a *perceptual situation*, an *activity* associated with it, and the *result* the activity is thought likely to obtain. Piaget derived this pattern from the traditional notion of the reflex, which is usually described as consisting of two elements: a stimulus and a fixed response. He was struck by a couple of things about this. First, in order to explain the phylogenetic development of reflexes, it was necessary to consider the result of the activities they trigger. To fit reflexes into the theory of evolution, their results had to favour survival or procreation. Second, he observed that the infant's reflexes were not nearly as immutable as they were said to be. Most of them are amenable to some modification, as the child grows up. He concluded that the three-step pattern of the reflex could be applied to sensorimotor action in general. All that had to be added, was the actor's expectation of the result. The pattern of the scheme therefore, in my view, looks like this:

1. Perceived situation → 2. Activity → 3. Expected result

Having thus become a goal-directed phenomenon, it provided a perfect context for the functioning of assimilation and accommodation. As in the reflex, every implementation of an action scheme requires the acting subject to recognise a triggering situation. Such a recognition is of course an assimilation, because no two situations in a subject's experience are ever quite the same.

Assimilation also plays a role in the third part of the scheme. If a scheme is to be considered successful, the actual result of the activity must be such that it can be assimilated to the expected one. If it is not, this is likely to cause a perturbation which may be disappointment or, if the unexpected result is in some way interesting, may be a pleasant surprise. In both cases, the perturbation may lead to a focusing of attention on the initial situation. If, then, a formerly disregarded characteristic of the triggering situation is taken into consideration, this may bring about a modification of the conditions that determine the triggering of the scheme; or it may bring about the formation of a new scheme. Both are instances of accommodation; and if the accommodation were done consciously, it would be an abduction, because, at the moment the changes are made, they are hypothetical in the sense that their usefulness has not yet been tested in further experience.

Children accommodate their action schemes by means of fortuitous choices quite some time before they begin to reflect on them consciously. However, the adult observer, who can and does reflect on the choices children make, can see in them the same abductive pattern as in later steps of cognitive development. Steffe cited the creation of non-Euclidean geometries as example, and many others can be found both in the historical and the individual development of mathematical thinking. I would therefore say that those who claim that non-inductively derived cognitive structures must be considered innate owe us an explanation of why some mathematical ones took so long to surface.

In his paper *L'épistémologie des régulations*, Piaget discusses the developmental transition from the most primitive regular behaviour patterns of biological organisms to "the self-regulation and self-organisation of cognitive systems that are able to engender their own programs and to create new ones" (Piaget, 1977, p. III). Only from the end of this development can it be seen as a "transition", because then the patterns can be "thematised" by reflection and considered qua "patterns" or "cognitive structures" irrespective of their individual content.

I would suggest that the pattern of abduction can be considered a mechanism (if not the principal one) that pervades cognitive development and makes it a relatively homogeneous progress. It appears in accommodations of action schemes on the sensorimotor level as well as in accommodations on the subsequent levels of concrete and formal mental operations. In my view, it is the mainspring of creativity.

CONCLUSION

The point I want to make in the present context, is that it makes no sense to claim, as Fodor, Bereiter, and others have done, that because hypothesis formation is an inductive process, there is a "learning paradox" concerning all theoretical conceptual structures that cannot be gleaned directly from experiential data. As I hope to have shown, every inductive inference involves the spontaneous creation of an idea that may turn out to fit the "data" but was not actually inherent in them. The same is true of conceptual accommodations and even of many elementary accommodations on the sensorimotor level. In both cases, there is a conceptual step that fits the pattern of abduction, a step that generates new knowledge whenever the abduction proves viable.

More important than all I have so far said may be an epistemological consideration. Scientific structuralism—that is, the attempt to analyse cognition, its processes and development in terms of mental structures—is neither a doctrine nor a philosophy, but, as Piaget put it, "essentially a method, with all this word implies with regard to technicality, obligations, intellectual honesty, and the progress of successive approximations" (Piaget, 1968, pp. 117–118). Consequently, we may conclude that the "learning paradox" springs from the technical assumptions that the formation of hypotheses is an inductive process and that induction cannot be the source of novel conceptual structures. I claim that these assumptions are unwarranted and as inappropriate in the domain of scientific explanation as they would be in philosophy or art.

Let me end by expressing my personal indebtedness to Bärbel Inhelder. Not having had the chance to talk with Piaget himself, I found in her an irreplaceable evaluator of my ideas. She was wonderfully open-minded and ready to discuss another's conceptions even if they did not always agree with her own. We are all constructivists, she once said, and we construct our own view of the world—what matters is that we try to be consistent in our thinking and that we are honest about it. The theory of schemes, she remarked, can be interpreted in more than one way —and this greatly encouraged me. I only hope that she would have considered what I have presented here as one of the possible interpretations.

REFERENCES

Bereiter, C. (1985). Towards a solution of the learning paradox. *Review of Educational Research, 55*, 201–226.

Chomsky, N. (1980). On cognitive structures and their development: A reply to Piaget. In M. Piatelli-Palmerini (Ed.), *Language and learning* (pp. 35–52). Cambridge, MA: Harvard University Press.

Fann, K.T. (1970). *Pierce's theory of abduction.* The Hague: Martinus Nijhoff.

Fodor, J. (1980). Fixation of belief and concept acquisition. In M. Piatelli-Palmerini (Ed.), *Language and learning* (pp. 143–149). Cambridge, MA: Harvard University Press.

Inhelder, B., & de Caprona, D. (1992). Vers le constructivisme psychologique: Structures? Procédures? Les deux indissociables. In B. Inhelder & G. Cellérier (Eds.), *Le cheminement des déscouvertes de l'enfant* (pp. 19–50). Neuchâtel, France: Delachaux et Niestlé.

Peirce, C.S. (1931–35). *Collected papers* (Vols 1–6) (Edited by C. Hartshome & P. Weiss). Cambridge, MA: Harvard University Press.

Piaget, J. (1947). *La psychologie de l'intelligence* [The psychology of intelligence]. Paris: Armand Colin.

Piaget, J. (1968). *Le structuralisme* [Structuralism]. Paris: Presses Universitaries de France.

Piaget, J. (1977). L'épistémologie des régulations [The epistemology of regulations]. In A. Lichnerrowicz, F. Perroux, & G. Gadoffre (Eds.), *L'idée de régulation dans les sciences* (pp. I–XIII). Paris: Maloine.

Steffe, L.P. (1991). The learning paradox: A plausible counterexample. In L.P. Steffe (Ed.), *Epistomological foundations of mathematical experience* (pp. 26–44). New York: Springer.

CHAPTER TEN

Culture and universals:
A tribute to Bärbel Inhelder

Patricia M. Greenfield
University of California, USA

In this chapter, I use a small-scale, homogeneous society to introduce a large theory of development. After introducing the theory, I then proceed to show the broad applicability of the theory by applying it to our own large-scale, heterogeneous society. The theory links culture and biological maturation to explain development. This is very much in the spirit of Bärbel Inhelder, who respected the contributions of both biology and culture to development. The chapter that follows is presented to honour Inhelder's cross-cultural research, notably her important collaborative study on sensorimotor development among the Baoulé (Dasen, Inhelder, Lavallé, & Retschitzki, 1978).

PIAGET/INHELDER, VYGOTSKY, DEVELOPMENT, AND CULTURE

Reinterpreting Genevan stages: Age-dependent sensitive periods for cultural learning

Beginning more than 30 years ago, cultural and cross-cultural developmentalists have severely criticised the Genevan school (e.g., Cole & Scribner, 1974; Greenfield, 1966). Considering the theory of Piaget and Inhelder from a cross-cultural perspective, this chapter aims to restore balance concerning the role of Genevan theory in cultural psychology. I here introduce the idea that the stage theory of Inhelder and Piaget has an important universal element as a theory of innate potentials and age-dependent sensitive periods for cultural learning.

The notion of age-dependent sensitive periods does lead to two important points of difference with Piaget and Inhelder (1966/1969). The first is that, whereas they emphasise minimal ages for certain developments, the notion of age-dependent

149

sensitive periods also implies constraints on the upper age for actualising these same cognitive capacities. The really important difference, however, has to do with the issue of stage specificity vs stage generality. The sensitive period idea is that the original capacity for a particular kind of development can be general, but that the way in which it is actualised through cultural learning makes it more specific. The analogy is to language: Human beings start out with a general capacity for language, but we learn specific ones. Once we have learned a particular language, we lose, to some extent, our capacity to learn different ones. I will make the case for this principle in the domain of concrete operations. The principle contrasts in a fundamental way with the Piagetian notion of domain-general stages.

By analogy with language, the sensitive period model of development leads to the hypothesis that, once culture-specific actualisations of a cognitive stage take place through experience during the optimal maturational window, other alternative actualisations become more difficult to acquire, even by the same experience later in development. This theoretical formulation leads to a definition of stages that is less general than Piaget and Inhelder posited. In my view, the sphere of application for a given stage becomes limited by the particular experiences that have actualised the maturational potential of that stage.

On the other hand, the concepts of innate potentials and age-dependent sensitive periods also have much in common with the view of Piaget and Inhelder (1966/1969) on the role of maturation in development: "Where we do have some data, we see that maturation consists essentially of opening up new possibilities and thus constitutes a necessary but not in itself a sufficient condition for the appearance of certain behaviour patterns" (p. 154). These maturationally given possibilities provide the possibility for particular sorts of active construction to take place. In other words, the concept of age-dependent sensitive periods is in no way a statement of maturational reductionism. I would also agree with Piaget and Inhelder's important point that "Organic maturation is undoubtedly a necessary factor and plays an indispensable role in the unvarying order of succession of the order of the stages of the child's development" (pp. 154–155).

Piaget and Inhelder (1966/1969; Piaget, 1972) note that acquisitions become more variable in their time of acquisition the further they are removed from their sensorimotor origins. I agree with this, but would also go two steps further: (1) Acquisitions become more variable (and therefore more culture-specific) *not only in their timing but also in their form*, the further they are removed from their sensorimotor origins. (2) As the forms of stage behaviour become more variable and culture-specific in the course of movement from sensorimotor to concrete operational to formal operations, so too do the forms of experience that are required to actualise each stage. The notion of stages as sensitive periods for cultural learning does entail a major modification of the theory: *no longer is the presence of a stage measured by its cross-domain applicability; stages are now by definition domain-specific*. Extrapolating from Piaget (1972), I believe that the culture- and experience-specificity of formal operations is greater than for the other stages.

However, I would also assert that the principle of specificity still applies to concrete and even sensorimotor operations, although in progressively lesser degrees. My examples later in this chapter relate to the transition from pre-operational to concrete operational thought.

The Western scientist as a culture-specific developmental outcome

Although Piaget and Inhelder's concept of maturation contributes to a biologically grounded universal stage theory, I also see Genevan theory in other respects as an ethnotheory, a formalisation of Western ethnotheories of development, that is, a folk theory of development. In using the term ethnotheory, I am asserting that scientists and lay people alike have some common cultural assumptions that enter implicitly and without awareness into the very foundation of both scientific and lay theories of development.

In the 1970s, I introduced the idea of Piagetian theory as a theory of the development of the Western scientist, rather than the universal individual (Greenfield, 1974/1976). I have since realised that Piaget himself asserted that understanding the basis for Western scientific thought was his most fundamental concern (Piaget, 1965a/1977). One can infer from this statement that Piaget saw his theory and research on child cognitive development as a way of understanding the developmental pathway to mature scientific thought. In *The growth of logical thinking from childhood to adolescence*, Inhelder took a leadership role in researching the cognitive development of the Western scientist (Inhelder & Piaget, 1955/1958). However, alternative endpoints could have been selected. The ethnotheoretic aspect of Genevan theory occurs in the aspect of the human condition that Piaget and Inhelder selected as the endpoint of development (Greenfield, 1974/1976), not in the sequence of stages leading up to this endpoint.

Piagetian theory, like the Western scientist, therefore emphasises the development of knowledge of the physical world, apart from social goals. This corresponds to an ethnotheory of development in which cognitive knowledge is valued for its own sake, apart from the social uses to which it is put. This is typical of European-derived cultures (Mundy-Castle, 1974).

Needed: A developmental theory that can include cultures that subordinate the cognitive to the social

Other cultures, however, have a different ethnotheory concerning the relationship between the cognitive and the social. They treat cognitive and social development as tightly integrated, with cognitive development *subordinate* to social development (Dasen, 1984; Wober, 1974). Such cultures see cognition not as a value in itself, but as a means to social ends. This is a view that is not encompassed in Genevan theory. Thus, in Piaget's treatment of social cognition (the work on moral judgement, Piaget 1932/1965b), the social is very much subordinated to the cognitive. The point here again concerns what is selected as the endpoint of development.

My assertion is that there are cultural differences in what constitutes the ideal, mature human being, and that the nature of the ideal in Western European culture involves a scientific rationality that is superordinate to or independent of social relationships and social feelings. Because this ideal endpoint is taken for granted as the only possibility, it then automatically becomes what needs to be accounted for in a developmental theory that is created within this type of culture.

But what about Vygotsky? This is a subject to which I now turn. Vygotsky (1962, part first published in Russian in 1934; 1978, most first published in Russian in 1956 and 1960) does, of course, have a sociocultural theory; it is the basis for the sociocultural component of the framework I am going to present. In Vygotsky's theory, the most important means to development is social interaction. Undoubtedly, one could link this difference in emphasis between Piaget/Inhelder and Vygotsky to cultural differences of the time. It does not seem coincidental that a greater emphasis on child development as a function of the sociocultural environment of the child arose in a communist country. This difference in learning mechanisms will be taken up in a moment.

However, for present purposes, I would like to emphasise the less obvious commonalties between Piaget/Inhelder and Vygotsky that stem from the fact that all were steeped in the epistemology and culture of Western Europe. Both Vygotsky and Piaget/Inhelder have selected the same endpoint of development to explain and, not coincidentally, it is a cognitive one. In other words, even for Vygotsky, social interaction functions as a means to cognitive development. Development itself is defined cognitively, in terms of language and conceptual thought.

What is needed in our field is a formal theory of development that is broad enough to be applicable to cultures in which the ethnotheory of development sees cognitive development as a means to social development, rather than vice versa. A first step would be to develop a theory of development for this alternative ideal endpoint: the person who has used his or her cognitive capacities to become wise in social relations and to achieve social goals. However, if we were to take that route, we would simply have a second ethnotheory of development in a different sort of culture from our own. What is really needed is a theory that includes mechanisms for the differentiation of these two major developmental pathways.

Mechanisms of cultural learning

Both Vygotsky and Piaget present models of learning as well as of development. Vygotsky (1956–60/1978) has an explicit model of socially guided learning. Piaget has an implicit model of discovery learning (Piaget, 1965a/1977). I hope to show that, as theories of environmental learning, both the implicit theory of Piaget and the explicit theory of Vygotsky are more tied to specific sociohistorical circumstances than either theorist realised. I will demonstrate that each model of learning describes adaptive responses to particular ecological circumstances. The notion is that both types of learning process are part of the universal *armoire* of developmental processes, but that each is selectively emphasised as a means of transmitting knowledge under different sociohistorical circumstances; sociohistorical circumstances are seen, in turn, as having a strong economic foundation. The model that is dominant at a particular place or time does have implications for the learning processes of the individual learner, as I hope to demonstrate. Where guided learning is dominant, my hypothesis is that the learner comes to rely more on guidance as a means to acquire new knowledge, and will tend to excel at learning and applying culturally normative modes of thought, action, and feeling. Where discovery learning is dominant, my hypothesis is that the learner becomes practised at discovering new knowledge, and will tend to develop individual creativity.

A THEORETICAL FRAMEWORK FOR DEVELOPMENT

The theoretical framework has the following four principal components:

Maturational component: Age-dependent sensitive periods for cultural learning (Fairbanks, 2000; Fischer, 1987; Newport, 1988). Part (although not all) of this component is supported by Genevan stages, which I will exemplify.

Sociocultural component: The maturational component is actualised through interaction with other members of the sociocultural milieu, often mediated by:

- Activities and cultural practices (e.g., Rogoff, Baker-Sennett, Lacasa, & Goldsmith, 1995; Saxe, 1991; Scribner & Cole, 1981).
- Tools (both concrete and symbolic) (e.g., Bruner, 1964, 1977–78; Bruner & Olson, 1973; Greenfield, 1993).
- Values (e.g., Greenfield, 1994; Rabain, 1979; Shweder & Bourne, 1982).

Ecological component: The sociocultural component is adapted to an ecological niche (e.g., LeVine, 1977; Super & Harkness, 1997; Weisner, 1984; Whiting & Whiting, 1975).

Historical component (Scribner, 1985; Vygotsky & Luria, 1930/1993): The ecological niche changes over time (Greenfield, 1999a, b).

Each component has been studied individually and draws heavily on the work of others, as the references indicate. The news, both theoretical and empirical, is the specification of their interactions. These interactions are specified in the very definitions of the components, each of which directly interacts with the next one down in the hierarchy.

1. *Culture is integrated with maturation*: What matures are abilities to acquire different elements of culture through the sociocultural component of the model. This idea builds on Inhelder's theoretical view: In 1982, in *Early cognitive development and malnutrition*, a sole-authored article on the Baoulé, she wrote (p. 26): "it is not necessary to choose one or the other of the alternative terms: innateness or cultural origins of behaviour. Would it not be preferable to envision a constructivist solution …?" Her notion of construction was in terms of individual activity. My model extends this notion to social construction carried out by a biological organism in a sociocultural environment, with the subject's own activity as one, but not the only, critical element.

2. *The sociocultural component is adapted to the ecological conditions.*

3. *Ecology changes over time.*

An interdisciplinary approach, drawing on methods and concepts from psychology, anthropology, and sociology is required to test the model.

Application in a small-scale, homogeneous society: Zinacantan, Chiapas, Mexico

Because the contextual components of the theory are so complex, the model can most easily be explored in a relatively small, relatively self-contained community over an extended period of ecological change. With my colleagues Carla Childs, Ashley Maynard, and Leslie Devereaux, I have been studying socialisation in just such a community: Nabenchauk, a Zinacantec Maya village in Chiapas Mexico, over a period of 26 years.

Interaction of the maturational and sociocultural components

Interaction of maturation and cultural practices.   I will begin by considering the interaction of the maturational and the sociocultural components; that is, the interaction of a universal age-dependent sensitive period with cultural practices. The activity domain selected for this analysis is weaving, the most complex technology in traditional Zinacantec life. (See Figure 10.1 for a photograph of the ancient Maya backstrap loom, photographed in Nabenchauk in 1995.) I will begin with a physical component of weaving in order to provide a very concrete illustration of the interaction between biological sensitivity and cultural experience. I will then use Piagetian stage concepts to move to a cognitive example, where the analysis is more abstract and inferential.

The physical example has to do with the uses of the body in learning to weave (Maynard, Greenfield, & Childs, 1999). Note in Figure 10.1 that while a post forms the top of the loom frame, the weaver's body in a kneeling position forms the other end. My focus is on the physical skill of kneeling.

Figure 10.1.   Woman seated at the ancient Maya backstrap loom. Note that a post (left side) forms one end of the loom frame, the weaver's body in a kneeling position forms the other end. Nabenchauk, 1995. Photo courtesy of Ashley Maynard.

Kneeling is a universal biologically given capacity that all human beings are born with. However, it can be maintained only by experience. This is demonstrated by Molleson's (1996) research in physical anthropology. By relating differential bone development in male and female skeletons to known gender differences in work activity at the same archaeological site, Molleson shows that culturally defined experience in kneeling for many hours from a young age shapes bone development (e.g., flattens bones of two first metatarsal bones of both feet), so that the capacity to kneel for long periods of time is maintained into adulthood.

Zinacantec cultural practices provide just such experience for girls. Girls grow up watching their mothers and other older females sitting in a kneeling position with their legs under them during weaving and many other daily activities (see Figures 10.2 and 10.3). Cultural values come into play too; these are highly valued

Figure 10.2.   Adult women kneeling to prepare tortillas. Nabenchauk, 1991. Photo courtesy of Lauren Greenfield.

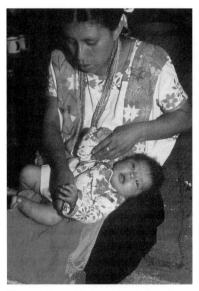

Figure 10.3.   Mother (Maruch Perez) kneeling to change her baby.

activities that define women's work. Girls learn to maintain this position through cultural activities. Starting at a young age, they kneel for many hours in a variety of situations and tasks, including play weaving at a toy loom (Figure 10.4) and drawing designs to embroider on their blouses (Figure 10.5).

The experience of my collaborator Ashley Maynard confirmed Molleson's conclusion that, without kneeling experience, the capacity to maintain a kneeling position for long periods of time can be lost with age (Maynard et al., 1999); Ashley was taught at age 23 to weave in Nabenchauk as part of an ethnographic study of weaving apprenticeship. Unlike Zinacantec girls, she had not had extended and repeated kneeling experience at a young age, and, indeed, she encountered problems in learning to weave because she was not able to kneel for long periods of time. Kneeling was very painful for her and she resorted to sitting cross-legged, much to the derision of the Zinacantecan teachers and other women who observed her weaving. The absence of culturally mandated kneeling experience at a younger age had caused her to lose her ability to kneel for the long periods required by weaving. Her experience showed that there is a sensitive period during which this experience must take place.

Figure 10.4.   Young girl, Rosy 1–209, kneels, as she engages in play weaving at a toy loom. Nabenchauk, 1993. Photo courtesy Patricia Greenfield. (The numerals are to identify families from our larger, two-generation study of weaving apprenticeships, e.g., Greenfield, 1999b; Maynard et al., 1999.)

Figure 10.5.   Girls (Loxa and Xunka 1–201) use the traditional kneeling position, even in newer activities such as drawing designs to embroider on their blouses. Nabenchauk, 1991. Photo courtesy of Lauren Greenfield.

Here I have used kneeling to demonstrate the interaction of biological sensitive periods with cultural practices. I now turn to more cognitive aspects of weaving, using Piagetian stage concepts. I am going to treat the timing of the transition from pre-operations to concrete operations as a sensitive period, a developmental window, that is actualised differently in different cultures.

Developmentally gradated tools.   My theme here is that cultures have sets of artefacts and practices that respect and stimulate sensitive periods for cognitive and neural development. I would like to make the argument that the developmental timing and order in which girls are exposed to various weaving tools show implicit knowledge of and respect for cognitive development. Specifically, these tools show implicit knowledge of progression from the pre-operational to the concrete operational stage and its time. Vygotsky (1934/1962; 1956, 1960/1978) noted how much cognitive history is contained in cultural artefacts and that these artefacts function, in turn, as tools for the stimulation of current cognitive development. I would like to take this line of thinking a step further: Not only cognitive history but cognitive development can also be contained in cultural artefacts. To provide evidence for this point, I analyse the cognitive requirements of a developmentally gradated set of weaving artefacts: the toy loom, the winding board, and the real loom.

Play weaving on the toy loom, illustrated in Figure 10.4, is widespread in Nabenchauk. It begins at age 3 or 4, in Piaget's pre-operational period. The toy loom is used several years earlier than the real loom and winding board, which are not used before age 6, the beginning of the concrete operational period. Using a winding board to prepare warp threads for the real loom is a concrete operational task, as I shall demonstrate later. Because the toy loom differs in just one respect from the real loom, it does not require concrete operational thinking to set up. The difference lies in the ropes between the two end-sticks, one rope on each side (Figure 10.6, functionally equivalent to the wide ribbons in Figure 10.4). By holding together the two end-sticks (shown at the top and the bottom of the loom in Figure 10.6), these ropes permit the warp or frame threads (the white threads in the middle of the loom in Figure 10.6) to be wound directly on the loom. Figure 10.4 shows how the end-sticks that constitute the loom are connected by a loop of ribbon (functionally equivalent to the rope in Figure 10.6) that goes around the weaver's back (hence the name *backstrap)* to the post; the tension necessary to keep the loom from collapsing is provided by the weaver, who leans back against the strap. Note that, unlike the real loom (Figure 10.7), the top and bottom end-sticks are connected by the ribbon or rope looped around them. The real loom (shown in Figure 10.7) does not have the side ropes (Figure 10.6) or ribbons (Figure 10.4) holding the loom frame (top and bottom end-sticks) together. Only the warp threads in Figure 10.7 hold the two end-sticks together. However, these threads cannot be wound

Figure 10.6. Toy loom. Note the side ropes that hold the two frame sticks together while the warp (white threads) is being wound. Photo courtesy of Lauren Greenfield.

Figure 10.7. Real loom. Note the absence of the side ropes; therefore the warp threads hold the loom together. However, they cannot be wound directly onto the loom, because the loom does not exist as connected sticks until the warp is wound. Nabenchauk, 1991. Photo courtesy of Lauren Greenfield.

directly because if the warp threads were not there, the loom would collapse; the loom has nothing to hold the two end-sticks together before the winding of the warp threads begins.

A real loom, must therefore have the warp pre-wound on an apparatus such as the *komen* or warping frame shown in Figure 10.8. My thesis is that winding the warp on a *komen* intrinsically involves concrete operational thinking. This is the case because winding on the *komen* requires mental transformation. The form of the warp threads on the warping frame (Figure 10.8) is quite different from the form of the threads on the final loom (Figure 10.7). Complex topological transformation is required to understand the connection between how you wind and how the threads end up on the loom. Let me illustrate with a sequence of photographs. Figure 10.9a shows a *komen* or warping frame, ready to begin winding. In Figure 10.9b, a girl has begun to wind the threads on the warping frame; in Figure 10.9c she has progressed a bit further. Figure 10.9d shows a close-up of the resulting configuration of threads. Compare this image with Figure 10.7, which shows how the warp might turn out (with additional winding and more colours) after being transferred to the loom. Note the difference in the configuration of threads between Figure 10.9d where warp threads are still on the warping frame, and Figure 10.7, where the warp threads have been transferred to the loom. Threads on the left side of the stick in the warping frame of Figure 10.9d go to one end of the loom (e.g., the top end-stick in Figure 10.7), while threads on the right side of the stick in the warping frame of Figure 10.9d go to the other end of the loom (e.g., the bottom end-stick in Figure 10.7).

This sequence illustrates an important cognitive point: that a complex series of mental transformations is required for a weaver to understand the connection between how the threads are wound on the warping frame and how they end up in the configuration shown on the loom in Figure 10.7. Because mental transformations characterise the Piagetian stage of concrete operations (e.g., Piaget, 1963/1977), winding a warp on the warping frame in order to set up a backstrap loom is a culture-specific concrete-operational task.

Figure 10.8.   *Komen* or warping frame. Nabenchauk, 1991. Photo by Patricia Greenfield.

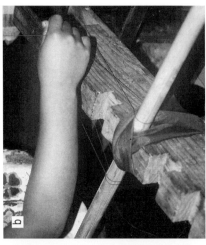

Figure 10.9. Creating a warp, using a warping frame. (a) The *komem* or warping frame, ready to begin. (b) A girl has begun to wind on the frame. (c) She has wound a few more threads. (d) A close-up of the resulting configuration of threads. Nabenchauk, 1995. Photos by Patricia Greenfield.

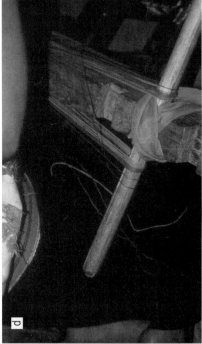

I now compare the cognitive level required to set up a real loom with that required to set up a toy loom. Whereas to set up a real loom demands the mental transformations of concrete operations, mental transformations are not required for the toy loom. Because of the extra supporting rope (Figure 10.6) or ribbon (Figure 10.4) on the side, the warp can be wound directly on the loom. The sequence in Figure 10.10 illustrates this point. In Figure 10.10a, a young girl has just started winding the warp directly on the loom, which is already set up. The top and bottom end-sticks (left and right in the photo) are being held in place by the tension between her backstrap, held by her body, and the rope attached to a rigid support, such as a tree or a house post. Unlike the real loom, the end-sticks are connected by white string; one of the two side strings is shown clearly at the top of Figures 10.10a and b. In Figure 10.10b, the young girl continues winding the warp between the end-sticks.

In Figures 10.10a and b, the warp threads are being wound into their final position between two end-sticks. This is similar to, for example, the way warp

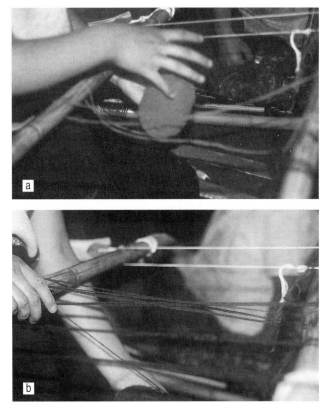

Figure 10.10.   (a) A young girl has just started winding the warp of her toy loom. (b) The girl continues winding the warp. Nabenchauk, 1995. Photos by Patricia Greenfield.

threads are stretched between end-sticks on the loom shown in Figure 10.6. Unlike winding the warp on a winding board, there is no mental transformation required to go from the winding process to the set-up loom.

The important conclusion from this analysis is that Piagetian theory is part of the Zinacantecs' implicit ethnotheory of development. Whereas Zinacantec girls start on the toy loom from age 3, they do not set up a real loom before age 6 at the earliest, the beginning of the normal age range of concrete operations. So, most interestingly, Piagetian theory is implicitly (but not explicitly) built into the developmental progression of Zinacantecan weaving tools.

If we think of Piagetian stages as age-dependent sensitive periods, then learning how to set up a real loom using a winding board can be seen as an activity that actualises concrete operations in a culture-specific form. This activity can also be seen as the kind of constructive problem-solving process emphasised by Inhelder. As Veneziano (1998) has pointed out, Inhelder had a great love for adaptive and contextualised tasks as a method for assessing cognitive development.

Cognitive stages as age-dependent sensitive periods. What is the evidence for Piagetian stages as age-dependent sensitive periods and how does play weaving fit into this picture? I should like to draw on a new theory of primate play by Fairbanks (2000) and propose that it applies both to human play in general and to play weaving in particular. Fairbanks (2000) has developed a theory of monkey play that posits its role in stimulating neuromuscular pathways that underlie a particular adult monkey skill. She contrasts her theory with the theory that play functions as direct practice of an adult behavioural skill. She observes that the height of each monkey play form occurs years before the adult behaviour (when it would not be very useful as practice). However, the playful form is most frequent just at the time the relevant neural substrate for that particular activity is developing. For example, play fighting in monkeys reaches its height just as the neural circuitry for adult aggression is developing—but years before aggression is required in adult monkey social life.

Could this analysis apply to play weaving? There are several parallels with Fairbanks' theory and data: First, there is the behavioural parallel: Just as play fighting occurs in monkeys several years before the real thing, so does play weaving on the toy loom occur several years before weaving utilitarian items on the real loom. Second, Thatcher (1994) presents EEG evidence for spurts in neural development. These spurts are periods of neural instability that serve as developmental transition points in the nervous system. One of these transition points or spurts is in the age range of play weaving (3–5).

My theoretical interpretation of these transition points in neural development is that they are sensitive periods—developmental windows—when stimulation (often in the form of culture-specific practices) actualises maturationally specific neural circuits. It follows from this that play weaving could stimulate neural and neuromuscular pathways that provide a foundation for the later cognitive development required to weave on a real loom. Hence, this spurt of neural development could provide a developmental window for the culture-specific actualisation of concrete operations.

Fischer and Rose (1994) identify a second spurt in neural development that occurs between 6 and 10 years of age. This is precisely the period in which weaving on a real loom begins for most Zinacantec girls. It is also Piaget's period of concrete operations, which, as I have tried to illustrate, are indeed required for setting up a real loom.

The role of values.   One aspect of values relevant to our theory is the ethnotheory of development to which Zinacantecs connect weaving. First, they are in agreement that development is important: A girl will weave when she has enough soul (implies that she is able to listen to instruction, follow instruction, do what is needed, and tolerate frustration), and this takes time to develop (Devereaux, field notes, 1991). However, there is something different here, different both from our ethnotheories of development and from our formal theories of development (specifically those of Piaget/Inhelder and Vygotsky): According to the ethnographic research of Leslie Devereaux, Zinacantecs do not value weaving as a technical skill; rather they value weaving for its social aspects: "the social interactional aspects of the learning process", the social utility of what is woven, and the enhancement of a girl's marriageability by being a good weaver.

To compare this with our ethnotheories and theories of development, the Zinacantecs do not have separate theories of cognitive and social development. For them, cognitive development is embedded in and subordinate to social interaction and the development of social activity. So, for example, one mother told us that her mildly retarded child (my observationally based diagnosis) would not be able to learn to weave. However, she explained, this was fine because the daughter had another useful job, putting thread on spools. It was not important to her that this job was cognitively much simpler than weaving. What mattered was that it made a contribution to the family. My point is the following: Cognitive development, as described by Inhelder and Piaget, may follow a common pattern across cultures, but the value attached to it does not.

This subordination of cognitive skills to social relationships and goals is part of a system of values that emphasises social interdependence in the definition of the self (Greenfield, 1994; Markus & Kitayama, 1991); this system of values is often called collectivism (Triandis, 1988). The emphasis on an individual's knowledge and technical expertise for its own sake is part of a system of values that emphasises independence and autonomy (Greenfield, 1994; Markus & Kitayama, 1991).[1] Consistent with this value system, we, in the United States or Switzerland for example, might value backstrap loom weaving if we thought it stimulated the development of concrete operational thought. However, this is not at all the way the Zinacantecs think about weaving. Instead, Zinacantecs are more interested in the social utility than in the purely cognitive value of weaving. Zinacantec culture contrasts with ours in this respect.

Weaving apprenticeship in sociocultural context. Let me illustrate the weaving apprenticeship practices in 1970, the year we did our first video study (Childs & Greenfield, 1980). As you will see, in the course of the apprenticeship process, maturational readiness for Genevan stages was met with Vygotskian scaffolding (Greenfield, 1984; Wood, Bruner, & Ross, 1978). The inter-individual activity theorised by Vygotsky (1956–60/1978) is beautifully exemplified by the following.

Katal, age 9, was videotaped as she learned to weave in 1970. Throughout our videotaping of her weaving apprenticeship, Katal's mother, serving as her teacher, was actively engaged in a process of scaffolding (Figure 10.11) (Greenfield, 1999 a, b). She was constantly anticipating her daughter's need for guidance and helping her to complete a weaving the daughter could not do on her own. For example, at one point, the mother entered the scene without being summoned, the teacher initiating help on her own. Figure 10.11 also shows four hands on the loom: Two belong to the learner, two to the teacher. This image symbolises a paradigmatic inter-individual process and demonstrates the interdependence of learner and teacher in weaving apprenticeship in 1970 (Greenfield, 1999a, b).

We also noted that this highly scaffolded process of apprenticeship left little room for error. In fact, errors were to be avoided because weaving materials were costly and difficult to obtain. This is one aspect of the ecological component, to which the socialising process of apprenticeship is adapted.

In addition, this highly scaffolded process of apprenticeship left little room for discovery. This was a quality well suited for the maintenance of weaving tradition in a society in which learning to weave meant learning to weave a closed stock of about four traditional patterns. Because the teacher was the mother, a member of

Figure 10.11. Video frame of Katal 1's mother, Xunka', helping Katal 1 to weave. Nabenchauk, 1970. Video by Patricia Greenfield.

the older generation, this example of weaving apprenticeship also illustrates the flow of authority from elder to younger (Greenfield & Childs, 1996). The collectivistic values of interdependence and respect for the authority of elders were implicit (although not explicit) in Zinacantec weaving apprenticeship.

Ecological component: The sociocultural component is adapted to an ecological niche

Reverence for stable tradition was related to the functionality of authority in agrarian societies, where the older generation controlled land, the essential means of subsistence and production (Collier, 1990). There was an absolute view of the world. For example, when I asked why a group of Zinacantecs were dressed like us rather than like them, the answer in Tzotzil was, "They don't know how to dress." Innovation was a negative. To be different was to gather opprobrium. This was a value judgement. Weaving was part of a collectivistic value system that emphasises the interdependence in social relations as well as respect for authority and cognitive skills in the service of social goals. This value system was well adapted to life in a subsistence, agriculturally based economy, in which the younger generation depended on the elders' land and in which co-operative exchanges of labour were required for the production of food and clothing.

Historical component: The ecological niche changes over time

In the decades from 1970 to the 1990s, there were significant economic changes in the culture of Nabenchauk. Zinacantecs moved from an agrarian, subsistence culture to a commercial society, from family- and community-held land to individually owned trucks and vans. Even woven textiles are sold—both to outsiders (see Figure 10.12) and to other Zinacantecs. In Figure 10.12, woven and

Figure 10.12.   Girls selling *servilletas* (used as tortilla covers, place mats, or hand towels) on the road at the edge of their village. Nabenchauk, 1991. Photo courtesy of Lauren Greenfield.

embroidered *servilletas* (napkins) are for sale to tourists and others who stop to buy; the *servilletas*, seen hanging in the background, are an item specially developed to sell to outsiders.

This type of entrepreneurship is part of a pattern of innovation and individualism. Innovation is seen in the change from a small closed stock of traditional woven patterns to a constant process of pattern innovation; each woven artifact is now unique, a mode of individual expression. For example, instead of a situation in which all males wear the same poncho (Figure 10.13), we found a large variety, giving a larger role to individual creativity and uniqueness (see Figures 14a, b, and c). Although the poncho shape and the background pattern of stripes have stayed the same, the woven and embroidered decoration is distinct for each poncho, and this decoration is getting increasingly elaborate (Greenfield, 1999a, b; Greenfield & Childs, 1996). Thus, the developmental outcome in terms of artistic expression has changed. Artistic expression has become more individualistic, less specified by social norms.

Commerce promotes individualistic practices because nuclear family members are regularly moving in every direction independently of each other. For instance, a child may go to a nearby market to sell fruit with a neighbour, or a father may drive 18 hours one-way to pick up some commodity to be sold. Members of a nuclear family operate more and more independently of each other as their involvement with commerce increases.

This societal level of historical change brought with it a change in the cultural practices concerned with weaving apprenticeship. This was revealed by our study of the next generation. Recall the case of Katal, who was learning to weave under her mother's tutelage in 1970. She grew up and had children of her own. In 1991, one of them, Loxa, was about the same age her mother had been in 1970, and we were able to study how she learned to weave. As with her mother's generation, we

Figure 10.13.   Parla brothers wearing virtually identical ponchos. Nabenchauk, 1970. Photo courtesy of Sheldon Greenfield.

Figure 10.14. Three distinctly different ponchos from the 1990s. (a) 1991, photo courtesy of Lauren Greenfield. (b) and (c) 1995, photos by Patricia Greenfield.

again made a videotape of her weaving apprenticeship. Figure 10.15 presents a frame from the video that is typical in many respects.

Comparing Figure 10.11 (mother learning to weave in 1970) with Figure 10.15 (daughter learning to weave at the same age in 1991), some differences are striking. Note that in contrast to the previous generation, Loxa's mother is not present in the frame. Instead, mother has designated Loxa's older sister, Xunka', to serve as teacher. This change in the generation of the weaving teacher is related to the historical increase in innovation; that is, weaving innovation is concentrated in teenage girls.

In addition, the learner has become much more independent. Unlike her mother's teacher, Loxa's teacher does not anticipate her need for help. Note that the older sister is paying no visual attention to the weaving learner in Figure 10.15; she is also much further away from the learner than the teacher in Figure 10.11. The learner must take the initiative to summon her teacher when help is required. The scaffolding process is directed by learner rather than teacher. There has been a movement from interdependence to independence of learner and teacher. In fact, the movement has been towards the independent discovery learning favoured by Piaget (1965a) and away from the scaffolded guidance described by Wood et al. (1978), based on Vygotsky's (1956, 1960/1978) theory (Gelman, personal communication, 1991).

This method is adapted to a situation where errors are less costly, and innovation and discovery are valued. Earlier I noted that innovation in woven patterns had come to be valued. In fact, errors had become less costly too. There had been a switch from the more expensive (to buy) cotton and the more expensive (to produce) wool to the cheaper acrylic, a petroleum-based product of the 1980s oil boom in Mexico. In addition, the development of a transport business, and the local commerce that followed, made the materials (thread) easier to get. Whereas in 1970,

Figure 10.15.   Video frame of Katal 1's daughter, Loxa 1–201, learning to weave in 1991. Loxa is about the same age as her mother was when she was videotaped learning to weave in 1970. Nabenchauk, 1991. Video by Patricia Greenfield.

cotton had to be purchased retail in the city of San Cristobal, acrylic thread could now be purchased wholesale in San Cristobal and resold retail in Nabenchauk. In other words, as materials became more plentiful, easier to get, and cheaper, errors became less costly over the same historical period in which apprenticeship changed (cf., Greenfield, 1984; Rogoff, 1990).

Theoretical conclusion and summary. A general theoretical conclusion follows: In circumstances where the goal of apprenticeship is to maintain tradition and avoid error, the Vygotskian model of socially guided learning is dominant. In circumstances where innovation is desired and errors are not too costly, the Piagetian model of independent discovery learning is dominant.

Note that there is still a process of sociocultural construction of weaving skill by which the maturational potential of a 9-year-old for learning and development is actualised in backstrap loom weaving. But the nature of the sociocultural process has been transformed in this particular family.

Testing generality and integrating levels of the theoretical model: Structural equation modelling

Was the observed historical change general? If so, was the change in fact mediated by the hypothesised change in ecological conditions? We used interview and demographic census data, plus structural equation modelling, to answer these questions affirmatively (Greenfield, Maynard, & Childs, in press). Such a model also takes account of within-culture individual differences in a way that a paradigmatic case study cannot.

Uneven social change and value conflict: Interaction between the sociocultural and ecological component

In a situation of uneven social change, some people have changed considerably towards the new more individualistic cultural practices; others have changed much less. Some members of the community have become merchants; others are still mainly in agriculture. In this situation, one might expect some conflict between the two models of learning and apprenticeship. I now want to present some ethnographic evidence for conflicting mental models of the apprenticeship process. Note that it is primarily in a situation of value conflict that values move from the implicit to the explicit level. In the conflict, we will see how underlying values are made explicit in the interpretive process of verbal discourse.

A little girl, Rosy, age 7, had spontaneously set up a toy loom. A teenage girl next door saw Rosy working, decided what she was doing was not good, and came over and undid everything. In Figure 10.16, the teenage neighbour is in the middle of taking out one set of threads in Rosy's warp (frame threads).

Figure 10.16.   A teenage neighbour taking out Rosy's warp threads because she thinks Rosy has done an inadequate job. Nabenchauk, 1995. Photo by Patricia Greenfield.

At this point it is important to present ethnographic evidence for conflicting mental models of the apprenticeship process: Clearly the teenage neighbour felt that Rosy should not make her own mistakes. Of Rosy's set-up she made the evaluative comment "bad". Rosy's mother had another model in mind: independent learning. "Let her do it by herself" said Rosy's mother Maruch. "She doesn't know how" replied the self-appointed teenage teacher. This reply reflected the older model of scaffolded, relatively errorless learning, in sharp contrast to the mother's model. Later, Rosy's mother elaborated her model even more explicitly. She told me that it was better for Rosy to learn by herself, as her older sister had done. She had neither helped nor talked to Rosy's older sister, said the mother.

Interestingly, Rosy's family was much more heavily involved in commerce than was the neighbour's family, so the conflicting models represented the two ecological niches present in Nabenchauk. Later, I asked Rosy about her own model of learning: Did she want to weave by herself or with help? She replied "by myself". Upon further questioning, she added that it was "worse" to have the girl help. So Rosy, like her mother, but unlike her self-styled teacher, had in mind the newer model of more independent apprenticeship.

We see learning to weave as but one example of two contrasting models of development mentioned earlier. These models, which I will call the interdependence script and the independence script (Greenfield, 1994), are very basic and generative. Each model is a value framework that guides development, socialisation, and behaviour across many domains.

Just as our model can explain cultural variability and value conflict in Nabenchauk, it can explain cultural variability and value conflict in Los Angeles. Here I will focus on the sociocultural level of values.

Extension of the theoretical framework to a multicultural society

Because change has been quite gradual in Nabenchauk and the Zinacantecs have kept changes pretty much under their own control in an intact community, this conflict between two models of socialisation is relatively recent and fairly mild. The Zinacantecs are just beginning their journey on the path to individualism. However, the path is much more abrupt and disruptive for the many immigrants who come from rural Mexico to the United States. Although they have been much more integrated into the modern Mexican commercial economy, more touched by formal education, and less collectivistic than the Zinacantecs, they carry with them an ancestral value system that, relative to urban Los Angeles, is very collectivistic. As our research has shown, these immigrants, many from rural backgrounds, come to the United States with an interdependent script of socialisation and development (Delgado-Gaitan, 1994; Greenfield, 1994; Tapia Uribe, LeVine, & LeVine, 1994). They meet a highly commercial, individualistic society that has a developmental script based on independence and autonomy (Greenfield, Raeff, & Quiroz, 1998; Raeff, Greenfield, & Quiroz, 2000).

This culture conflict is expressed in many ways. For example, relative to the dominant culture, these immigrants experience parallel struggles to those of Rosy —between a model that stresses helpfulness and one that stresses doing it yourself.

Here is an example: We arrived to start a study in an elementary school in West Los Angeles serving low-income Latino families. There had just been a major conflagration in the school involving the federally funded school breakfast programme. The problem, as seen by the school, was that immigrant Latino mothers were accompanying their children to school, having breakfast with them, and helping their school-age children to eat. When the school locked the families out of the schoolyard at breakfast, there was a major blow-up (Quiroz & Greenfield, 1996).

One of the problems, as seen by the school personnel, was that these mothers were literally spoon-feeding their school-age children instead of letting them eat by themselves. Such behaviour was seen as leading to dependency, rather than to the self-sufficiency advocated by the schools. On the other hand, helping the children eat their food also reflected Latino cultural values: Being helpful towards one another is a highly desirable trait. Part of this conflict between the two value systems sets independence over and above helpfulness.

How general was this conflict over school breakfasts? Would it be correct to say that it reflected two contrasting cultural models of development? With Catherine Raeff and Blanca Quiroz, I conducted experimental research to investigate these questions (Raeff et al., 2000). We administered a set of scenarios concerning social dilemmas at home and at school in two different schools. Each dilemma could be solved in a number of different ways, some consonant with an individualistic model of development and socialisation, some consonant with a collectivistic model. Parents, teachers, and children were tested in two schools. In the school I am going to talk about here, the families were Latino immigrants from Mexico and Central America.

Here is an example of a dilemma that relates to the school breakfast example (Raeff et al., 2000). In this dilemma, which takes place at school, the issue is whether to help or not:

> It is the end of the school day, and the class is cleaning up. Denise isn't feeling well, and she asks Jasmine to help her with her job for the day which is cleaning the blackboard. Jasmine isn't sure that she will have time to do both jobs. What do you think the teacher should do?

Figure 10.17 shows the results. Just as the school was unified in the opinion that mothers should not help their school-age children to eat, so teachers were in broad agreement that Jasmine should not help Denise (Figure 10.17). Most often they thought a third person should be found to do the job (see Figure 10.17). The point, often, was to get someone who would volunteer to do the job by choice. They did not want to infringe on Jasmine's autonomy in achieving completion of her own job. Latino immigrant parents, in sharp contrast, were quite unified in their view that Jasmine should help Denise (Figure 10.17). This response paralleled their desire to help their children eat breakfast.

This pattern of results shows a strong conflict between helpfulness and independent autonomy, with Latino immigrant parents supporting helpfulness, and teachers (representing dominant societal culture) prioritising Jasmine's right to autonomy and Denise's individual responsibility for her job. The Latino children (like Rosy) are often in between, constructing their own values out of two disparate

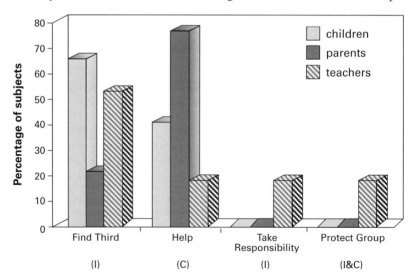

Figure 10.17.   Distribution of responses to the "jobs" scenario by Latino immigrant parents, their children, and teachers. I = individualistic, C = collectivistic.

and conflicting value systems. Here for example, they are in between parents and teachers on helpfulness (Figure 10.17).

As we saw for the Zinacantecs, another aspect of the collectivistic worldview is an ethnotheory of development in which cognitive skills are in the service of social goals. In the Latino immigrant ethnotheory, cognitive development is subordinated to social relations—just as it is for the Zinacantecs. This can lead to other kinds of cross-cultural value conflicts and misunderstandings in the individualistic schools.

Here is an example: During one of our observations of a Los Angeles pre-kindergarten class made up of mostly Hispanic children, the teacher was showing a real chicken egg that would soon hatch. While teaching the physical properties of the egg, she asked children to describe eggs by thinking about the times they had cooked and eaten them. One child tried three times to talk about how she cooked eggs with her grandmother, but the teacher disregarded these comments in favour of a child who explained that the insides of eggs are white and yellow (Greenfield, Raeff, & Quiroz, 1996, p. 44).

From the Latino point of view, the first child's answer was typical of the associations encouraged in her home culture of interdependence. That is, objects are most meaningful when they mediate social interactions. The child therefore acted on this value of interpersonal relations in answering the teacher's question. The teacher, however, did not recognise this effort on the part of the child and considered the social descriptions of the time they had eaten eggs as irrelevant; only physical descriptions of these occasions seemed to be valued (Greenfield et al., 1996). Here, the ethnotheory of development that places knowledge of the physical world as a means to social relationships is not valued or understood. Cognitive development expressed in this context is devalued.

CONCLUSION

I have tried to present a model that features a new idea: age-dependent sensitive periods for cultural learning. Because of the actualisation of these bio-logically grounded developmental windows by the sociocultural component, the implication is that the same cognitive stage will take different forms in different cultures. Just as we would not expect concrete operational children in the United States to set up a backstrap loom, so we might not expect concrete operational children in Nabenchauk to solve a problem in cross-classification (and in fact in an experiment I tried, children of concrete operational age could not do this).

Another theoretical idea that builds on Inhelder and Piaget's description of cognitive stages of development is that particular stages of cognitive development are built into various tools and that the order in which the tools are presented can implicitly respect the stages of Inhelder and Piaget. This "developmental sequence" of cultural tools illustrates how the notion of cognitive construction through individual activity, developed so richly by Inhelder, can be expanded to incorporate the notion of cultural construction of cognitive development.

My theoretical model also explains development as an interaction among various levels: the maturational, the sociocultural, the ecological, and the historical. Thus, biological concepts are integrated with sociocultural ones. I have tried to illustrate the complex interactions among the various levels by using findings from a relatively simple, homogeneous society, a Zinacantec Maya community in Chiapas, Mexico. I have selected a part of the model, the level of symbolic value interpretations, to test in Los Angeles, where we have found the same opposition between two different ethnotheories or models of development; a more collectivistic model stressing helpfulness and a more individualistic one stressing autonomy.

Integrating theories of social and cognitive development

In the West, there is a split between theories of social and cognitive development. This reflects a split in our goals for development, a split in our ethnotheories of development. True to European-derived cultures, Inhelder has had a critical role in developing the most influential theory of cognitive development. This was an amazing accomplishment that we must now build upon as we remember Bärbel Inhelder with great admiration. In taking the next theoretical step, we need to keep in mind that, in many cultures, such a split between the cognitive and the social is not the norm; cognitive skills are seen as a means to social goals. I propose that our formal theories are only as universal as the ethnotheories they presuppose. Therefore, we need a formal theory of development that does not presuppose the dominance of cognitive development nor the split between the social and the cognitive. In conclusion, we need a universal theory that transcends culture-specific ethnotheories of development. This requires a higher-order theory that integrates different ethnotheories as alternative paths in a more universal theory of development.

ACKNOWLEDGEMENTS

This paper was originally presented at the Annual Symposium of the Jean Piaget Society, Santa Monica, CA, June 1997 under the title Culture and Universals: Integrating Social and Cognitive Development. This version was adapted from a chapter that will appear in L. Nucci, G. Saxe, & E. Turiel (Eds.), *Culture, thought, and development* (Mahwah, NJ: Lawrence Erlbaum Associates Inc.). The research on which it is based was supported by the Spencer Foundation, the Wenner-Gren Foundation, the Fogarty International Center of NIH (Steven Lopez, PI), ECOSUR, San Cristobal de las Casas, Chiapas, Mexico, the UCLA Urban Education Studies Center, the Harvard Chiapas Project (Evon Z. Vogt, Director), the Harvard Center for Cognitive Studies (Jerome S. Bruner, Co-Director), the Milton Fund of Harvard University, and the Radcliffe Institute. I would like to express my appreciation to our participants in Chiapas and Los Angeles and to my collaborators Carla Childs, Ashley Maynard, Leslie Devéreaux, Catherine Raeff, and Blanca Quiroz. Thanks to my lab group and to Larry Nucci, Elliot Turiel, and Geoffrey Saxe for their very useful and important feedback on earlier versions.

NOTE

1. Piaget recognises these two cultural systems in a talk originally given in 1947 and just recently published in French (Piaget, 1998). He distinguishes societies that emphasise autonomy (which he terms "modern") versus those that emphasise "heteronomy", i.e., social conformity and the authority of elders (which he terms "primitive"). The difference between his theoretical framework and the present one is that he interprets the latter system through the lens of the former. This approach leads to the construction of a developmental hierarchy in which heteronomy is a lower, less valued developmental stage of both cultures and individuals than is autonomy. In contrast, I have tried to see each system from its own perspective, emphasising the developmental goals of each, rather than using the goals of one to negatively evaluate the other.

REFERENCES

Bruner, J.S. (1964). On the course of cognitive growth. *American Psychologist, 19*, 1–15.

Bruner, J.S. (1977–78). Symbols and texts as the tools of intellect. *Interchange, 8*(4), 1–15.

Bruner, J.S., & Olson, D.R. (1973). Learning through experience and learning through media. In G. Gerbner, L.P. Gross, & W.H. Melody (Eds.), *Communications technology and social policy* (pp. 209–212). New York: Wiley.

Childs, C.P., & Greenfield, P.M. (1980). Informal modes of learning and teaching: The case of Zinacanteco weaving. In N. Warren (Ed.), *Studies in cross-cultural psychology* (Vol. 2, pp. 269–316). London: Academic Press.

Cole, M., & Scribner, S. (1974). *Culture and thought: A psychological introduction.* New York: Wiley.

Collier, G.A. (1990). *Seeking food and seeking money: Changing productive relations in a Highland Mexican community* (Discussion Paper 11). United Nations Research Institute for Social Development.

Dasen, P.R. (1984). The cross-cultural study of intelligence: Piaget and the Baoulé. In P.S. Fry (Ed.), *Changing conceptions of intelligence and intellectual functioning: Current theory and research* (pp. 107–134). Amsterdam: North-Holland.

Dasen, P.R., Inhelder, B., Lavallé, M., & Retschitzki, J. (1978). *Naissance de l'intelligence chez l'enfant baoulé de Côte d'Ivoire* [The growth of intelligence in Baoulé children]. Berne: Huber.

Delgado-Gaitan, C. (1994). Socializing young children in Mexican-American families: An intergenerational perspective. In P.M. Greenfield & R.R. Cocking (Eds.), *Cross-cultural roots of minority child development* (pp. 55–86). Hillsdale, NJ: Lawrence Erlbaum Associates Inc.

Fairbanks, L.A. (2000). Behavioral development of nonhuman primates and the evolution of human behavioral ontogeny. In S. Parker, J. Langer, & M. Mackinney (Eds.), *Biology, brains, and behavior: The evolution of human behavior* (pp. 131–158). Santa Fe, NM: SAR Press.

Fischer, K.W. (1987). Relations between brain and cognitive development. *Child Development, 58*, 623-632.

Fischer, K.W., & Rose, S.P. (1994). Dynamic development of coordination of components in brain and behavior: A framework for theory. In G. Dawson & K.W. Fischer (Eds.), *Human behaviour and the developing brain* (pp. 3–66). New York: Guilford Press.

Greenfield, P.M. (1966). On culture and conservation. In J.S. Bruner, R.R. Olver, P.M. Greenfield (Eds.), *Studies in cognitive growth* (pp. 225–256). New York: Wiley.

Greenfield, P.M. (1974). Cross-cultural research and Piagetian theory: Paradox and progress. *Dossiers Pedagogiques*, 34–39. [English version in K.F. Riegel & J.A. Meacham (Eds.), *The developing individual in a changing world: Vol. 1. Historical and cultural issues* (pp. 322–333). The Hague: Mouton, 1976.]

Greenfield, P.M. (1984). A theory of the teacher in the learning activities of everyday life. In B. Rogoff & J. Lave (Eds.), *Everyday cognition: Its development in social context* (pp. 117–138). Cambridge, MA: Harvard University Press.

Greenfield, P.M. (1993). Representational competence in shared symbol systems: Electronic media from radio to video games. In R.R. Cocking & K.A. Renninger (Eds.), *The development and meaning of psychological distance* (pp. 161–183). Hillsdale, NJ: Lawrence Erlbaum Associates Inc.

Greenfield, P.M. (1994). Independence and interdependence as developmental scripts: Implications for theory, research, and practice. In P.M. Greenfield & R.R. Cocking (Eds.), *Cross cultural roots of minority child development* (pp. 1–37). Hillsdale, NJ: Lawrence Erlbaum Associates Inc.

Greenfield, P.M. (1999a). Cultural change and human development. In E. Turiel (Ed.), Development and cultural change: Reciprocal processes. *New Directions for Child and Adolescent Development*, *83*, 37–59.

Greenfield, P.M. (1999b). Historical change and cognitive change: A two-decade follow-up study in Zinacantan, a Maya community in Chiapas, Mexico. *Mind, Culture, and Activity*, *6*, 92–108.

Greenfield, P., & Childs, C. (1996, November). Learning to weave in Zinacanta: A two-decade follow-up study of historical and cognitive change. In I. Zambrano & E.Z. Vogt (Chairs), *Microcosms of the social world: Formal and informal education in the Maya area of Chiapas*. Symposium conducted at the American Anthropological Association, San Francisco.

Greenfield, P.M., Maynard, A., & Childs, C.P. (in press). History, culture, learning, and development. *Cross-Cultural Research*.

Greenfield, P.M., Raeff, C., & Quiroz, B. (1996). Cultural values in learning and education. In B. Williams (Ed.), *Closing the achievement gap: A vision for changing beliefs and practices* (pp. 37–55). Alexandria, VA: Association for Supervision and Curriculum Development.

Greenfield, P.M., Raeff, C., & Quiroz, B. (1998). Cross-cultural conflict in the social construction of the child. *Aztlán*, *23*, 115–125.

Inhelder, B. (1982). Early cognitive development and malnutrition. In R.V. Garcia & J.C. Escudero (Eds.), *Drought and man: Vol. 2. The constant catastrophe: Malnutrition, families, and drought* (pp. 24–29). Oxford, UK: Pergamon Press.

Inhelder, B., & Piaget, J. (1958). *The growth of logical thinking from childhood to adolescence*. New York: Basic Books. [Also published the same year in London by Routledge & Kegan Paul. (Original work published 1955)

LeVine, R.A. (1977). Child rearing as cultural adaptation. In P.H. Leiderman, S.R. Tulkin, & A. Rosenfeld (Eds.), *Culture and infancy: Variations in the human experience* (pp. 15–27). New York: Academic Press.

Markus, H.R., & Kitayama, S. (1991). Culture and the self: Implications for cognition, emotion, and motivation. *Psychological Review*, *98*, 224–253.

Maynard, A., Greenfield, P.M., & Childs, C.P. (1999). Culture, history, biology, and body: Native and non-native acquisition of technological skill. *Ethos*, *27*, 379–402.

Molleson, T. (1996, March). The physical anthropology of role specialization from neolithic times. In *Culture and the uses of the body*. Fondation Fyssen Colloquium, St. Germain-en-Laye, France.

Mundy-Castle, A.C. (1974). Social and technological intelligence in Western and non-Western cultures. *Universitas*, *4*, 46–52.

Newport, E.L. (1988). Constraints on learning and their role in language acquisition: Studies of the acquisition of American Sign Language. *Language Sciences*, *10*, 147–152.

Piaget, J. (1963). Intellectual operations and their development. [Reprinted in H.E. Gruber & J.J. Vonèche (Eds.), *The essential Piaget: An interpretive reference and guide* (pp. 342–358). New York: Basic Books, 1977.]

Piaget, J. (1965a). Developments in pedagogy. [Reprinted in H.E. Gruber & J.J. Vonèche (Eds.), *The essential Piaget: An interpretive reference and guide* (pp. 696–719). New York: Basic Books, 1977.]

Piaget, J. (1965b). *The moral judgment of the child*. New York: The Free Press. (Original work published 1932)

Piaget, J. (1972). Intellectual evolution from adolescence to adulthood, *Human Development*, *15*, 1-12.

Piaget, J. (1998). *De la pédagogie* [About pedagogy]. Paris: Odile Jacob. [Original papers published 1930–1957, edited by S. Parrat & A. Tryphon.]

Piaget, J., & Inhelder, B. (1969). *The psychology of the child*. New York: Basic Books. (Original work published 1966)

Quiroz, B., & Greenfield, P.M. (1996). *Cross-cultural value conflict: Removing a barrier to Latino school achievement*. Unpublished manuscript, Department of Psychology, University of California, Los Angeles.

Rabain, J. (1979). *L'enfant du lignage. Du sevrage à la classe d'âge chez les Wolof du Senegal* [Child of the lineage: From weaning to age-graded peer group among the Wolof of Senegal]. Paris: Payot.

Raeff, C., Greenfield, P.M., & Quiroz, B. (2000). Developing interpersonal relationships in the cultural contexts of individualism and collectivism. In S. Harkness, C. Raeff, & C.R. Super (Eds.), *The social construction of the child: The nature of variability* (pp. 59–74). San Francisco: Jossey-Bass.

Rogoff, B. (1990). *Apprenticeship in thinking: Cognitive development in social context*. New York: Oxford University Press.

Rogoff, B., Baker-Sennett, J., Lacasa, P., & Goldsmith, D. (1995). Development through participation in sociocultural activity. In J. Goodnow, P. Miller, & F. Kessel (Eds.), *Cultural practices as contexts for development* (pp. 45–65). San Francisco: Jossey-Bass Publishers.

Saxe, G.B. (1991). *Culture and cognitive development: Studies in mathematical understanding*. Hillsdale, NJ: Lawrence Erlbaum Associates Inc.

Scribner, S. (1985). Vygotsky's uses of history. In J.V. Wertsch (Ed.), *Culture, communication, and cognition: Vygotskian perspectives* (pp. 119–145). Cambridge: Cambridge University Press.

Scribner, S., & Cole, M. (1981). *The psychology of literacy*. Cambridge, MA: Harvard University Press.

Shweder, R.A., & Bourne, E.J. (1982). Does the concept of the person vary cross-culturally? In R.A. Shweder & R.A. Levine (Eds.), *Culture theory: Essays on mind, self, and emotion* (pp. 158–199). New York: Cambridge University Press.

Super, C.M., & Harkness, S. (1997). The cultural structuring of child development. In J.W. Berry, P.R. Dasen, & T.S. Saraswathi (Eds.), *Handbook of cross-cultural psychology: Vol. 2, Basic processes and human development* (2nd ed.). Boston: Allyn & Bacon.

Tapia Uribe, F.M., LeVine, R.A., & LeVine, S E. (1994). Maternal behaviour in a Mexican community: The changing environments of children. In P.M. Greenfield & R.R. Cocking (Eds.), *Cross-cultural roots of minority child development* (pp. 41–54). Hillsdale, NJ: Lawrence Erlbaum Associates Inc.

Thatcher, R.W. (1994). Cyclical cortical reorganization: Origins of human cognitive development. In G. Dawson & K.W. Fischer (Eds.), *Human behaviour and the developing brain* (pp. 232–266). New York: Guilford Press.

Triandis, H.C. (1988). Collectivism vs. individualism: A reconceptualization of a basic concept in cross-cultural social psychology. In C. Bargley & G.K. Verma (Eds.), *Personality, cognition, and values: Cross-cultural perspectives of childhood and adolescence.* London: Macmillan.

Veneziano, E. (1998, September). *Early language uses and their relation to young children's "know-how" about the mind.* Poster presented at the 15th advanced course of the Jean Piaget Archives, Geneva, Switzerland.

Vygotsky, L.S. (1962). *Thought and language.* Cambridge, MA: MIT Press. (Original work published 1934)

Vygotsky, L.S. (1978). *Mind in society: The development of higher psychological processes.* Cambridge, MA: Harvard University Press. (Original work published 1956, 1960)

Vygotsky, L.S., & Luria, A.R. (1993). *Studies on the history of behavior: Ape, primitive, and child* (V.I. Golod & J.E. Knox, Trans.). Hillsdale, NJ: Lawrence Erlbaum Associates Inc. (Original work published 1930)

Weisner, T. (1984). A cross-cultural perspective: Ecocultural niches of middle childhood. In A. Collins (Ed.), *The elementary school years: Understanding development during middle childhood* (pp. 335–369). Washington, DC: National Academy Press.

Whiting, B.B., & Whiting, J.W.M. (1975). *The children of six cultures: A psychocultural analysis.* Cambridge, MA: Harvard University Press.

Wober, M. (1974). Towards an understanding of the Kiganda concept of intelligence. In J.W. Berry & P.R. Dasen (Eds.), *Culture and cognition.* London: Methuen.

Wood, D., Bruner, J.S., & Ross, G. (1978). The role of tutoring in problem solving. *Journal of Child Psychology and Psychiatry, 17,* 89–100.

CHAPTER ELEVEN

Bärbel Inhelder and the fall of Valhalla

Terrance Brown
Chicago, USA

Alles! Alles!	All things, all things,
Alles weiss ich:	All things I know:
alles ward mir nun frei!	All things are clear now!
…	…
Mein Erbe nun	My legacy
nehm' ich zu eigen.	I now reclaim.
Verfluchter Reif!	Accursed Ring!
furchtbarer Ring!	Dreadful Ring!
dein Gold fass' ich	I seize the gold,
und geb' es nun fort.	And give it away.

—Richard Wagner (1865)
Brünhilde's *Immolation*

In the late 1980s, Jack Meacham, then editor of *Human Development*, asked me to review the Genevan school's work on strategies and procedures (Brown, 1988a). Four years later, Bärbel Inhelder asked me to prepare an English translation of *Le cheminement des découvertes de l'enfant* (Inhelder & Cellérier, 1992), the final summary of that work. In 1997, Jacques Vonèche, director of *Archives Jean Piaget*, invited me to review this subject once again for a *Cours avancé* paying homage to Inhelder's life and work. I was honoured by that request. However, rather than report Inhelder's clarifications and unravel Cellérier's fascinating new theoretical tangles in light of the final book, I thought that it might be more appropriate, given the occasion, and more realistic, given the space available, to try to place the work on strategies and procedures within the context of Inhelder's collaboration with Piaget and, to an extent consistent with her privacy, to try also to place it within the context of her personality. She was, after all, a mentor and friend for 20 years.

As far as Inhelder's contributions are concerned, there is no doubt that *Le cheminement* constitutes a valedictory. Like all great farewells, it attempts to make sense of a certain piece of history. In the present case, the history at issue is not just a chronicle of the Genevan school in which she was so intimately involved. Nor is it only an exposition of how the structure–function bifurcation developed into the beginnings of a reconciliation between epistemological and psychological approaches. If one is willing to read between the lines, it also tells the story of how Inhelder, as a person, sought to follow her functional interests, to distinguish herself from Piaget's structural approach, and to develop her own identity as a scientist.

Although it is almost certain that Bärbel Inhelder would not have been comfortable with the parallels I am about to draw,[1] it is my conviction that, taken in concert with her *Autobiography* (Inhelder, 1989), her chapters in *Le cheminement* are in many ways analogous to Brünhilde's *Immolation*. In her own valedictory, Brünhilde recounts the story of a great hero, ponders his faults and virtues, evaluates his successes and his failures, and in the end establishes her identity through an act that accomplishes both her father's and the hero's goal: the re-establishment of the proper relation between love and power. To my mind, Inhelder's case is similar. In her *Autobiography* and in *Le cheminement*, Inhelder who, like Brünhilde, gave up her godhead—her place in Valhalla—in order to defend a great figure and his ideals, came in the end to reclaim her heritage, psychology, through an act announcing a new world order: the reconciliation of Piagetian epistemology with cognitive psychology. But the parallels must not be pushed too far. Brünhilde, like her father Wotan, saw an opposition between love and power and believed that power was evil. In contrast, Inhelder never conceived an opposition between psychology and epistemology, and never condemned the study of how universal knowledge is constructed. Although it seems likely that she suspected for many years (if not from the very beginning) that Piaget's epistemic subject was not what psychology was all about, she did not say so until the very end. Only after decades of studying how universal categories and rational knowledge are constructed did she voice her doubts. What she concluded was that epistemology, by itself, could not explain discovery and that cognitive psychology, by itself, could not explain rationality. She sought, therefore, to find what Piaget would have called a *tertium quid* (an intermediate term), but not by restoring epistemology to philosophy as Brünhilde restored the Rhinegold to the Rhine. Her tack was, rather, to suggest a world in which the gods of Genevan epistemology and the gnomes of American cognitivism would, through some sort of licit union, give rise to a psychology that had the universal traits of Piagetian epistemology and the individual traits of real people with real histories living real lives. That, essentially, is what the work on strategies and procedures was all about.

SHIPS IN THE NIGHT

When I wrote *Ships in the night* (Brown, 1988a), four key references were available to me: Inhelder and her team's paper *Des structures cognitives aux procédures de découverte* (Inhelder et al., 1976), Cellérier's two papers *Structures cognitives et schèmes d'action, I et II* (Cellérier, 1979a, b), and the last paper that Inhelder and Piaget wrote together, *Procédures et structures* (Inhelder & Piaget, 1979). From those, I teased the following account.

In the 1970s Inhelder, Cellérier, and a team of young researchers decided to deviate from the epistemological project of discovering the great structural and functional laws that rule the construction of reason and to search out the principles of teleonomic organisation that rule the construction of effective action. Not only would this help reconcile the approach of the Genevan school with American "cognitive science", but it would also supply Piaget's epistemology with something it sorely needed—a theory of what Inhelder called "discovery", by which she meant a theory of how the schemes out of which structures were constructed were invented.

The point of attack, identified by Cellérier, was Piaget's equivocation about the notions of scheme and structure. On the one hand, according to Piaget, knowledge construction begins with schemes of action, with *savoir-faire*, i.e., with knowing how things can be accomplished. At all levels, schemes enjoy a goal–means or teleonomic organisation, although it is only at the level of intelligence where intention comes into play that means may be combined and recombined in various ways until the goal is reached. On the other hand, and again according to Piaget, knowledge construction ends in structures, in *savoir*, i.e., in knowing pure and simple. Although much knowledge never becomes structured (and not all knowledge can), at levels where it does, structures enjoy logical or operational rather than teleonomic organisation. They are, in fact, formed through exhaustive co-ordination of action possibilities. Whatever goal is set, these possibilities will have to be employed in combinations allowable within the system in order for effective action to be taken.

Where Cellérier saw equivocation was in the fact that structures are sometimes labelled schemes even though such "schemes", strictly speaking, are really structures. For example, "the scheme of the permanent object",[2] is not really a scheme of a particular action organised around a goal. Rather it is what one might call a sensorimotor "protocategory" or "protostructure" created by exhaustive co-ordination of actions possible on a particular set of objects.

The reason that Cellérier believed this equivocation to be so important rests on two further distinctions that need to be elaborated. The first has to do with the distinction between what is *sufficient* and what is *necessary*. While the organisation of a scheme is sufficient in so far as it is effective in reaching the goal, it is necessary only in the vanishingly few cases where there is only one way to reach a goal. In contrast, the organisation of a structure is both sufficient and necessary for the simple reason that structures are comprised of all effective schemes of action held in simultaneous relation—there are no other ways to reach any goal to which the structure applies. This leads, then, to a final distinguishing wrinkle. Because structures are not organised around any particular action or goal—or conversely, because they are applicable to every action and to every goal—they are devoid of temporal direction. Time comes into play only when a scheme of action specifies a specific path through the exhaustive maze of an action structure.

These clarifications in place, Cellérier goes on to distinguish Piagetian epistemology from cognitive science in the following way. Piagetian epistemology, concerned solely with the construction of reason, studies how atemporal structures are derived from schemes of action—the epistemic transformation. In contrast, American cognitive science more or less takes reason as a given and studies how structures of knowledge are used to create schemes of action—the pragmatic transformation. The unseemly realities of human motivation aside, there is no reason why these ships should have passed so silently in the night. Both epistemic and pragmatic transformations are essential to understanding human conduct. Without the first, logical necessity cannot be understood; without the second, the dialectics of discovery remain a mystery. How then, to bring the two schools together?

Cellérier's attempts to do so, reported in my former review, were based on revising the production system hypothesis that once dominated cognitive science. In *Part II* of *Le cheminement des découvertes de l'enfant* (Inhelder & Cellérier, 1992), Cellérier rejects his previous formulations. I shall not, therefore, recall them here.

LE CHEMINEMENT DES DÉCOUVERTES DE L'ENFANT

The story told in *Part I* of the work that I have called Inhelder's valedictory (Inhelder & Cellérier, 1992) is not vastly different from the story I pieced together from diverse articles to write *Ships in the night* (Brown, 1988a). What is new and valuable about this section of the book is that it brings together the theory and methods developed by Inhelder and her colleagues in more systematic and coherent fashion, and provides novel and interesting experimental illustrations. In contrast, Cellérier's reworking of the interface between genetic epistemology and cognitive psychology in *Part II* was not anticipated in *Ships in the night*, and represents new and far-reaching insights into the interface between genetic epistemology and cognitive science. Because of the highly complex and abstract nature of Cellérier's ideas, it is not possible to analyse *Part II* here. I shall, therefore, concentrate on Inhelder's conceptual contributions and only indicate how she evaluated Cellérier's new synthesis.

In the Preface, in Chapter 1 (written with de Caprona), and in the "Final remarks" (written with Cellérier, de Caprona, and Ducret), Inhelder presses hard on the point that her intention in taking up the work on strategies and procedures was to create a "genetic psychology" consistent with and complementary to Piaget's "genetic epistemology". This was not just an empty bow in Piaget's direction. Rather, it reflected the fact that everyone involved in the new project was convinced through long and intimate acquaintance with Piaget's ideas that they offered by far the best extant explanation of the phenomenon central to epistemology, i.e., the creation of rational (in the logical sense) models of "reality". At the same time, they were convinced of two other things. First, they were convinced that it was not possible to make Piaget's epistemology, by itself, a basis for developmental psychology. Piaget's "epistemic subject" was too narrowly conceived and left out too many categories central to psychology, e.g., values, intention, motivation, self and self-esteem, etc., for it to serve in that capacity. And worse, Piaget's theory did not explain convincingly how structures were used to create new schemes of action, although *Experiments in contradiction* (Piaget, 1974/1980), *The equilibration of cognitive structures* (Piaget, 1975/1985), and *Les formes élémentaires de la dialectique* (Piaget & García, 1980) all groped in that direction. At the same time, Inhelder and her group were equally convinced that it was not possible to make any extant psychology, in particular cognitive psychology or artificial intelligence, a basis for epistemology. An obvious reason was, of course, that most of these psychologies deal more with manifestations of knowledge than with its construction. More central to Inhelder's concerns, however, was the fact that even those psychologies dealing with knowledge construction failed to address the problem of how logical norms or the feeling of necessity is created. All of this led Inhelder to believe that a new and synthetic theory was needed.

In order to understand why Inhelder did not believe that Piaget's epistemology could ground a psychology and why, therefore, she went off in search of something new, three issues need to be considered: (1) Piaget's conception of psychology; (2) Piaget's conception of the epistemic subject; and (3) Inhelder's question—a second-level heading in Chapter 1 of *Le cheminement*—"What subject for psychology?". However brief the discussion of these topics, it will, I think, help in understanding what was unique and original about Inhelder's thought.

PIAGET'S CONCEPTION OF PSYCHOLOGY

Piaget's conception of psychology is very little known. What is better known and usually assumed to be his psychology is his epistemology. The reasons for this conflation seem straightforward.

Piaget's goal, established early in his life, was to create an epistemology based on evolutionary theory and under empirical control. That, he believed, was how all sciences of fact, all empirical sciences, worked—and he had no illusions that epistemology could ever be a completely formal science. As a relation between the knowing subject and its environment, there would always be a contingent factor that eluded pure deduction. The stumbling block was that knowledge construction—particularly in its scientific form—takes place over generations and is not, even for someone who lived as long as Piaget, amenable to longitudinal study. True, one could try to reconstruct history, as Brunschvicg had done, but history is hard to know. What Piaget sought, in addition to historical reconstructions, was a domain of observation where the growth of knowledge could be observed directly by individual scientists within their lifetimes. His bold hypothesis was that, at some level, all knowledge construction must be the same and that the way knowledge is built up in children must at some abstract level map onto the way knowledge is constructed by adults. In other words, the ontogenesis of knowledge must inform epistemology.[3]

No doubt it was this adducing of psychological facts to solve epistemological questions that accounts for the conflation of his epistemology with developmental psychology. Piaget, however, never claimed to be a psychologist or supposed that knowledge construction was all there was to developmental psychology. The idea that his theory was a complete theory of psychological development was never expressed by Piaget. In fact, he explicitly claimed that, at best, it was only one part of one aspect of conduct (1947/1967b, pp. 10–13):

> Conduct, conceived in terms of functional exchanges, itself presupposes two essential and deeply interdependent aspects: an affective aspect and a cognitive aspect … Intelligence … is not an isolable and discontinuous category of cognitive process. It is not, properly speaking, just one structuration among others: it is the form of equilibrium toward which [the functioning of] all structures tends, and its formation is to be sought from the beginning of perception, habits, and the elementary sensorimotor mechanisms.

At best, then, Piaget's epistemological theory was only half a psychology and, to this author's mind, not the most important half (see Brown, 1996).

Even so, to the extent that psychology has scientific pretensions, it makes knowledge claims and becomes subject to epistemological scrutiny. It is from this viewpoint that we can discover how Piaget conceived psychology. Despite a certain lack of fervour, Piaget tried here and there in bits and pieces to deal with psychology as a science. His most systematic treatments can be found in six texts: *La psychologie de l'intelligence* (Piaget, 1947/1967b); *L'explication en psychologie* (Piaget, 1950); *Explanation in psychology and psychophysiological parallelism* (Piaget, 1963/1968); *Le système des sciences* (Piaget, 1967a); and *The place of the sciences of man in the system of sciences* (Piaget, 1970). His views on this subject evolved very little over the 23 years involved, so I shall concentrate on the first and most detailed statement.

In *L'explication en psychologie*, Piaget argues that because psychological phenomena are peculiar to living beings, they must be rooted in biology, the most empirical and, therefore, the most "objective" of the sciences. At the same time, because one of the goals of psychology is to explain mental operations, it must deal with logic and mathematics, the most "subjective" of the sciences. Psychology, then, stands as a bridge between the objective and the subjective.[4] There being no way to "perceive" the subjective, a science of psychology could not be conceived, as it had been conceived during the first half of the twentieth century, as a science of observable behaviour. Knowledge is not drawn from perception alone. At the same time, there being no way to "objectify" the subjective, a psychology concerned, as it had been before Watson, with consciousness alone could not claim to be science.[5] Faced with this dilemma, Piaget reasoned that psychology had to be conceived as a science of *conduct*, a term that, for him, included both observable behaviour and states of consciousness. Under this definition, psychologists find themselves in the presence of two series of phenomena: the organism's observable behaviour and its subjective experience. The problem is to figure out the relation between the two.

For Piaget this tension between the organic and the subjective constituted a general class of problems exemplified by the relation between experiment and deduction in mathematical physics. It is a fundamental tension between causal and implicative relations. Organic facts involve causal series just as much as physical facts do, whereas both in psychology and physics, states of consciousness involve systems of implications to which, properly speaking, the concept of cause does not apply. Piaget opted, therefore, for an epistemological conception of psychology based on the principle of psychophysiological parallelism: Consciousness runs parallel to empirical biology but is not reducible to it. In particular, as neurophysiology can never explain the phenomenon of logico-mathematical necessity, the psychological and physiological are parallel and irreducible. All that can be established about the relation between these two levels of phenomena is that implication appears to stand in relation to causality as psychology stands in relation to physiology.[6] Only by joining the principle of psychophysiological parallelism to the notion of equilibrium, could the epistemologist get around the ineluctable division between the causality inherent in the organic, observable, objective aspect of conduct and the implication inherent in the conscious, unobservable, subjective aspect of conduct. Because the principle of equilibrium applied both to causal and implicative domains, it could be used to move between biology and logic. That is why Piaget held psychology to be operatory in nature and why his developmental theory became a theory of transitions from one form of equilibrium to another.

The problem with all of this for Inhelder was that it had to do only with the epistemology of psychology and not with psychology itself. What and where, exactly, were the categories necessary to psychological explanation, i.e., motivation, intentionality, etc.? On these subjects, Piaget, even in his discussion of explanation in psychology, was largely silent.

PIAGET'S EPISTEMIC SUBJECT

If this overview of what Piaget saw as the problematics of psychology seems to leave out many of the concepts central to that science, it must be remembered that he was interested in the "epistemic" rather than the "psychological" subject. Put more bluntly, he was not interested in people or personalities as psychologists understand those terms. Moreover, Piaget would not even have studied the epistemic subject if such study had not been forced upon him by the fact that structures of knowledge are not static. If they were—if they were furnished ready-made and did not change—there would have been no need to speak of a subject at all. That not being the case, it was necessary to allow some such concept to enter, be it "the 'structure of structures', the transcendental ego of *a priorist* theories, or, perhaps, more modestly, the 'self' of psychological theories of synthesis". But, Piaget continues, "lacking this overarching power of synthesis and having no structures at its disposal until it constructs them, the subject will, more modestly but also more realistically, have to be defined in the terms we earlier proposed, as the centre of activity" (Piaget, 1968/1970, p. 70). Elsewhere in the same text Piaget emphasises that he had no interest in the subject in so far as individual "lived experience" was concerned (p. 68). Because the fundamental categories of knowledge are universal, the subject necessary to explain knowledge construction could not be individual. It had, in fact, to be average, so average "that one of the most instructive methods for analysing its actions is to construct, by means of machines or equations, models of 'artificial intelligence' for which a cybernetic theory can then furnish the necessary and sufficient conditions" (p. 69).

No wonder then that Inhelder, a psychologist devoted to the study of the growth of scientific knowledge in children, was discontent. Many passages in *Le cheminement* make clear that her decision to give back the gold—to cease searching for the universal knowledge structures of the epistemic subject—was in large part motivated by a growing conviction that, if Piaget's epistemology was to be convincingly linked to living, breathing subjects, it would have to deal with creatures of a different sort. That is why not far into the first chapter of *Le cheminement*, she asks the question: "What subject for psychology?" (Inhelder & Cellérier, 1992, p. 20).

WHAT SUBJECT FOR PSYCHOLOGY?

To understand Inhelder's answer to this question, it is important, first, to look at her reasons for initiating the research into strategies and procedures. What was it that Piaget's structural approach lacked? What else was needed?

Recall in this respect that the epistemic transformation concerns how certain of the general categories of knowledge, e.g., space, time, causality, number, etc., were constructed, first through the co-ordination of sensorimotor schemes, and then in thought through the co-ordination of their semiotic counterparts. One general question raised by this phenomenon—the question that most interested Piaget— was how such "structures" are created and stabilised, but from the very first Inhelder was interested in going the other way. Piaget wanted to know how structures are created out of schemes; Inhelder wanted to know how schemes are created out of structures. How to bring these two interests together?

It seemed inherent in Piaget's thinking that there was some sort of reciprocal arrangement, that the functioning of structures created new schemes and that co-ordination of the new schemes created new structures. Inhelder's questions were: Why study only half of this cycle? Why study only structuration? Would not a complete epistemology require that one also understand what I will by symmetry call "schematisation", (by which I mean the creation of new schemes through the functioning of structures)?

As history played out, despite her early and ongoing interest in the functional aspects of knowledge, Inhelder spent the bulk of the first 40 years of her career studying its structural aspects. True, even as early as two years after her collaboration with Piaget began, she was applying what had been learned in the structural studies to studies of children at risk for mental retardation (Inhelder, 1943/1968), but this early functional research was constantly interrupted by Piaget's structural projects and proceeded only by fits and starts (Inhelder, 1954, 1955, 1972; Inhelder, Sinclair, & Bovet, 1974). Only with the work on strategies and procedures, begun in the 1970s, was she able to turn her attention full-time to functional studies.

In addition to Piaget's abiding structural interests, there was a second and correlative reason that Inhelder was slow to take up a purely functional approach. This had to do with Piaget's aversion to the idea of finality, a concept he avoided until the development of cybernetics legitimised the concept of finalised processes (Piaget, 1967/1971, p. 189—French edition). Recall in this respect that in *The origins of intelligence in children* (1936/1952, p. 15—French edition), Piaget denounced the doctrine of finalism (which he associated with Aristotle's doctrine of "final cause") and denied that any of the categories in his table linking the categories of understanding to adaptive functions had anything to do with finalised processes.[7] In this, of course, he only fooled himself, as "Goals and Means", listed among the categories of internal organisation, are the heart and soul of functional processes. Even so, 30 years would have to pass before he would grudgingly admit that, in its cybernetic incarnation, the concept of finality had scientific meaning (Piaget, 1967/1971, p. 189—French edition). For Inhelder, the great impediment posed by this struggle with the concept of finalised processes delayed her functional work because the concept of finality is an organiser for many of the concepts necessary to the study of function and many of the concepts central to intuitive psychology, e.g., the concepts of goal, means, intention, etc.

Finally, however, Inhelder's long-standing interest in the functioning of knowledge and the rehabilitation of the notion of finality convinced her to assert that the psychological subject was not identical with or reducible to Piaget's epistemic subject.[8] Because of its structural characterisation, Piaget's strangely unfinalised being did nothing but understand[9] and that in timeless fashion. What psychological explanation required was a goal-directed, motivated agent. What it needed was a subject conceived in functional, teleonomic, and temporal as well as in structural terms.

INHELDER'S CONCLUSIONS

Were space available, it would be interesting to examine some of the experiments reported in Inhelder and Cellérier's book. All that I can do here is to describe the paradigm situation and then move on to a hurried discussion of Inhelder's conclusions.

The basic experimental question posed by Inhelder and her team was, given a child's knowledge structures at some point in time, how did that child use those structures to formulate specific actions in concrete situations and why were children's actions so different in identical situations? The methods employed varied but were all limited to the microgenetic level, that is, to detailed observations of children's reactions to experimental situations. Particular foci of interest were how children interpreted the problems presented, the goal–means structures they set up, the specific means they used to reach the goal, and the way they evaluated progress towards their goal. Just how all of this differed from Piaget's epistemological investigations can perhaps be most succinctly exhibited by posing three oppositions: Where Piaget sought to grasp each subject's nomothetic characteristics, Inhelder and her team sought to capture each child's individual characteristics; where Piaget sought to lay bare the ateleonomic and atemporal structure of the subject's understanding, Inhelder and her team sought to expose the teleonomic and temporal unfolding of each child's action; where Piaget sought to illuminate the construction of knowledge on the macrogenetic level, Inhelder and her team sought to elucidate the construction of know-how on the microgenetic level.

CONCLUSION

Although Inhelder considered the work on strategies and procedures to be unfinished and the problem of discovery unresolved, she also believed that certain things had been achieved, that Piaget's theory had been extended and enriched, and that signposts had been put in place that could guide future investigations. With regard to the achievements, she felt that the way action is guided and the way successive cognitive centrations are controlled had been delineated by experiment. She summarised the central empirical finding as follows: "All children's practical procedures … give evidence of two types of organisation. On the one hand, they are organised top-down, descending from planning to observable 'realities'; on the other, they are organised bottom-up, ascending from observable realities to new heuristics" (Inhelder & Cellérier, 1992, p. 15). With regard to the extension and enrichment of Piaget's theory, she wrote: "Guy Cellérier lays the foundations for psychological constructivism from the interdisciplinary perspective opened up by Piaget's conception of an epistemology founded on biology with psychology as an intermediary. This is a ground-breaking synthesis that … comes directly out of the … switch to functional analysis … In my view, [Cellérier's] theoretical conceptions constitute the most authentic and original extension of Piagetian thought" (Inhelder & Cellérier, 1992, pp. 15–16). And with regard to the future, she ends her work on strategies and procedures with a daring question: "Would it be too audacious to hope that a constructivist cognitivism ought to do two things:

on the one hand, it ought, in the future, to orient thinking about and research on the construction of machines with psychogenetic architecture; on the other hand, it ought to provide an always deeper knowledge of the processes of guidage, of regulation, and of evaluation that underlie children's journeys to discovery?" (Inhelder & Cellérier, 1992, p. 306). In this manner, less dramatic than Brünhilde's, Inhelder renounced the old world order—a decontextualised epistemology opposed to a metaphysically pragmatic cognitive psychology—reclaimed her heritage as a psychologist, and spurred her steed into the flames.

NOTES

1. Inhelder believed that metaphors have no place in science. Still, I like to think that she might accept the correspondences I establish here as "partial morphisms" (see Piaget, 1990/1992).
2. The reader needs to distinguish "schemes" (*schèmes*) from "schemas" (*schémas*) from "schemata". Piaget (1961/1969) distinguishes the first two terms in his foreword to *The mechanisms of perception* where he says: "In our usage, [the terms *schème* and *schéma*] correspond to quite distinct realities, the one operative (a scheme of action in the sense of instrument of generalisation) and the other figurative (figural or topographical schema)" (p. ix). The third term, often used by English and American translators to render *schémes* in English, comes from Kant and actually refers to "categories" which are structures.
3. The definitive exposition of this thesis is found in a posthumous work, *Psychogenesis and history of science* (Piaget & García, 1983/1989).
4. Because of the relation he conceived between psychology and sociology, Piaget also assigned sociology the same bridging function. For Piaget, just as there is no evolutionary biology of individual organisms, there is no ontogenetic development of individual subjects. Evolutionary biologists envision biological adaptation as the result of interactions among individuals within a population and with an environment. That is how Piaget conceived psychosocial adaptation (Piaget, 1967/1995). That some scholars mistakenly believe that Piaget's theory is a theory of individual construction stems from his insistence on the fact that individuals have to be able to make sense of their experience through the use of the assimilatory structures at their disposal (see Brown, 1988b).
5. It is true that Helmholtz, Wundt, and others had begun an empirical psychology of lower mental processes like perception long before Watson, but they did not, in principle, limit psychology to the study of observable behaviour.
6. In the text under examination, Piaget appears to have accepted too readily the then reigning conflation between the conscious (as subjective) and the organic (as objective) and did not carry through his already clearly formulated ideas about the nature of formal and empirical knowledge. In later and better worked-out texts (e.g., Piaget, 1961/1969, 1974), he clearly recognises that both subjective (formal) and objective (empirical) knowledge require consciousness. The distinction rests not on whether consciousness or subjectivity is involved—all knowledge begins in subjective experience—but on what is known. Formal knowledge is no more subjective than objective knowledge is; empirical knowledge is no more objective than formal knowledge is. The difference is that formal knowledge is knowledge of properties of action, while empirical knowledge is knowledge of resistances to action, data out of which the subject constructs the properties of "objects". But these taxonomic problems were never fully worked out, and Piaget, to my mind, never fully understood the nature of psychology or psychological explanation. (For further discussion of these issues, see Brown, 1997.)
7. From the contemporary point of view, all of this is confusing. When Piaget wrote *La naissance de l'intelligence* the idea of goal–means organisation was considered teleological and unacceptable to science. But at the same time that he denied the possibility of final causes, Piaget invoked intentionality—a phenomenon central to psychological finality identified by the recombination of means to reach a goal—as the criterion of intelligence. In 1976, Cellérier (1976/1983) made clear

that this confusion arose from a conflation of the levels of cause and morphogenesis (also see Brown, 1997). Despite his interest in cybernetic ideas and in the work of Papert and Cellérier, Piaget never sorted all of this out in a systematic way and these confusions continued to plague him to the very end.

8. Inhelder lists a third factor that influenced her decision to study strategies and procedures, i.e., the advent of a rambunctious and daring group of students willing to break with the past and strike out in new directions. Because this influence was more of a sociological than an epistemic order, I will not discuss it here.

9. It goes without saying that understanding itself involves finality. Piaget admitted as much in his distinction of presentative, procedural, and operatory *schemes* in the Introduction to *Possibility and necessity*, written at the end of his career (Piaget, 1981/1987, p. 4–5).

REFERENCES

Brown, T. (1988a). Ships in the night. *Human Development*, *31*, 60–64.

Brown, T. (1988b). Why Vygotsky?: The role of social interaction in constructing knowledge. *The Quarterly Newsletter of the Laboratory of Human Cognition*, *10*(4), 111–117.

Brown, T. (1996). Values, knowledge, and Piaget. In E. Reed, E. Turiel, & T. Brown (Eds.), *Values and knowledge* (pp. 137–170). Mahwah, NJ: Lawrence Erlbaum Associates Inc.

Brown, T. (1997). ¿Es la teleonomía una categoría del entendimiento?: La teoría de las atribuciones causales de Piaget y García. [Is teleonomy a category of understanding?: Piaget and García's theory of causal attribution]. In R. García (Ed.), *La epistemología genética y la ciencia contemporánea: Homenaje a Jean Piaget en su centenario* (pp. 297–314). Barcelona: Gedisa.

Cellérier, G. (1983). The historical genesis of cybernetics: Is teleonomy a category of understanding? (T. Brown, Trans.). *Nature and System*, *5*, 211–225. (Original work published 1976)

Cellérier, G. (1979a). Structures cognitives et schèmes d'action. I [Cognitive structures and action schemes. I]. *Archives de Psychologie*, *47*(180), 87–106.

Cellérier, G. (1979b). Structures cognitives et schèmes d'action II [Cognitive structures and action schemes. II]. *Archives de Psychologie*, *47*(181), 107–122.

Inhelder, B. (1954). Les attitudes expérimentales de l'enfant et de l'adolescent [Experimental attitudes in children and adolescents]. *Bulletin de Psychologie*, *7*(5), 272–282.

Inhelder, B. (1955). Patterns of inductive thinking. *Acta Psychologica*, *11*, 217–218. [Proceedings of the 15th international congress of psychology, Montreal, 1954.]

Inhelder, B. (1968). *The diagnosis of reasoning in the mentally retarded* (B. Stephens, Trans.). New York: The John Day Company. (Original work published 1943)

Inhelder, B. (1972). Information processing tendencies in recent experiments in cognitive learning—empirical studies. In S. Farnham-Diggory (Ed.), *Information processing in children* (pp. 103–114). London: Academic Press.

Inhelder, B. (1989). Bärbel Inhelder (autobiography). In G. Lindzey (Ed.), *A history of psychology in autobiography* (pp. 208–243). Stanford, CA: Stanford University Press.

Inhelder, B., Ackermann-Valladão, E., Blanchet, A., Karmiloff-Smith, A., Kilcher-Hagedorn, H., Montangero, J., & Robert, M. (1976). Des structures cognitives aux procédures de découverte: Esquisse de recherches en cours [From cognitive structures to discovery procedures: An outline of ongoing research]. *Archives de Psychologie*, *44*(171), 57–72.

Inhelder, B., & Cellérier, G. (Eds.). (1992). *Le cheminement des découvertes de l'enfant*. Neuchâtel: Delachaux & Niestlé. [To appear in English as *Children's journeys of discovery*, T. Brown, E. Ackermann, & M. Ferrari (Eds.), Hillsdale NJ: Lawrence Erlbaum Associates Inc.]

Inhelder, B., & Piaget, J. (1979). Procédures et structures [Procedures and structures]. *Archives de Psychologie, 47*, 165–176.

Inhelder, B., Sinclair, H., & Bovet, M. (1974). *Learning and the development of cognition* (S. Wedgwood, Trans.). Cambridge, MA: Harvard University Press.

Piaget, J. (1950). L'explication en psychologie [Explanation in psychology]. In J. Piaget, *Introduction à l'épistémologie génétique, Tome III: La pensée biologique, la pensée psychologique, et la pensée sociologique* (pp. 133–186). Paris: Presses Universitaires de France.

Piaget, J. (1952). *The origins of intelligence in children* (M. Cook, Trans.). New York: International Universities Press. (Original work published 1936.)

Piaget, J. (1967a). Le système des sciences [The system of sciences]. In J. Piaget, (Ed.), *Encyclopédie de la Pléiade. Logique et connaissance scientifique* (pp. 1151–1224). Dijon: Éditions Gallimard.

Piaget, J. (1967b). *The psychology of intelligence* (M. Piercy & D.E. Berlyne, Trans.). London: Kegan Paul. (Original work published 1947)

Piaget, J. (1968). Explanation in psychology and psycho-physiological parallelism (J. Chambers, Trans.). In P. Fraisse & J. Piaget (Eds.), *Experimental psychology: Its scope and method. I. History and method* (pp. 153–191). New York: Basic Books. (Original work published 1963)

Piaget, J. (1969). *The mechanisms of perception* (G.N. Seagrim, Trans.). New York: Basic Books. (Original work published 1961)

Piaget, J. (1971). *Biology and knowledge* (B. Walsh, Trans.). Chicago: University of Chicago Press. (Original work published 1968)

Piaget, J. (1970). *Structuralism* (C. Maschler, Trans.). New York: Basic Books. (Original work published 1967)

Piaget, J. (1970). The place of the sciences of man in the system of sciences. In *Main trends in psychology* (pp. 1–57). Paris: UNESCO.

Piaget, J. (1974). *La prise de conscience* [The grasp of consciousness]. Paris: Presses Universitaires de France.

Piaget, J. (1980). *Experiments in contradiction* (D. Coltman, Trans.). Chicago: University of Chicago Press. (Original work published 1974)

Piaget, J. (1985). *The equilibration of cognitive structures* (T. Brown & K. J. Thampy, Trans.). Chicago: University of Chicago Press. (Original work published 1975)

Piaget, J. (1987). *Possibility and necessity: Vol. 1. The role of possibility in cognitive development* (H. Feider, Trans.). Minneapolis, MN: University of Minnesota Press. (Original work published 1981)

Piaget, J. (1992). *Morphisms and categories* (T. Brown, Ed. & Trans.). Hillsdale, NJ: Lawrence Erlbaum Associates Inc. (Original work published 1990)

Piaget, J. (1995). *Sociological studies* (L. Smith, Ed., T. Brown et al., Trans.). London: Routledge. (Original work published 1967)

Piaget, J., & García, R. (1980). *Les formes élémentaires de la dialectique* [Elementary forms of dialectics]. Paris: Éditions Gallimard.

Piaget, J., & García, R. (1989). *Psychogenesis and the history of science* (H. Feider, Trans.). New York: Columbia University Press. (Original work published 1983)

Wagner, R. (1865). *Götterdämmerung.*

CHAPTER TWELVE

The experimental approach of children and adolescents [1]

Bärbel Inhelder
Bulletin de Psychologie, 1954, 7(5), 272–282

Translated by Trevor Bond, James Cook University, with the permission of the editor of *Bulletin de Psychologie.*

1. THE PROBLEMS

The problem that has occupied us for a number of years is that of the formation of inductive reasoning. Yet another research project devoted to the origin of knowledge, you are going to say! Hasn't the Genevan School, guided by the theories of M. Piaget, already explored the origins of the principal cognitive instruments of the child, such as its logic, its conception of number and space, its notions of physical quantities, of speed and time, its understanding of chance and probabilities? Actually, we know in general terms the child's conception of the world and the instruments of its adaptation to the real world, however, we are fully conscious of the fact that this picture contains two considerable gaps which concern, on the one hand, the functional aspect of thought, and adolescent reasoning, on the other.

In reality, it is not enough for the child to acquire the instruments of knowledge; he must still know how to put them to work. And yet, if today we understand the structures of the child's thought, in large part we ignore its functioning.

How is the child going to use these intellectual instruments, the ideas and mental operations in an experimental situation, that is to say, in situations where the child itself is going to experiment, and not just to respond to the questions that are posed by an investigator? How is he going to actualise the structures, and what role will each particular step in reasoning play in the whole process? The work on operational analysis calls for an essay on functional synthesis as well.

But there is more. The research on the origin of reasoning should not stop at childhood. It is clear that the forms of reasoning evolve beyond childhood and are subjected to profound transformation at the onset of adolescence. What is exactly the nature of the reasoning process which links the thought of the child with that of the adolescent and how do we explain its evolution?

In order to make our contribution to filling these two gaps, we have undertaken, with the collaboration of the research assistants and several groups of students of the Institute Jean-Jacques Rousseau, a collection of investigations into the origins of induction. We now know that the achievement of inductive method is contemporaneous with the formation of the deductive structures of formal thought. There appears to be mutual reliance and integration between the functional aspect, characterising the inductive method, and the structural aspect of formal deduction. It is, actually, the study of induction, which has led us to the heart of the operational mechanisms of formal thought, and, inversely, it is the operational analysis, which clarifies the techniques of the experimental method. The two aspects of our study then become one and finally converge towards the same, single goal: to analyse the workings of the intellectual instruments.

2. DEFINITION

How can one define the inductive method? It is a general experimental approach and is not merely a particular system of operations opposed to deduction. All perfect and rigorous reasoning is necessarily deductive. As Piaget showed in his *Introduction to Genetic Epistemology*, induction is sometimes preparation for deduction, sometimes a method tht calls upon an *ensemble* of particular deduction. According to the convincing argument of Lalande, induction is an experimental approach which consists of closely examining the real world about its deductibility: an approach which is expressed in the language of our adolescents in the following fashion: "there must be a relationship, but it's necessary to experiment in order to know what sort", or even: "I want to see if what I think is correct". We will call inductive the method of the child or adolescent, which organises an experiment for the purpose of working out laws and verifying experimentally their generality.

The question then is to know how the child and the adolescent go about this experimental organisation which consists of carefully examining the real world.

3. METHODS OF INVESTIGATING AND ANALYSING INDIVIDUAL CASES

The psychological study of the origins of inductive reasoning requires the use of tasks which provoke the free discovery of laws and causes. Far from suggesting the solution to a problem, each type of experiment elicits active research. Given that our purpose is the knowledge of inductive processes rather than their products, the tasks must encourage the invention and organisation of the experiment, the interpretation of its results and their verification.

What is important for us to know, is the psychological process of the research. Consequently, the tasks allow the discovery not only of the one correct solution, but all the levels of partial solution going from practical success to the elaboration of partial laws and culminating in the discovery of the general law. As well, the tasks stimulate the whole range of verification procedures from simple repetition of one event to the demonstration or proof of a law.

In order to be suitable for all developmental levels the tasks are easily handled but at the same time amenable to allowing complex discoveries.

In all inductive processes, the transfer of one discovery to the next plays an essential role. This is why we have arranged groups of tasks, which permit the generalisation of partial discoveries by way of analogy and transfer.

The inductive elaboration of the facts and laws occurs by way of a continual confrontation of reasoning with the data from the experiment. Reasoning in physics cannot proceed without this mutual reliance between thought and things. Therefore, we have chosen our tasks from several domains of physics (optics, hydrostatics, mechanics) and chemistry.

The tasks are the background upon which the psychological approach to induction unfolds. We have used them to examine individually more than 1,600 children and adolescents drawn from the public schools of Geneva and the International School. It goes without saying that no subject knew in advance the laws to be discovered nor the appearance of the devices. But it is clear that the solution to each problem implies an undeniable cultural and educational contribution.

We will now describe several types of tasks and analyse by their means certain features of the experimental approaches of adolescents of 14–15 years.

The first group of tasks permit us to study the *discovery of physical invariants*. According to common sense, the elementary laws of physics are discovered by observation and generalisation. But it is easy to show that the discovery of a physical law presupposes much more than observation and generalisation: it always presupposes the construction of invariants, that is to say, the discovery of a new relationship which is not given as such in the experiment.

A. The equality of angles of incidence and reflection

It seemed interesting to us to study this law of optics by transposing it into the domain of mechanics. How does the child, by means of games of billiards, go about discovering that the angle of incidence which the trajectory of a marble forms with a projection wall is equal to its angle of reflection? The problem, of course, is posed in a concrete fashion. We successively place a little target figure at various positions of the game and simply ask the children and adolescents to aim at it. The marble is projected by a propelling device against the reflecting wall. For the young children, the game is limited to aiming at the figure. For those from 7 to 11 years, it permits the discovery of the covariation of causes and effects, while the adolescents succeed in extracting the constant, i.e., the law of equality of angles.

Actually, towards 14–15 years, the adolescent from our *milieu* goes beyond the interpretation of facts by genuine construction. He constructs and imagines a line perpendicular to the plane of reflection. As a boy of this age put it: "If there were a line here (he traces a perpendicular line), the marble would come back on itself. There would be zero angle. The more the figure approaches the launcher, the more the launcher must also approach the figure. It's necessary to think in straight lines, whatever distance the lever moves in one direction, you find the same distance in the other direction, the two angles are equal."[2] To the construction of the perpendicular add also the hypothesis of a reciprocal implication of the two inclinations, leading to the construction of a constant: the equality of angles.

B. The inclined plane

The experiment of the falling bodies along an inclined plane poses an analogous problem. It is presented in the form of a game: Marbles of different masses roll down the length of a plane where the angle of the incline is variable. By the action of a springboard, the marbles make a parabolic trajectory and fall into one of the compartments, which the child can open or close at will.

For the young children, the experiment consists simply of getting the marbles into one or other of the compartments. For those from 7 to 11 years, it is about relating the starting and finishing points of the trajectory, that is establishing the correspondences one by one between causes and effects. Without working out the mathematical law, all the adolescents succeed, at least, in understanding that the length of the trajectory of the marble is a function of the height of its fall, by excluding variations in its mass. That was expressed by a lad of 16 years of age in the following fashion: "To always end up in the same compartment, whatever the slope, it (the marble) must always leave from the same height."

C. The conservation of motion in a horizontal plane

Without expecting the adolescents to make a completely spontaneous discovery of the principle demonstrated by Galileo and Descartes,[3] we observe however that the basic premise of the conservation of motion can impose itself virtually as a necessity in certain experiments of which the following one is very easy to organise.

Take a ball rolling along a horizontal plane propelled by a spring device. Without any external hindrance to slow its progress, it will maintain uniform rectilinear motion. The hindrances are the factors of friction: friction as a function of the weight of the marbles, friction due to the resistance of the air, itself a function of the size of the marbles and, finally, the irregularities of the plane itself. Children and adolescents can also launch pairs of marbles differing in weight or in volume, in order to discover the factors of friction on the one hand and to postulate the principle of conservation of motion on the other.

The young ones—even those of school age—look for thousands of reasons to explain the marbles' movements. At the level of formal thought, conversely, an explicit reversal of the problem takes place. Certain adolescents do not ask why the ball moves, but rather why it stops. A 14½-year-old boy said to us, for example: "Theoretically, the marbles should go to the end, but in practice you never see that." Astonished by the dispersion of the balls along the horizontal plane, he seeks to explain the different factors of friction: "If you launch all the marbles with the same momentum, their stopping depends on weight, air friction, and the plane, which is not always truly horizontal. If these factors didn't interfere, the marbles would continue to roll." It is clear that such explanations result from a rather diffuse environmental contribution. However, the personal elaboration is undeniable. Perhaps the recent discoveries in physics have brought about in our environment what Koyré calls a sort of intellectual mutation.[4]

A *second group* of tasks is designed for children and adolescents to discover the *notions of the equilibrium of forces*, or the systems of actions and reactions.

A. The balance experiment

The law of levers, arranged in the form of a set of scales, has the advantage of being known by children of all ages. In our school playgrounds and parks, young children already play on the see-saw and discover from personal experience the elementary laws of equilibrium.

We have arranged the experiment into two different forms, the first adapted for young children, the second more interesting for adolescents. For the young children, we have constructed a set of wooden scales, from the lever-arms are suspended cradles in which one or more dolls of different weights can be seated to make it balance. The young children then go about finding the conditions for balancing in the case where one doll would like to act as the counterbalance for several others, and the case where two dolls of different weights would like to balance the scales together. For the older children and the adolescents, we have constructed Meccano scales and provided a series of packets, identical in appearance but having differing weights, with our subjects having to determine the relative weights. The two types of experiments allow the children and adolescents to discover, partially or completely, the law of levers and even to uncover the principle of the equality of work. While the young children do not succeed in dissociating the respective roles of weight and distance, the children from 7 to 11 years of age succeeding in dissociating the two notions, but only the adolescents discover the general law. As a 14-year-old boy said, a little confused: "The bigger the distance is, the smaller the weight should be. You put the heavier weight at the fraction that represents the lighter weight; it stays in place, the forces compensate." Adolescents also succeed in conceptualising the law of levers as a unique system of transformations. Engaging an integrated whole of operations of inversion and reciprocity, they often show themselves even capable of discovering the equality of work.

B. Equilibrium of mechanical forces on an inclined plane

The equilibrium of weight on an inclined plane is frequently arranged as a trolley drawn by means of a string up an inclined plane of variable height and held in place by means of a counterweight. The system is in equilibrium when P = M.sin alpha.

The children as well as the adolescents amuse themselves by filling and emptying the trolley, making it ascend and descend the track, and finally determining the conditions of equilibrium. It is towards 14–15 years, but not before, that a certain number of adolescents first succeed in discovering that the system is in equilibrium when h/H = p/M (the partial height of the rail [h] is to its maximum height [H] as the weight [p] is to the mass of the trolley [M]).

A 15-year-old girl says: "The trolley, which weighs 4 units, is in equilibrium with 1 single counterweight when the rail is at a quarter of the maximum height, the ratios are then equal."

C. Two experiments incorporating hydrostatic equilibrium

1. *Connected vessels.* The experiment of the connected vessels appeared to us, at first glance, too easy for adolescents. To our astonishment, the general law and a rough explanation were discovered only towards 13–14 years of age. Our game consisted of a system of moveable vessels. In the first instance, the child has to make the water reach a particular floor of a house.[5] The child, after experimenting with the uncovered display, must find a way to make the water reach an exact level, even when that level is hidden. The water containers can be changed; sometimes they contain the same quantity of water, sometimes different quantities.

2. A second device is copied from a model of an *hydraulic press.* Children and adolescents have at their disposal a system of connected vessels and a piston to which weights from a graduated series can be added. In addition, they have two liquids with different densities, such as water and alcohol. They study the displacement of the liquid as a function of the weights placed on the piston. The pressure exerted by the weights and the piston is directly proportional to the displacement of the liquid, and the displacement of the liquid is inversely proportional to its density.

Again, it is the adolescents, and they alone, who understand that the equilibrium in this hydrostatic experiment constitutes a system of forces acting in opposition. Towards the age of 14–15 years, certain adolescents explain the principles of equilibrium in a clear and simple fashion: "The apparatus doesn't descend or ascend. The pressures in the bottom of the tube are equal. A larger weight on the piston is balanced by a larger column of water. The pressure transmits itself completely. When the liquid is lighter (one of lower density), the piston encounters less resistance and pushes more." The principle of reciprocity between actions and reactions is then discovered.

A *third group* of tasks prompt the discovery of *proportional ratios*. Although implicit in each of the preceding experiments, proportionality can be studied in an explicit fashion in the experiment of the projection of shadows. We provide several rings which have diameters of 5, 10, 15, and 20 cms mounted on stems. The child is asked to project a single shadow on the screen. In order to do this, he must place the stems of the rings in holes in a metre long board. For young children, of course, the task consists of just making the single shadow, while the adolescents have, as well, to discover the general law according to which a classmate could succeed at once with the experiment, without any prior trials. Actually, adolescents of 14–15 years reveal themselves capable of discovering the law of proportionality. As one of them expressed it: "You can take any distance, providing that there is the same ratio between the diameters and the distances." Certain adolescents work out the law according to which the shadow is directly proportional to the diameters of the rings, and inversely proportional to their distance from the light-source.

Proportionality is a general schema, which forms only at the level of formal thought. Does the schema occur independently of experience? We do not believe so, because the schema has been suggested by it and really seems to be the result of a long series of experimentations and concrete manipulations. However, the operational scheme of proportionality for its part, goes beyond concrete experience for its structure.

A *fourth group* of tasks, finally, is aimed at allowing children and adolescents to discover the method of experimental verification, which relies on the variation, and systematic combination of the factors in play.

A. Flexibility

By what experimental methods and thought processes is the adolescent going to discover that the flexibility of a metal rod depends on several factors (its composition = coefficient of elasticity, length, thickness, cross-sectional shape and force applied)? It goes without saying that you do not ask that question in the abstract. Only tasks, which are easily managed and amusing, interest children and adolescents. The child is given a large basin of water, a game of metal rods which differ in quality (there are rods of steel and brass), in length, in cross-sectional shape and area (there are thick and thin rods, round and square rods). The child or adolescent is also given three little figures of different weights. For the young children, all this represents a lake with moveable bridges and fishermen, while the same device gives the adolescent the possibility of experimenting and verifying his hypotheses. The rods can be fixed on the edge of the basin in a horizontal position. Figures attached to the free end of the rods exert a flexing force perpendicular to the surface of the water. We simply ask the children and adolescents to experiment until each of the bridges touches the level of the water. By way of example, we move a figure to the water level. We observe the manner in which the child chooses the rods and adjusts them, and we seek to know if he succeeds in making a series of bridges according to their flexibility. If the child or adolescent invokes several flexibility factors, we ask him to provide an experimental proof. We stick close to this language: "I will believe you only when you have proved to me that the length is a factor in flexibility, or that the shape of the rod plays a role, etc." We leave the maximum of initiative to the children and adolescents, and record carefully the manner in which they organise the experiment and spontaneously execute the proof.

Towards 15 years of age, but not before, the majority of adolescents, without any special introduction, succeed in the execution of a rigorous proof. Here are, for example, the intentions of an adolescent, who verbally states each of the steps of his thoughts: "I am trying to see if shape plays a role. From amongst all the rods, I have chosen two, which are the same length, the same metal, the same thickness. I attach them both in the same way. Of course, I have each rod the same weight. So I push with the same force. You see: the round rod touches the water level. You can easily see: either the square rod will do the same, and then shape is not important, or the square rod remains below the water-level, which will prove that shape is important." He experiments and exclaims: " Ah! I see: the square rod remains below the water level, I conclude from that, that the squares are more flexible than the rounds, all the other factors being equal." He proceeds in the same manner for each of the five factors.

This behaviour shows us that the adolescent is capable of acquiring a rigorous experimental method, which consists of varying only one single factor at a time. Why does this method, so simple in appearance, form so late? It is because it requires a more advanced level of formal thought. The adolescent at this advanced level knows how to carefully examine the experiment [see Note 1]. In order to test if the length is a factor determining flexibility, the adolescent chooses rods that differ only in length; everything else is held equal. To test if the sectional shape of a rod plays a role in flexibility, he chooses two rods with different sectional shapes, everything else is held equal, and so on, for each of the factors. The experimental method and rigorous verification presupposes two mechanisms of thought: on the one hand, the systematic combination of all the factors in play, and, the neutralisation or compensation of these factors, on the other.

B. The pendulum

An analogous, but much simpler, experiment can be arranged by means of a pendulum. The intention is for children or adolescents to discover that the frequency of a pendulum is a function of its length, to the exclusion of all other invoked factors, such as, for example, the suspended weight, the momentum imparted or even the height of its drop.

Towards 14–15 years, but not earlier, adolescents correctly test all the possible hypotheses by combining them methodically. In varying the length, they take care to maintain the weight, the amplitude and momentum constant. In varying the weight, they hold constant the length of the string, as well as all the other factors, etc. The famous method, familiarly called "method of all other things equal",[6] then always has recourse to combinatorial operations on the one hand and neutralisation or compensation of factors on the other.

C. The mixture of liquids

We have incessantly underlined the importance of the combinatorial method, the acquisition of which appears to us as characteristic of the level of adolescence. It seems then interesting to examine this method in its own right, and for that, we have used a chemistry problem. We present to the children or adolescents five flasks all containing colourless liquids: 1 concentrated sulphuric acid,[7] 2 water, 3 oxygenated water, 4 sodium thiosulphate crystals, 5 potassium iodide.

The mixture of three of these liquids (1+3+5) produces colouring, while liquid 4 is a reducing agent and liquid 2 is neutral. Without the child's knowing how, we make a coloured sample and simply ask him to reproduce it by means of some of the liquids at his disposal. The experiment then allows the children and adolescents a whole range of easy and concrete manipulations. With the solution found either empirically or methodically, we ask the children or adolescents to indicate to us the role of each of the five liquids.

While the children have a tendency to mix unsystematically the different liquids, the adolescents seek to determine the role of each and to this purpose they devote themselves to establishing the complete set of possible combinations. In order to explore, for example the role of the neutral element and that of the reducing agent, one of the young girls investigated made two successive hypotheses: "Either they are neutral or they have a colouring effect." She immediately took the initiative to verify the two hypotheses and compare then the two mixtures: on one hand 1+3+5+4 and on the other 1+3+5+2. This comparison actually allowed her to come to the decision: 4 is the decolouring agent and 2 is neutral.

The combinatorial method has been well and truly suggested by the concrete experience of the mixtures. However, it goes beyond experience, by the fact that it consists of drawing up an exhaustive table of all the possible combinations. More or less fortunate trial and error can, in certain cases, already result in the effective mixture; but when this trial and error fails, or when it becomes too complicated to memorise each of the successive mixtures, all that is left is to adopt a methodical procedure which, although it appears more demanding at first glance, reveals itself as more rational in the long term. But there is more: each time that the goal is not only to succeed in making the colour but also to determine the factors at work, it is necessary to have recourse to a combinatorial scheme, which alone permits (the experimenter) to envisage the whole set of possible combinations.

After having reviewed several of the tasks and analysed some of the reasoning typical of the level of adolescents of 14–15 years, we will now discuss the results as a whole.

4. DISCUSSION OF THE RESULTS

The experimental approaches can be analysed from two complementary view-points: that of the functioning of inductive reasoning, and that of the operational structures.

A. Functional analysis

To give a true picture of the formation of experimental approaches we are going to proceed by cross-sectional and longitudinal analyses.

Cross-sectional analyses

The cross-sectional view shows us that within each of the phases of development, several interdependent factors are at work. In each child's experimenting, one can distinguish the motives of action, an experimental strategy,[8] an interpretation of the data, and methods of verification.

By motives, we mean the purposes of the research activities that a child or adolescent adopts in the course of its successive experimental trials.

The strategy refers to all of the steps intended to organise the experiment.

The interpretation, which is, from the outset, an interpretation of reality, consists of elaborating facts and laws from the results of the actions which a child or adolescent exercises on the objects.

Verification, finally, has the role of confronting expectations with the interpreted results.

These four factors: motive, strategy, interpretation, and verification are not merely juxtaposed but always united. The motives orient the strategy; the strategy determines the interpretation, and this necessitates the steps of verification. It goes without saying that this has nothing to do with some rigorous temporal order. An observation or interpretation can be the starting point for research or can spark new motives for action. These four factors are going however to facilitate for us the developmental analysis.

Longitudinal analyses

Although the evolution of experimental behaviour is revealed as continuous, we observe however moments of profound transformation which marks the appearance of a new stage of development. Three important stages can be distinguished.

The first, called the stage of *imaginative (play) techniques* extends from 4 to about 6½ or 7 years.

The motives for action are activity for effect, accompanied often by the pleasure of being the cause. In the chemical colouring experiment, the child mixes several liquids in a single container, simply to see what is produced. In the inclined plane task, the child rolls the marble along the groove, excited to be the cause of the flight of the ball which he then recovers from one of the compartments. However, he does not seek to change the course of events: each result enchants him, what happens, must happen.

Strategy, at this lower level, corresponds to a sort of global intervention into the real world. In the billiard task, the child shoots more and more strongly by means of the spring action, convinced that without having to change direction he would hit the little figurine. In the same spirit again, he projects the marble along the horizontal plane in the hope that by dint of magic and patience, all of them will get to the end-goal.

The interpretation of the experiment consists essentially of finding in the real world the ideas that the young child has already has of it. Sure, he is already capable of noting the success or failure of a global action. But he is not yet capable of objectively interpreting the experiment. Thus, in the game of billiards, he sees whether or not he has hit the figurine, but he sometimes seems incapable of seeing the rectilinear trajectory of the propelled marble.

Verification must be called pseudo-verification, because the child remains more or less impermeable to the experiment. He does not feel any need to confront the different outcomes obtained; he explains each particular result by itself. If a natural explanation is not obvious, the child invokes the caprices of nature. On the inclined plane, a marble jumps more or less distant, because it is more or less tired; the child refuses to admit the equality of the levels of water in the connected vessels.

During the first stage, the child also feels, for the greater part of the time, a lively pleasure in acting on the device and seeing what happens, but he learns nothing more as a result of the experiment itself.

The second stage is characterised by the formation of concrete techniques. It extends from 7 to 10½ or 11 years.

The motives of action are oriented toward the discovery of practical laws. The child longer acts just to see what happens, but in order to find a new relationship. It is no longer his need to play, which takes precedence, it is his need to intervene effectively in the external world. He then uses the device with a view to producing a technical (precise) action. More and more often, the child says, "I would like to know how the machine works." For example, in the experiment of the inclined plane, he asks himself how to make the marble jump into a chosen compartment. The need for effective action orients research towards the discovery of partial laws.

The strategy at this level, becomes a differentiated and no longer global intervention in the experiment. The child seeks more and more often to establish the relationships between causes and effects. The search for causality orients him to the establishment of co-variations. For example, in the experiment of the transmission of forces across a liquid, the child discovers that the more the piston is loaded the more the level of liquid is displaced in an open system of connected vessels. He does not yet discover general laws, but a series of particular relationships.

The interpretation of the experiment gains in objectivity. Actually, interpreting the experiment represents a whole group of concrete operations such as establishing correspondences, classifications, seriations, counting and measuring. The child is capable of saying that the biggest rings project the biggest shadow, and conversely, that the more the rings are moved away from the light source, the smaller is their shadow. It is between 8 and 10 years of age that the child is found to be closest to the facts. At an earlier age, he has a tendency to deform them; at a more advanced age, he tends to go beyond them.

At this level, verification corresponds to the degree of generalisation of the discovered laws. The child is no longer satisfied in observing a single fact or a single causal relation. He seeks to generalise and to reproduce the same phenomenon under the same conditions. For example, after having rolled a single marble along the inclined plane, he would take a second and a third marble of different weights in order to verify if each has the same effect or if the effect varies as a function of mass. Verification at the level of the second stage consists then of passing from the particular case to the general case and taking account of the exceptions. But what is still missing at this level is the systematic variation of the factors in play.

Experimentation at the level of the concrete techniques is already very rich. The child is capable of working out the partial laws for himself, of confronting his predictions with experience and to learn anew from an error. But you cannot expect a systematic process of experimentation or a view of the entire problem. He can act and intervene in the experiment, make a series of observations, but he cannot yet direct the research.

The third stage will be characterised by *techniques*, which one can without exaggeration call *scientific*. This third stage really begins with pre-adolescence but it reaches its completion only towards 14–15 years. It is, above all, characterised by the transformation of motives, strategies, interpretation, and verification procedures.

The motives consist of searching for truth and not only dominating the experimental device. Actually, the majority of adolescents do not rush into action but think about it before intervening. They say to us, for example, "I have a theory but I cannot reveal it to you yet. I would like to verify it." There are those who outline a group of implications: "If my idea is correct, this or that must happen." The experimental device becomes more and more an occasion for reasoning. It prompts demonstration.

The experimental strategy becomes optimised only at the level of adolescence. In effect, only the adolescent is capable of plotting a plan of action and making an inventory of the possible factors. Take the experiment of the combination of liquids. While the child at the second level made a series of trials and errors, the adolescent straightaway seeks to draw up a plan, which embraces all of the possible combinations. He endeavours to exhaust all the combinations of two, then all the combinations of three, and finally all the combinations of four elements. It is due to this systematic strategy, embracing all the possibilities, that he will be capable of methodically and rapidly reaching the solution to the problem. In other experiments, the strategy or the action-plan consists of seeking not to experiment on all the cases but to make a choice of the crucial situations or the convincing cases. Think about the experiment of the trolley on the inclined plane. It will be actually useless, not to say impossible, to proceed successively to research all of the equilibrium positions of the trolley. The better strategy consists of extrapolating: put the rail in the horizontal position and, even if that means having to look at the intermediate positions.

The interpretation corresponds to translating the concrete data into abstract notions. The adolescent seeks, for example, to use geometrical systems of reference to translate the physical data. It is the way that, in the experiment of the falling bodies, he succeeds in considering an inclined plane, not only as a function of its infinitely variable angle of inclination, but also as a function of its height. The interpretation finally takes account of the experimental fluctuations. In the experiment called the "piston", the adolescent works out very well the displacement zones for each of the liquids of different densities. He succeeds also in establishing not only general laws, but also allowances for their probable fluctuations.[9]

The methods of verification are particularly important during the third phase of development. They consist essentially of not being limited to a global interpretation of the facts but to proceed to a complete dissociation of all the factors in play. Thus in the flexibility experiment, the adolescent no longer contents himself with noticing that one rod is more flexible than another; he takes care to work in conditions such that each of the factors will be isolated by neutralising all the other interdependent factors. This systematic variation of factors is actually acquired only very late. What takes precedence in the whole of the verification procedures is the rigorous research, which seems to be absent at the preceding levels.

In résumé, the transformation of behaviour, which takes place during adolescence, is marked by a noteworthy change in the motives of action. Compared to the child, the adolescent intervenes much more actively in the experiment. He questions (cross-examines) the device, from the start with a series of questions. His research takes more and more the form of a dialogue with the experiment. One can even say that the motives of the research consist of deducing reality and, if reality resists, of questioning it about its deducibility. Seeking to deduce reality means discovering its constants. But in this search, the global interpretation of the experiment does not always answer the question that was posed. The facts are often intertwined. Confronted with experimental complexity, the adolescent does not give in so easily. He often imagines a genuine strategy. He draws up an inventory of the possible factors. He systematically dissociates the interdependent factors and varies them one by one. The interpretation then plays a more restricted but so much more precise role. It consists of selecting existing factors and excluding absent factors. The interpretation answers 'yes' or answers 'no' or it even replies 'the question was badly put'. Not satisfied with having selected the possible factors, the adolescent seeks to demonstrate or to prove the necessity of their presence. He is smitten with verification. Thus, he discovers at some point the method of systematic variation of factors, all other things being equal. In certain cases, without any specific instruction at school, he searches to discover proportional relationships. The procedures of demonstration and proof always rely on an exhaustive combination of all the experimental variables. The command of this combinatorial method seems to be a good indicator of the accomplishment of formal thought.

B. Structural analysis

Without wishing to redraw the picture of the concrete and formal operations put to work in the course of the experimentation, we will content ourselves in asking if the more highly evolved discoveries made by adolescents of 14–15 years with regard to our tasks, are supported by a core common structural nucleus, comparable to that which confers coherence on the concrete operations of the child, but, however, different from it.

Let us take up again in this regard the forms of reasoning characteristic of the level of adolescence, the proportionality schemes, the notions of equilibrium of forces and combinatorial analysis.

The adolescent, as opposed to the child, succeeds in using the operational scheme of proportions. The workings of this scheme are revealed as a new thought structure, a structure inaccessible to the child. In the experiment on projection, the children succeed only in effecting the concrete operations such as seriating the diameters of the rings from smallest to largest and even that of seriating the distances, which separate the rings from the light-source. The adolescent goes much further and becomes capable of making a new synthesis in establishing a relationship between these two ordered series. The proportionality scheme is supported by a separate operation, which synthesises the previously elaborated concrete operations. By this fact, it corresponds to an operation of the second power. The proportionality scheme, as M. Piaget has shown in his work on *The transformations of logical operations*,[10] is a consequence of the notion of a group of four transformations of propositions, in which all the operations of a system can be transformed, each into the others, according to the laws of reciprocity and inversion.

The formation of the notion of physical equilibrium, such as the system of action and reaction of forces, is supported in the same way by a four-group of transformations composed of the identity, reciprocal, inverse, and correlative operations. In the experiment of the transmission of forces through liquids, there is indeed a direct operation when you place the weighted piston on one of the arms of the connected vessels. There is an inverse action (= negation) when you lift it off. The inverse operation nullifies the direct action and vice versa. There is a reciprocal operation when you understand the reaction of the liquid as a force of resistance working in the opposite direction. Hydrostatic equilibrium is then a reciprocity (equal and opposing actions). There is, finally, a correlative operation (by definition, the inverse of the reciprocal) when one understands that the density, on the one hand, increases or decreases the resistance (inversion), but on the other hand remains distinct from the resistance.

It goes without saying that the adolescent who shows himself as being capable of understanding by himself such a system of operations is not conscious of the group structure. However, everything happens as if there exists a sort of congruence between the available operations of the mental structures and the system of physical operations that the adolescent attempts to separate and understand. At the very least, we can make the hypothesis that the adolescent assimilates the physical operations in play to a system of possible transformations—a system, which corresponds to the general structures of his formal reasoning.

The schema of operations that the adolescent uses each time he seeks to establish a complete picture of the possible factors, or associations with a view to making an experimental proof, calls upon combinatorial analysis in its qualitative form. In the example of the chemical colourings, the child still proceeds only by empirical mixtures or by juxtaposed pairings, but the adolescent embraces the entirety of the possible combinations and succeeds, sooner or later, in forming a system of combinations. In the same fashion the adolescent who handles the method of the systematic variation of factors, all other things being equal, has recourse to a combinatorial system. We already know that a combinatorial system relies upon a network or lattice structure, a structure homologous with, and yet distinct from, the group structure.

But we can go further and admit that all hypothetico deductive thought is governed by the logic of propositions and which, by this same fact, go beyond the real in order to embrace the possible, rely on the formal structures of the group and lattice. We can then conclude that the operational schemes characteristic of the experimental approaches of the adolescent rely on a core of structures, which, according to M. Piaget, obey a law of double reversibility, reuniting in one whole, all the operations of inversion and reciprocity which, in the concrete reasoning of the child from 7–11 years, exist only in a separated and juxtaposed state (simple reversibility). Thus, the structures of the experimental reasoning of the adolescent are also larger and more mobile than those characterising the reasoning of the child. They integrate the concrete operations in a new synthesis which confers on thought almost unlimited possibilities of construction and a progressive detachment in relation to content, from which their formal character is derived.

5. CONCLUSION

It results from these facts that the acquisition of the experimental method is due to the interdependence of two factors: the cultural climate and schooling on the one hand, and the formation of a new psychological behaviour, on the other. We do not intend to reduce the role of the *milieu*, which seems to us of prime importance in the elaboration of objectivity. It is clear that experimental behaviour develops only in a cultural and social milieu, which favours the exchange of ideas and invites confronting points of view. But, on the other hand, it really seems that even in favourable conditions, a scientific, experimental approach appears only late, because it presupposes the prior elaboration of a whole group of elementary intellectual instruments. The possession of these concrete instruments is not always enough to allow an adolescent to run his own experiments without problem. A new behaviour imposes itself: that which Poincaré called the 'game-plan' (when comparing the progress of deduction to that of a game of chess, he contrasted the 'game-plan' with the rules determining any particular move). This game-plan presupposes an organisation of cognitive instruments as a function of new goals, which give rise to new intellectual structures. These structures are formed only towards the age of 14–15 years. Our results lead us to believe that there is interdependence between the goals assigned to actions and the instruments put to work. In other words, the curiosity of the adolescents for scientific truths calls upon an ensemble of formal operations, which pose, in their turn, new problems. Towards 14–15 years gifted adolescents seem then to possess the psychological dispositions necessary for the acquisition of the inductive experimental method—it's up to the school to create a climate favourable to their realisation!

Bärbel Inhelder

Professeur à l'Institut des Sciences de l'Education de Genève

(Institut Jean-Jacques Rousseau)

AUTHOR'S NOTE

The content of this article, in a slightly different form, was the subject of a conference at the Ecole Normale Supérieure at Saint-Cloud. We are happy to be able to offer it to the *Bulletin de Psychologie* which is read (with sympathy) in Geneva, and to be able on this occasion to thank the school of Saint-Cloud. The ideas presented in these pages will be developed in a following work.

TRANSLATOR'S NOTES

1. I would be the first to agree that the qualities required to translate this sort of work from its original French into English are the following: ability to write clearly in English, knowledge of the subject matter, and more than passing comprehension of the French language. I will leave the critics to determine if I should score any points at all on any of those three criteria. My aim has not been to make a free translation of Inhelder's 1954 ideas into 1990s English but to attempt to capture somewhat both the style and the content of the paper in a way that represents the essence of her presentation at St Cloud.

    Students of the Genevan *oeuvre* will know the problems caused by the misunderstandings over the various translations of *décalage* into English; problems that persisted until the term decalage was just appropriated into English-language texts. There are a number of similar language-specific problems inherent to this paper of Bärbel's as well. The one that has been the greatest stumbling block has been the verb *dégager* which usually presents as "to free" (your trapped leg) or "to clear" (the road of snow) but which Inhelder uses in the sense of the adolescent's intellectual process of liberating and understanding the general scientific laws from the physical experiment in which their operation is detected. However, the last line of this 1803 stanza from Erasmus Darwin about Isaac Newton carries this meaning of "dégager" perfectly:

NEWTON's eye sublime
Marked the bright periods of revolving time;
Explored in Nature's scenes the effects and cause,
And, charm'd, unravelled all her latent laws.

—Michael White (1997) *Isaac Newton: The last sorcerer*
(London: Fourth Estate)

Dégager is translated variously as "work out", "separate and understand" as seems appropriate in the context.

Interroger le réel/le dispositif/l'experience: The English language does not seem to support very well the notion of an investigator interrogating/cross-examining the real/the device/the experiment in order to see if constants might be deduced. The idea includes the close and careful examination of all the details and the posing of questions which are answered by the results of experimental actions on the equipment.

Attitude: *Les attitudes experimentales* of children and adolescents incorporates the disposition of the subjects to behave in more (or less) scientific ways when confronted with problems instantiated as tasks. The term "approaches" is used here to include both the cognitive and behavioural orientations of the subject to problem-solving by experimentation.

While I am sure this paper does not present a theory of formal operational thinking (see Chapter 4, this volume), it does provide a systematic description of adolescent problem-solving behaviour which will appeal to secondary school teachers and others who work with adolescents.

2. Possibly DEF(14;8) see *The growth of logical thinking from childhood to adolescence (GLT)*, Inhelder & Piaget, 1958, p.11; see Chapter 4 for full reference.)

3. "Society had to wait for Galileo and Descartes with the 'intellectual mutation', as A. Koyré called it, which resulted from their discovery" is the reference in *GLT*, p. 129.

4. See note 3.

5. The device for this task remains on display at the Archives Jean Piaget in Geneva.

6. Bärbel Inhelder claimed in her Autobiography: "I was lucky to work with a particularly enthusiastic group of students … One of the questions we asked was how the method of ceteris paribus (all other things being equal) was discovered. … The results of a series of experiments … were highly promising and in the corridors of the Institute one could hear excited discussions about how we had discovered a new stage: formal thought is not achieved before the age of fifteen or so!".

7. Dilute sulphuric acid is both sufficient *and* safer.

8. Strategy (tactique) does not have exactly the same meaning in the 1950s research as it does in the Genevan work of the 1970s.

9. What we would now call "error" estimates.

10. Probably "Le groupe des transformations de la logique des propositions bivalentes"/The group of logical transformations of two-valued propositions (Piaget, 1949/n.t., see Chapter 4).

Author index

Author index

Subject index

Subject Index